Refounding the Church

Other books by
Gerald Arbuckle

Out of Chaos: Refounding Religious Congregations
(Paulist Press/Geoffrey Chapman)

Earthing the Gospel: An Inculturation Handbook for Pastoral
Workers (Geoffrey Chapman/Orbis Books)

Grieving for Change: A Spirituality for Refounding Gospel
Communities (Geoffrey Chapman)/
Change, Grief, and Renewal in the Church: A Spirituality for a
New Era (Christian Classics)

Refounding the Church

Dissent for Leadership

Gerald A. Arbuckle SM

GEOFFREY
CHAPMAN

Geoffrey Chapman
A Cassell imprint
Villiers House, 41/47 Strand, London WC2N 5JE

First published 1993

British Library Cataloguing-in-Publication Data
A catalogue record for this book is available from the British Library.

ISBN 0-225-66678-2

Cover illustration by Jim Bray

Typeset by Colset Private Ltd, Singapore
Printed and bound in Great Britain by
Biddles Ltd, Guildford and King's Lynn

For:
Mary, Joseph, Michael, Jim, Gerard and John

Zealous as they were for souls and for the welfare of holy Church . . . they offered me . . . eager longing and constant humble prayer.

(St Catherine of Siena)

Refounding is a faith journey into the paschal mystery for mission today according to the Spirit of the original Founder.

Contents

xi   **Acknowledgements**

1   **Introduction**
2   Loyal dissent is essential for mission
3   Contemporary restorationism: contrary to Vatican II values
5   The Church can learn from elephants
6   'Authority' and 'pathfinding' dissenters
7   Case study analysis: religious life — the Church in miniature
9   'Dissent' as a pejorative term

15   *Part One   Dissent, Leadership and Refounding in the Church*

15   **1 A refounding stalled: the problem explained**
16   Identifying today with the pain of Jeremiah
21   The need for 'continual reformation' or refounding
22   Historical background to the paradigm shift
25   The structures of the pilgrim Church
29   Action for refounding the Church: some reflections
33   Summary

36   **2 The Church in chaos: an inevitable experience**
37   Understanding culture and mythology
39   The Church: tensions within its creation mythology
43   Life-cycles of cultures: application to the Church
43   *Model 1: Into chaos — Vatican II and revitalization*
55   *Model 2: The Church — from a 'growing' to an 'ageing' culture*
62   Summary

66   **3 Secrecy, orthodoxy and 'witch-hunting'**
68   Understanding 'witches' and 'witch-hunting'
73   Application of theory to the post-Vatican II Church
78   Orthodoxy, witch-hunting and models of the Church
78   *Understanding 'authority', and 'power'*
80   *Cultural models of Church*
81   *Model 1: Strong group/strong grid culture —*
     pre-Vatican II Church
84   *Model 2: Strong group/weak grid culture — the*
     restorationist Church
88   *Model 3: Strong grid/weak group culture — the*
     accommodation Church
90   *Model 4: Weak grid/weak group culture — intentional Chris-*
     tian communities
93   Summary

98   **4 The transforming leadership of 'authority dissenters'**
95   Defining leadership
101 Transforming leadership
101 *1. The need for a vision, strategies and accountability*
106 *2. The need to empower people*
108 *3. The need for personal authenticity*
108 *4. The need for community-oriented innovators*
110 *5. The need to foster responsible dissent*
114 *6. The need to claim one's authority/power*
118 *7. The need for appropriate knowledge/skills*
119 *8. The need to apply the axiom 'the new belongs*
     elsewhere'
120 *9. The need for reflection and 'not-knowing'*
121 *10. The need for rituals of mourning*
122 A spirituality for leadership in refounding
125 Summary

129 *Part Two   The Church in Miniature: The Refounding of*
     Religious Congregations

131 **5 Challenging restorationism: refounding religious**
     congregations
132 Religious life: mirrors the chaos in the Church
134 Refounding in religious congregations: overview of model
146 Refounding persons as dissenters: clarifications

149   Applying the axiom 'the new belongs elsewhere'
155   Summary

158 6 Living community: essential for refounding
158   Understanding community in religious life
159   *Model 1: The 'ascetical' community*
159   *Model 2: The 'relational'/'mobile' community*
161   *Model 3: The 'mission' community*
163   Case studies: importance of discernment
166   Community, congregational refounding and Roman
       restorationism
168   The 'therapeutic' model of religious life: individualism over
       community
174   Community and group-oriented cultures
175   Fostering refounding communities: practical insights
177   Summary

180 7 Denial, grieving and leadership
181   Understanding resistances to change
183   The stages of cultural/individual grieving
184   Understanding the need for rituals of mourning
187   Denying loss in Western cultures
188   Loss and congregational cultures
193   The leader's role: to challenge denial ritually
197   A ritual of group grieving
198   Summary

**201 8 Collaborative government: practical hints for authority
       dissenters**
202   Collaborative government: definition and some practical
       insights
205   Achieving collaborative leadership: practical hints
216   Summary

220   Epilogue
225   Index

Acknowledgements

I am particularly grateful to Ruth McCurry, of Geoffrey Chapman, and Bill Burrows, of Orbis Books, for the encouragement to write this book, and to my colleagues Michael Mullins SM and Jane Blaxland for their helpful insights, particularly into leadership. I thank the editors of *The Way*, *Review for Religious* and *Human Development* for their permission to quote from articles of mine that they have published.

21 November 1992

Introduction

*You must bear in mind that, if I speak strongly in various places . . .
against the existing state of things [in the Church], it is not wantonly, but
to show I feel the difficulties which certain minds are distressed with.*
                                                    (John Henry Newman)[1]

When leaders in the Church or other organizations are concerned for the
future they foster a reasonable degree of diversity and dissent. Dissent is a
confusing and at times a highly emotive word, especially for those people
who are irrevocably wedded to the status quo or who fear any form of
change whatsoever. The reality, however, is that there can be no constructive change at all, even in the Church, unless there is some form of dissent.

By *dissent* I mean in this book simply the *proposing of alternatives* – and
'a system that is not continuously examining alternatives is not likely to
evolve creatively'.[2] Open organizations encourage people who propose
alternative ways of doing things because they know that organizations (or
cultures) age and produce deadwood. New ideas and ways of doing things
may guarantee that life and vitality will continue. They are the seedlings
out of which the future is born. However, seedlings are very fragile; they
can be smothered long before they have had the chance to develop and
become vigorous plants. So also with proposals for alternative ways of
thinking or acting. Organizations, the Church included, are built to
administer, maintain and protect from harm that which already exists; in
contrast, creative or dissenting people are designed to give birth to that
which has never been in existence before. Thus dissenters threaten the well-
oiled structures of an organization's process. The alternatives they propose
are seen as chaotic, something to be vigorously avoided by those taking
comfort in the predictable and safe ways of tradition.

Confronted with the possibility or reality of chaos, and the anxiety it
evokes, people usually act to reaffirm their culture's or organization's
traditional identity, structures and boundaries. Groups develop their own
set of sanctions – that is, reward and punishment mechanisms – intended
to keep the members in line. Pressure is placed on individuals to conform;
if they do not, the sanctions escalate. It is then that witch-hunts (see

Chapter 3) flourish with high levels of intolerance, bitterness and anger, searching out dissenters or non-conformists, branding them as the causes of the chaos, and excluding them from any effective involvement in the group. At times this exclusion process actually results in death, for example in the days of the Inquisition or the show trials in the Soviet Union under Stalin. In these witch-hunts, in which conformity or orthodoxy is the major concern, the group consumes energy that should be creatively directed to helping the group relate to the wider world and to issues of far greater importance for its survival and growth.

Nations are capable of a dramatic surge of change following an authoritarian-led revolution, but it is short-lived because such systems cannot tolerate people who freely offer alternative ways of reacting to changing needs. Creative people are anathema to totalitarian systems. Eventually these totalitarian systems collapse, killed by their own refusal to accept needed innovation under the inspiration of dissenters at all levels of society. The recent sensational break-up of the Soviet Union aptly illustrates this point.[3]

Dissenters in open societies have rights, but they also have duties. They need to propose and pursue their options for action with respect, patience and tolerance, gifts of course so brilliantly exemplified in the prophets of old. Jesus Christ was such a principled dissenter. With patience, courage and love he challenged the religious and cultural status quo of his times by proposing an alternative way of life and by living what he preached. Gradually people came to accept him and his message either directly through himself or indirectly through his disciples. Martin Luther King was another responsible dissenter. He challenged the nation through non-violent action based on frequently stated principles of human equality; eventually many came to accept what he did and said, thus changing the nation's way of life. However, there had to be a degree of openness within the American political system to allow King to continue to function as he did. In the case of Jesus Christ the political and religious hierarchical system of Palestine finally could tolerate dissent no longer, for its leaders realized the chaos this would lead to in their own lives and the organization they supported. Their witch-hunting led to the death of Christ.

Loyal dissent is essential for mission

Back in 1950 Pius XII recognized the urgency for the Church to be a body open to responsible or principled dissent. Speaking first in general terms about organizations, he said that 'wherever there is no expression of public opinion, above all, where it has been ascertained that no public opinion exists, then one is obliged to say that there is a fault, a weakness, a sickness, in the social life of that [group]'. He then applied this to the Church: 'For she too is a living body, and there would be something missing from her life if there were no public opinion within her, a defect for which pastors as well as the faithful would be responsible'.[4] Thirteen years earlier the same Pope spoke sympathetically of dissidents: 'we must be solicitous for them and ceaselessly concerned ever to understand them better . . . we must beware of too hastily attributing perverseness to them'.[5] For him, principled dissenters are a blessing of the Lord because they help to prevent the Church from becoming excessively introverted:

> [The Church] welcomes and hallows all that is truly human . . . [she] cannot shut herself up, inactive, in the privacy of her churches and thus neglect the mission entrusted to her by divine Providence, the mission to form people in their fullness and so ceaselessly to collaborate in building the solid basis of society. This mission is of her essence.[6]

John Paul II reiterates this need for openness. As archbishop of Krakow, he said with estimable bluntness that 'Conformity means death for any community. A loyal opposition is a necessity in any community.'[7] Also, he insisted that an organization must 'not only allow the emergence of the opposition, give it the opportunity to express itself, but also must make it possible for the opposition to function for the good of the community'.[8] And it is through dialogue that opposition is to work for the good of the whole group. As Pope, he stated in 1979 that 'Truth is the power of peace . . . . What should one say of the practice of combating or silencing those who do not share the same views?'[9] In his 1990 encyclical on the revitalization of missionary activity, the Pope at least indirectly approves of loyal dissent in the Church since he keeps encouraging evangelizers to 'new and bold endeavours' in their pastoral life.[10] 'New and bold endeavours' apostolically are alternative pastoral ways of acting; this assumes of course that a loyal opposition is allowed to develop, otherwise traditional ways of pastoral care cannot be challenged by the new and the bold.

Contemporary restorationism: contrary to Vatican II values

However, these statements of quite radical support for a principled opposition as a way of fostering an open Church do not describe what in fact is generally happening. Various members of the Church's hierarchy are so insistent on theological and apostolic orthodoxy or conformity within the Church that it is not the open society as desired by Pius XII, Vatican II and the statements of John Paul II. There are well-orchestrated attempts to restore the Church to the cultural ghetto or opposition-to-the-world mentality of the pre-Council times. Restorationism is an ill-defined, but none the less powerful, movement within the Church towards the *uncritical* reaffirmation of pre-Vatican II structures and attitudes in reaction to the stress resulting from the theological and cultural turmoil generated by the

3

changes of the Council and the modern world at large. Restorationism takes many forms, some fanatically aggressive and others less so. It is marked by degrees of intolerance to any form of opposition; dialogue is rarely possible with individuals or institutions adhering to its beliefs. As long as this state of affairs exists there is what Pius XII above refers to as 'a fault, a weakness, a sickness' within the body of the Church.

In Part One of this book I examine the reasons for the contemporary restorationist drive within the Church. I argue that the efforts to take the Church back to a pre-Vatican II period is one of the culturally predictable, but theologically unacceptable, options in reaction to the chaos precipitated to a significant extent by the theological/cultural revolution of Vatican II (see Chapter 2). By *chaos* I mean the generally sudden cultural breakdown in which a people's network of meaning systems (symbols, myths and rituals) disintegrates.[11] As a result of the insecurities and uncertainties evoked by the chaos, people feel numb, confused, angry and lost.

This chaos can still be the catalyst for an immense surge of faith-inspired evangelization, because it can force us to look for radically new ways to preach the Good News as the old pastoral methods are simply no longer effective. The Gospel must be drawn into a dynamic interaction with contemporary issues, for example secularism, world poverty, ecological crises; we desperately need new organizations, structures and methods of evangelizing a constantly changing world. So enormous is the task and the risks involved that no longer is the phrase 'renewal of the Church' adequate to convey the immensity of the challenge facing us. A fresh expression is necessary. Hence I speak of the process of *refounding the Church*, that is, of finding and implementing new forms of bringing the faith/justice Good News to the world. This is more akin to the phoenix – a rebirth – than the gentle, refreshing breeze that 'renewal' has come to connote; those who lead this rebirth I refer to as refounding persons.[12] People committed to refounding the Church are not anti-tradition. On the contrary, they recognize that the most fundamental challenge confronting the Church's leaders is to guide the awkward, uneven and unending movement of adapting the Gospel message to an ever-changing society without at the same time brokering or blowing away the sense of continuity with the past that provides us with the roots of our identity.

However, dogmatic restorationists, that is those who would uncompromisingly pull the Church back from the values of Vatican II into 'the privacy of her churches and thus neglect [her] mission', fear the disorder or malaise of chaos, because they cannot cope with the unpredictability and messiness that are the inevitable accompaniment of the anxiety-evoking new and bold pastoral endeavours. Order that is seen as synonymous with retreat from the world of change, they assert, must be immediately re-established and all must conform to it. Anyone daring to question this thrust only intensifies the Church's anxiety, so they must be marginalized as rapidly and as firmly as is possible!

The Church can learn from elephants

All organizations, including the Church, can be likened to elephants because both come to see their own worlds through a process of conditioning.[13] Fully grown elephants are conditioned to remain in place because when young they are shackled to stakes deeply rooted in the ground; mature elephants could pull the stakes up, but their conditioning is so strong that they do not attempt to move. As they were trained to act, so they do. Cultures of organizations are like this; once dynamic and mobile like young elephants, they later become conditioned to the status quo. The axiom is: 'We have always done it this way, so why change!' Any chaos experience makes the secure ways of the past even more enticing. A contemporary example of the dangers of falling victim to elephant-like conditioning is the IBM computer company. The production of mainframe computers made this a powerful organization, but by 'clinging to its beloved mainframe business, and the ways of selling computers that went with it, the biggest computer company of them all has jeopardised its future'. World interest in proprietary mainframe computing has faded and 'open-systems computing – networks of workstations and personal computers' have become their substitutes.[14] IBM, initially so innovative, has failed to keep pace with changing needs and new technological inventions.

What can elephants and IBM teach the Church? Jesus, who liked to use examples familiar to his audiences to illustrate his message (e.g. Lk 7:24–27), would answer, 'a lot'! The way many local churches have reacted to the post-Council chaos is no better than the manner IBM has related to changes in the business market. They have neglected to keep in touch with the needs of people. Reflect on the laudable success of Catholic schools in the past that were established for poor Catholics and run relatively cheaply because of the abundant supply of religious as teachers. Now the costs to parishes of maintaining these schools in many areas exclude the poor. Yet we continue to hold on to these expensive establishments, calling them Catholic schools – somehow believing that we are providing Catholic education for the poor! We are old elephants conditioned and blinded by the success of the past.

Perhaps we can take heart from the fact that even in Old Testament times elephant-like conditioning flourished with rather predictable results. Once the Israelites took possession of the promised land they fell victim to a false conditioning that the more goods they possessed the more Yahweh loved them, failing to see the greed and complacency eating into their hearts. The prophets stormed for generations with little success against this and it would need the dramatic chaotic experience of the Exile, the loss of all possessions – especially the kingship, Jerusalem and the temple – before some could see how crippling their conditioning had become. They discovered the dangers of taking comfort in outward expressions of religion or observance rather than in a living, risk-oriented creative faith.[15]

So many in the Church today are consciously or unconsciously assenting to the restorationist movement, like older elephants conditioned to remain comfortably and uncritically shackled to the stakes of the past ghetto-style Church. If the Church is to become young again, as Christ and Vatican II would wish, we need hope-filled dissenters at all levels in the Church. We require leaders, in the smallest Basic Christian Community to the highest pastoral positions in the Church, gifted with 'charismatically inspired, creative imagination[s]', as Karl Rahner incisively reminds us.[16] These people have a vision of the new Church modelled on the values of Vatican II and they are pained by what Paul VI refers to as the 'split between the Gospel and culture'. This is 'the drama of our time. . . . Therefore every effort must be made to ensure a full evangelization of . . . cultures.'[17] They appreciate the deep causes of the Church's elephant-like conditioning to the status quo and that change is essential and possible, though the steps forward be small and halting. For them, 'Things that are impossible by human resources, are possible for God' (Lk 18:27). And they readily acknowledge the general formula for any innovation, even within the Church: a willingness to question the status quo, pragmatic imagination, an idea, initiative, courage, and a few friends to help the project off the ground.

'Authority' and 'pathfinding' dissenters

There are two major categories of refounding persons or dissenters required in the Church if the formula for innovative pastoral action outlined in this book is to be put into effect: 'authority' dissenters and 'pathfinding' dissenters. It is rare that the two types are found in the one person in everyday life, though they are commonly combined in founders of religious congregations. People in the first category, unlike pathfinding dissenters, hold officially appointed positions of authority – for example, bishops, pastoral directors and congregational leaders have the power to open and close doors to new and bold pastoral endeavours. As 'friends' of pastoral innovators they can make the structural changes necessary for the 'pathfinding' dissenters to use their gifts for the Church. This book is particularly about the qualities needed in these 'authority' dissenters and the type of obstacles they encounter in their apostolic work. Authority dissenters have a transformational style of leadership – that is, they aim to create an entirely new order of things through creative or imaginative pastoral quantum leaps. Understandably, restorationists fear such people for they prefer a managerial style of leadership through which order or the status quo is maintained or re-established.

The primary task of the authority dissenters demands that they discover and use the gifts of the pathfinding dissenters for the benefit of the Church. Gifted with pragmatic imaginations, a shrewdness for timing and organizing, pathfinding dissenters devise pastorally alternative ways for the bridging of the gap between the Gospel and cultures. Not only do they dream up appropriate pastoral strategies, but they actually move to implement them. They are dreamers who *do*! For people comfortably attached to outdated pastoral methods, pathfinding dissenters are annoying because they refuse to settle for the mediocre. They are what the poet T. S. Eliot refers to as 'another voice', the carriers of the Gospel vision through radically new language and action in response to ever-changing apostolic needs. The voices of the past cannot do this:

> . . . Last season's fruit is eaten
> And the fullfed beast shall kick the empty pail.
> For last year's words belong to last year's language
> And next year's words await another voice.[18]

As carriers of 'another voice' and alive with the power of Christ, they yearn to draw others to him in believing, worshipping and social justice-oriented communities through which the Gospel is lived and presented in ways relevant to the ever-changing needs of our times. Every time the Gospel is brought into critical and evaluative interaction with the world of today, I believe this is an act of responsible or prophetic dissent.

Case study analysis: religious life – the Church in miniature

Part One of this book explains why principled authority and pathfinding dissenters in the Church today are both so needed and at the same time so unpopular. Since a religious congregation ideally should be the people of God or the pilgrim Church in miniature, an in-depth study of contemporary religious life can throw light on what is happening within the Church as a whole. A case study is a detailed perception of connected processes in individual and collective experience of a particular section or group within a wider society; through case-study analysis we are able to see quite sharply the tensions and movements characteristic of the larger group. Hence Part Two of this book is a case-study review of contemporary religious life; for example, I reflect on the reasons why religious congregations are so sluggish in responding to the call for refounding and why creative religious rarely experience support for their pastoral initiatives. As religious life is, so is the Church. So many of the tensions and crises within today's religious congregations are to be found in every section of the wider Church's life (e.g. dioceses, parishes, episcopal conference). A thorough reflection on religious life provides Church leaders and evangelizers everywhere with a more nuanced grasp of the problems they are confronting.

In previous writings I have focused on the qualities and role of the refounding person as the pathfinding dissenter.[19] In this book I concentrate particularly and in practical terms on the role of the *authority dissenters* in religious congregations – namely, the official congregational leaders. What is said of them can be usefully applied to leadership throughout the Church.

Religious congregations historically evolved as dissent movements to challenge society and the Church to measure up to Gospel values. In fact, the most dramatic growth points for religious life have been those stages when society and Church were particularly corrupt. While there are many examples of corruption of power in contemporary society, it might at first sound a little dramatic and exaggerated to point to corruption of power in the Church. In fact, a Church that is uncritically restorationist has the sickness referred to above by Pius XII, because power is being used to turn the Church excessively inwards away from its primary task of evangelizing the world. This *is* a corruption of power. Religious, as in earlier times of decay in society and the Church, are desperately needed as prophetic witnesses or dissenters for Gospel values. By their lifestyles and their bold apostolic initiatives they will dissent from a culture of restoration developing within the Church. Inevitably this will lead to tensions with the hierarchical structures within the Church for the latter are primarily concerned with order and unity. In fact, as the history of religious life illustrates, the more religious are doing their job correctly the greater the tensions and conflicts will be with the hierarchical Church. The fear of suffering must not dissuade them from their primary task of being 'martyrs of prophecy' within society *and* the Church.[20]

Religious life today, however, mirrors the chaos in the Church as a whole. All too few religious and communities are prepared to take up the challenge to refound. There are religious who want a quick fix to their chaos, anything in fact that would allow them to avoid the pain and darkness integral to conversion to radical Gospel values. Some nostalgically and undiscerningly seek a return to old religious life symbols or customs to satisfy a fundamentalist craving for security and identity. They refuse to ask the awkward question for fear that the answers will demand too much of their courage and faith: what is the mission of religious life today? Others have become so identified with the surrounding culture of materialism, individualism and self-fulfilment that they have lost contact with the ascetical and counter-cultural roots of religious life. Much in religious life today is so sick or encased in escapist denial that concerned religious find it difficult to find support for their efforts at authentic refounding. Congregational leaders are often at a loss to know what to do or else they are themselves trapped in the culture of denial of their religious communities. The 1992 summary of a major survey of religious life in the United States significantly concludes that 'In many cases, leaders [of religious congregations] lack the necessary competencies or training to function effectively. . . . The most striking weakness among current leaders is their inability to formulate a strategy to achieve a purpose or mission.' The authors noted that 'One of the first issues to surface [in the survey findings] . . . was the urgency of selecting and training leaders who not only can manage the complexity of religious life . . . but who also can focus the attention of their communities on a vision that will unite individual efforts inspired by the mission of their founder or foundress'.[21]

Responsible dissenting religious and their communities recognize that prayerful asceticism and prophetic action are at the very heart of religious life, demanding of them an inner/outer conversion to radical Gospel values. They know in faith that the chaos has provoked crises of immense importance for themselves personally and for their communities. For them, as for the ancient Greeks, the present crises can be likened to a turning point of an illness 'in which it is decided whether or not the [individual] organism's self-healing powers are sufficient for recovery'.[22] Recovery for them means first and foremost the entering by communities and individuals into Christ's paschal mystery for mission; it is discerning what God wants and doing it, not what a congregation or individuals desire. They are aware that the process of refounding could lead to the death of a religious community, but because it is accepted in faith, though painful, it becomes a salvific or grace-filled act, prophetically contributing to the building of the Kingdom. The process of self-healing means that we acknowledge the chaos within ourselves personally and within contemporary religious life. Only by accepting our inner brokenness, poverty and powerlessness do we begin to discover the mystery of God's all-powerful love and compassion. Then we realize as never before that any constructive movement out of the present malaise is impossible without the call and power of the Holy Spirit.

'Dissent' as a pejorative term

I realize there is a danger of being misinterpreted as a result of using the word 'dissent' in the book's title. The term 'dissent' for many, since the publication in 1990 of the Roman document *Instruction on the Ecclesial Vocation of the Theologian*, connotes disrespect for, and even repudiation of, the authoritative magisterium. The document, which is essentially a disciplinary one, formulates a code of behaviour severely restricting the work of theologians in ways that Vatican II did not.[23] Despite this highly restrictive and debatable use of dissent, I still believe we can continue to use the word in the sense I have already described – namely, the prophetic move by people who genuinely love the Gospel and the Church to offer responsibly alternative ways of preaching the Good News to the world of our time. Jesus Christ himself and all the prophets throughout history have all acted as dissenters. Because 'dissent', 'dissenting' and 'dissenter' have taken on particularly pejorative meanings in the minds of some in the Church, this is no reason for us to drop such tradition-sanctioned terms.

Of course, the manner in which dissent is done must always be according to the Gospel and with due respect for the divinely established structures of the Church. Authentic dissent is not synonymous with withdrawal from the Church, the un-Gospel-like use of coercive power or the harsh condemnation of those who differ from one's views. On the other hand, those who head the hierarchical structures of the Church must themselves be open to dialogue. If they are not, then they should not be surprised if dissenters continue to speak more insistently for the channels of communication to be opened up.

Though this book draws on several disciplines – for example, history, theology and scripture, and social psychology[24] – the main models of analysis are derived from cultural anthropology. This little-known discipline helps us to look at familiar issues through different eyes so that we can get a quite unexpected perspective on them. Like a surprising move on a chessboard, anthropology offers a new way of looking at the contemporary Church. Anthropology is about how people feel and communicate with one another within and across cultures. It is often about laying bare the cultural forces that motivate people, though they are so often unconscious of these forces' existence and their power to control behaviour.[25] Since the best way to grasp the power of human communication is to record what people actually say, at times I quote in case studies what people say about their experiences in the Church and religious congregations in order to give flesh to the principles enunciated.

I hope also that readers will be helped by the practical nature of several chapters on leadership (Chapters 4 to 8). The mass of contemporary literature on leadership is a quagmire for the non-professional, so I attempt to highlight those points in the material available that have particular practical relevance to this book's theme. Every Christian – not just the religious – is called to prophetic or pastorally innovative leadership, so the mistakes and successes of religious congregational leaders as set out in Part Two offer lessons for *all* ecclesial leaders. As evangelizers ponder these lessons it is my hope that they will experience the promise of Jesus: 'every scribe who becomes a disciple of the kingdom of Heaven is like a householder who brings out from his storeroom new things as well as old' (Mt 13:52).

Notes

1. J. H. Newman, letter to J. Keble, 6 September 1843, cited by J. I. Gonzalez Faus, *Where the Spirit Breathes: Prophetic Dissent in the Church* (Maryknoll, NY: Orbis Books, 1989), p. 103.
2. J. W. Gardner, *On Leadership* (New York: Free Press, 1990), p. 128. I am grateful to Gardner for several insights in this introduction.
3. See ibid.
4. Pius XII in *L'Osservatore Romano* (18 February 1950), as cited by K. Rahner, *Free Speech in the Church* (London: Sheed & Ward, 1959), p. 5.

5. To bishops of France, December 1937; cited by Y. Congar, *Lay People in the Church* (London: Bloomsbury, 1957), p. 444.
6. To new cardinals, cited ibid., p. 446.
7. Cited by L. Swidler, 'Democracy, Dissent, and Dialogue' in H. Küng and L. Swidler (eds), *The Church in Anguish* (San Francisco: Harper & Row, 1987), p. 312.
8. Cited by D. Dorr, *Option for the Poor: A Hundred Years of Vatican Social Teaching* (Dublin: Gill & Macmillan, 1983), p. 246.
9. Cited by Swidler, op. cit., pp. 312f.
10. John Paul II, *Mission of the Redeemer* (Boston: St Paul Books, 1991), para. 66.
11. See G. A. Arbuckle, *Earthing the Gospel: An Inculturation Handbook for Pastoral Workers* (London: Geoffrey Chapman / Maryknoll, NY: Orbis Books, 1990), pp. 26–78.
12. Ibid., pp. 208–20 and G. A. Arbuckle, *Grieving for Change: A Spirituality for Refounding Gospel Communities* (London: Geoffrey Chapman, 1991), pp. 5f.
13. See J. Belasco, *Teaching the Elephants to Dance: The Manager's Guide to Empowering Change* (New York: Plume, 1991), p. 2.
14. *The Economist* (UK) (14 December 1991), pp. 69f.
15. See W. J. Harrington, *A Cloud of Witnesses: Creative People of the Bible* (Wilmington, DE: Michael Glazier, 1988), p. 37 and *passim*.
16. K. Rahner, *The Shape of the Church to Come* (New York: Seabury Press, 1974), p. 47 and *passim*.
17. Apostolic Exhortation, *Evangelization in the Modern World* (Sydney: St Paul Publications, 1982), para. 20.
18. 'Little Gidding' in *Four Quartets* (London: Faber & Faber, 1959), pp. 53f.
19. See G. A. Arbuckle, *Strategies for Growth in Religious Life* (New York: Alba House, 1986); G. A. Arbuckle, *Out of Chaos: Refounding Religious Congregations* (New York: Paulist Press / London: Geoffrey Chapman, 1988).
20. See Congregations for Religious and Bishops, *Directives for the Mutual Relations between Bishops and Religious in the Church* (Sydney: St Paul Publications, 1978), para. 12 and *passim*.
21. D. Nygren and M. Ukeritis, 'Future of Religious Orders in the United States: Research Executive Summary', *Origins*, vol. 22, no. 15 (1992), p. 267.
22. J. Habermas, cited by J. O'Connor, *The Meaning of Crisis: A Theoretical Introduction* (Oxford: Basil Blackwell, 1987), p. 55.
23. See *Origins*, vol. 20, no. 8 (1990), pp. 117–26, and comments by R. A. McCormick and R. P. McBrien, 'Theology as a Public Responsibility', *America*, vol. 165, no. 8 (1991), pp. 184ff.; also L. Örsy, 'Priests and People', *The Tablet* (London) (9 June 1990), p. 726, 'The Limits of Magisterium', ibid. (25 August 1990), pp. 1066–9, and 'Magisterium and Theologians: A Vatican Document', *America*, vol. 163, no. 2 (1990), p. 32.
24. For a psychological / scriptural analysis of contemporary restorationism, see M. H. Crosby, *The Dysfunctional Church: Addiction and Codependency in the Family of Catholicism* (Notre Dame, IN: Ave Maria, 1991); V. C. Hoffman, *The Codependent Church* (New York: Crossroad, 1991).
25. For an introductory overview of the role of cultural anthropology, see J. L. Peacock, *The Anthropological Lens: Harsh Light, Soft Focus* (Cambridge: Cambridge University Press, 1986), pp. 4–7 and *passim*.

PART ONE
Dissent, Leadership and Refounding in the Church

'[The] structure must not only allow the emergence of the opposition, give it the opportunity to express itself, but also must make it possible for the opposition to function for the good of the community . . .
(Karol Cardinal Wojtyła, 1969)

1 A refounding stalled: the problem explained

Catholicism has an incomparable intellectual, cultural, mystical, and spiritual heritage. Why then does it appear so stagnant, so lacking in self-confidence, enthusiasm, and purpose? What can be done to mobilize the religious potential in its tradition?

(Avery Dulles)[1]

[There is] an undeniable negative tendency [within the Church]. . . . Difficulties both internal and external have weakened the Church's missionary thrust.

(John Paul II)[2]

This chapter explains:

- the type of pain people experience on seeing the restorationist movement within the Church;

- why we are committed to continual reformation or refounding of the Church;

- why Vatican II symbolizes a major theological paradigm shift;

- the phrase 'refounding the Church' further;

- why the Church's charismatic structures are essential for the refounding process;

- some actions to begin the refounding process.

In any great venture there comes a time when the will to press ahead falters in the face of the enormity of what must be done. Leadership becomes frightened, paralysed, even retreatist, when confronted by the risks that must be taken if the momentum is to be maintained. This precisely describes what is happening in the Church today. Now over twenty years have passed since the Vatican II Council, and the reforms it called for are stalled. So many of our leaders are seemingly paralysed when they are challenged to take the risks that are imperative if the reforms of the Council are to be implemented.

Identifying today with the pain of Jeremiah

My work brings me into contact with many priests, religious and laity in widely differing parts of the world. They repeatedly express a deep sadness or anguish at what they see happening in the Church they dearly love. Readily do they identify with the cry of Jeremiah as he contemplates the destruction of all that is dear to him and to Israel. His sadness is all the more intense because few official leaders understand it or sympathize with him:

> In the pit of my stomach how great my agony!
> Walls of my heart!
> My heart is throbbing!
> I cannot keep quiet . . .
> Ruin on ruin is the news.
>
> (Jer 4:19, 20)[3]

Committed evangelizers feel the lethargy, the pastoral inertia and apathy, the loss of opportunities to evangelize a world where people are yearning for meaning, the pulling back by so many of our Church's leaders from the challenge to listen to and evangelize cultures from within. They are in pain because they see their friends walking away from the Church as it fails to speak compassionately to them. They are distressed when ecclesiastical authorities, whom they have traditionally been taught unconditionally to trust, are seemingly bent on restoring the Church to pre-Vatican II attitudes and structures. This history of trust and the discovery that it is often misplaced tears their hearts asunder. While Rome speaks of the need for justice in the world, they feel it discourages any reasonable critique of its own structures and secretive methods of governing and financing.

I believe that people have very good reasons to feel distressed about what they see happening within the Church today. Regrettably, Walbert Bühlmann's evaluation has truth: the central leadership is out to 'install a conservatism such as never before seen'.[4] The Church is becoming again introverted, withdrawing within its old ghetto boundaries. Ecclesiastical structures that should be encouraging communication up and down and sideways are reverting to the pre-Vatican II style of highly selective listening. Bishops are very often being appointed without adequate consultation of priests, religious and laity within the dioceses they are to serve. Collegiality – a foundational emphasis in the Council – is being downplayed and it is increasingly difficult for local churches to develop and sustain that diversity so clearly called for in the Council. The bishops of Southern Africa in their 1992 *ad limina* report complained to the Pope that they are gravely worried about 'the apparent erosion of the responsibility of the local church in matters such as inculturation of the liturgy, sacraments and religious life'.[5] Uniformity is 'in', unity and communion in diversity are not to be fostered.

16

Everywhere I go I find fear. People deeply devoted to the Gospel and to the outward evangelizing thrusts of the Council hesitate to express their sadness or criticism of what they see happening, lest they be named and marginalized. Hence issues of concern to all in the Church, such as the possibilities of women as ordained ministers and of married clergy, cannot be discussed openly. Rome fails to understand that people are not asking that they decide on such matters, but they wish their informed views to be listened to and considered without prior condemnation.

Figure 1.1 sets out in summary form the reasons for the pain and fear I have been describing. The three columns are three anthropological typologies or models of the Church. An anthropological typology is not a perfect representation of the real world, but it is the highlighting of the major emphases or symbols of a particular culture or group of people. Nuanced explanations or details are omitted to allow us to grasp a little more clearly what is in reality a highly complex situation. There is no problem about this provided this limitation inherent in all typologies is kept in mind. Today it is common for theologians to use the word *paradigm* rather than typology or model, though in practice there is little significant difference in meaning. A paradigm is 'the entire constellation of beliefs, values, techniques . . . shared by members of a given community'.[6]

However, theologians speak of a 'paradigm shift', which means that there is a fundamental break with preceding theological paradigms. This is well illustrated in Figure 1.1. I have listed there in the left-hand column the major characteristics or symbols of the pre-Vatican II Church; the centre column contains the qualities that should mark the Church according to the Vatican II documents. In the right-hand column there are the qualities that the Church should possess according to the restorationists. People who have interiorized Vatican II values are developing a way of being Church that powerful restorationists fear and are determined to undermine. The latter yearn for the return of many of the symbols and authority structures of the pre-Council Church and are doing all they can to see that this happens. They even invoke the term 'reform' to sanction their actions, though it is often not what the Council had in mind in using the word. Among restorationists, however, there are many inconsistencies. For example, on the one hand there are papal social encyclicals that penetratingly uncover the evils within contemporary society and assert the need for social justice. But on the other hand, there is such an emphasis on the maintenance of orthodoxy that people, particularly priests and religious, fear to risk the prophetic witness that these encyclicals demand. The atmosphere is simply not conducive to boldness of apostolic initiative.

	Pre-Vatican II typology	Vatican II+ typology	Restorationist typology
The culture of the Church	Closed to dialogue	Open to dialogue	Closing to dialogue; fear of dissent
Foundations of Catholicism	Revelation of God in Jesus	Same	Same
Model of Church	Fortress: perfect society	Pilgrim: community of sinners journeying with Jesus	Desiring to return to fortress model
	Church from top down	People of God: Church from top down/ from down up	Return to pre-Vatican II
	Universal/ Eurocentric	World Church/ multicultural	Ideologically open to cultures; in practice, restorationist
Structure and authority	Hierarchical— vertical authority structures, under Pope; centralization of papacy, Curia; 'creeping infallibility'	Hierarchical— collegial authority: Pope and bishops; local churches restored; collaborative emphasis at all levels	Desiring a milder form of pre-Vatican II structures
Leadership style	Directive; dominative; secretive; no accountability to faithful	Servant style	Directive; dominative; secretive; little/no accountability to faithful
Leadership aims	Uniformity; orthodoxy; submission	Creative evangelization in changing world	Emphasis on: evangelization, inculturation, but limited by centralization ideology
Bishops	Delegates of Pope	Disciples of Christ/ successors of apostles	Institutionally overshadowed by Pope
Appointment of bishops	Minimal/no consultation	Wide consultation	Pro forma consultation; opinions often bypassed

Figure 1.1 Theological typologies/mythologies

	Pre-Vatican II typology	Vatican II+ typology	Restorationist typology
Curia	Extension of Pope	At service of and accountable to whole Church	Extension of Pope
Episcopal conferences	Unofficial gatherings	Formal establishment to teach/serve local churches	Disempowered
Liturgy: Sacraments Rites Office	Latin; theatrical; congregation passive; uncreative; legalistic/rubrical	Vernacular; simple; congregation active; creative	Creativity not encouraged
Popular religiosity	Clerical domestication	Lay encouragement	Theoretical encouragement; in practice, to be domesticated by local bishops
Evangelization	Primary concern: souls; little/no concern for social justice; concern for works of charity	Integral salvation: justice is constituent part of mission of Church	Inconsistencies between dynamic social teaching and inability/refusal to take risks
World	Evil; Church protects faithful; other-worldliness	World is created by God; it is both good and sinful	Dynamic statements for involvement in the world, but clergy and religious need to withdraw
Relations with cultures	Eurocentric; not concerned with other cultures	Dialogue; cultures to be evangelized; inculturation	Dialogue encouraged, but inability to accept consequences for Church structures/theology
Theology	Theocentric; eschatological; dream/fiction of perennial universal theology	Human experience in history; incarnational; Christocentric; biblical	Tension with non-European theologies; hesitancy to dialogue with emerging theologies
Moral concerns	Legalist; personal morality; particular concern for sexual morality	Personalist; social sins/social justice	Concern for social social sins/social justice; but involvement in social action discouraged for clergy/religious

Figure 1.1 (contd)

	Pre-Vatican II typology	Vatican II+ typology	Restorationist typology
Priesthood	Cultic	Preacher of Word; builder of believing/ worshipping/ justice-oriented community	Role: confused
	Relating to laity: superior	Relating to laity: co-operation	Relating to laity: confused
Seminaries	Removed from evil world/ closed to use of social sciences; training for cultic role; uniformity	Personal formation; use of any science to preach Gospel; stress on diversity of gifts; concern for option for the poor	Conflicting emphases: reflecting confusion re role of priest
Eucharist	Holy Communion/ Mass/Sunday obligation	Union of faithful, centred on the Eucharist, symbol and source of unity	Vatican II directions not developed; fear of inculturation at local levels
Laity role	Passive; ministries closed to them; participation in apostolate of hierarchy, e.g. Catholic Action	Active; admission of baptismal apostolic obligations; involvement in appropriate ministries	Setting limits to involvement in ministries; fears about experiment- ation lead to minimalism and new forms of clericalism
Religious	Spiritual elite; withdrawn from evil world; institutionalized; apostolates restricted, e.g. education, hospitals	Prophetic: to Church/world; committed to boldness of apostolic initiative; option for the poor	Attempts by hierarchical authorities to assimilate religious charisms into institutional models and discourage prophetic initiatives
Prophetic action/ responsible dissent	Strongly discouraged/ seen as unnecessary; lay involvement in political action, e.g. political parties	Encouraged/ integral to realize the Church's mission	Increasingly discouraged; emphasis on orthodoxy evokes atmosphere of distrust and conformity to the status quo
Gender	Unquestioned patriarchy	Implicit mutuality	Reiteration of patriarchal values

Figure 1.1 (contd)

The need for 'continual reformation' or refounding

The Council recognizes the Church is a community of sinners, requiring on-going purification and renewal.[7] While acknowledging that the Church is of divine origin, it asserts it is also human and thus prey to all kinds of failings:

> Christ summons the Church, as she goes her pilgrim way, to the continual reformation of which she always has need, insofar as she is an institution of men and women here on earth. Therefore, if the influence of events or of the times has led to deficiencies of conduct, in Church discipline, or even in the formulation of doctrine (which must be carefully distinguished from the deposit itself of faith), these should be appropriately rectified at the proper moment.[8]

This significant statement cannot be ignored whenever we begin to reflect on why principled or responsible dissent is necessary in the Church.

The Council in the above text refers to 'deficiencies' in the Church. In fact, the Council was called by Pope John XXIII because he felt that the Church, at least since the French Revolution, had become gravely deficient in its willingness to move out and evangelize the world. The Council called the Church to share the 'joys and hopes, the griefs and the anxieties of the people of this age, especially those who are poor or in any way afflicted'.[9] This is a radical shift in thinking, a theological paradigm or mythological shift that would demand equally dramatic attitudinal and structural changes at *all* levels of the Church's life. Where once the Church had sought to remove itself from history, now following the Council it is faced with the evangelical imperative to enter into the lives of people, their cultures, both to give *and* to be changed by them. The Council speaks of this process as a living exchange; today we call this 'inculturation' or 'earthing the Gospel'.[10] The theological paradigm shift is such that the Church must continually be involved in reforming itself. Ways of evangelizing and government structures suitable for the maintenance of a fortress Church, that is a Church isolated from the world around it, are totally inadequate for a Church committing itself to the task of preaching the Gospel to the world. The world is changing so rapidly that what is pastorally suited for today's needs is inadequate in tomorrow's world. Never will the Church be able to claim that it is fully reformed; it must always be in the state of becoming and reforming.

Another way of expressing the need for continual reformation is to say that the Church must be ever *refounding* or transforming itself. Like the term 'reformation', the phrase 'refounding the Church' can evoke needless fears. An analogy will help to explain what I mean. When I have a punctured tyre on my car I either repair it, replace it with a spare, or buy a new one so that I can restore the vehicle to its primary task of getting me from A to B. If I choose any of these options I become involved in 'renewing' the car. In order 'to refound the car', however, I would need to invent a form of transport that is radically different, for example a hovercraft that has no wheels and so does not get punctures. This necessitates a quantum or mega-leap in creative thinking and action. So also, when thinking of the Church's primary task of preaching the Kingdom within an ever-changing world we need apostolic creativity of quantum-leap proportions.

In other words, renewal or the refurbishing of existing pastoral strategies is insufficient. Rather we require *radically* different and as yet unimagined ways to relate the Good News to the pastoral challenges of the world, for example secularism, materialism, secularization, environmental destruction, political and social oppression. That is, we need pastorally creative quantum leaps in our thinking, structures and action. Thus prophetic people or 'apostolic quantum-leap' persons are needed within the Church to critique, or dissent from, the conventional and ineffective pastoral wisdom of the present. Without these courageous people the Church simply cannot fulfil its mission. I believe the word 'refounding', not 'renewal' or even 'reformation', best conveys the dramatic nature of what Vatican II is asking of us. The phrase 'refounding the Church', therefore, means the ongoing process whereby Gospel values are applied to the most urgent, non-ephemeral needs of today, under the inspiration of persons who see and can make it happen. Refounding connotes not just palliative care, but primarily a radical inventiveness directed at the causes of today's pastoral problems. For example, refounding persons are primarily concerned not with the symptoms of poverty but with its structural and attitudinal causes. Ultimately only a profound love for Christ and the Church can sustain people in such a challenge, because their involvement in the refounding process commonly leads to its own particular type of suffering and marginalization.[11]

Historical background to the paradigm shift

At the close of the eighteenth century the French Revolution helped to destroy the stable socio-political order with which the Church had been allied for centuries. Napoleon aimed to place the Church directly under the control of the state, thus modelling for the rest of Europe a new form of state–Church relationships. As the nineteenth century developed the Church had to confront an entirely different and anxiety-evoking situation at all levels of human endeavour: the vigorous power of an anti-clerical state system, the growing impact of the Industrial Revolution on society, the Enlightenment values of naturalism, rationalism, liberalism, democracy and the growing fascination of the world for the new empirical sciences and historical research methods. The efforts to turn back these radical ideas and movements and to restore the pre-Revolutionary alliance of throne and altar failed irrevocably in the revolutions of 1830 and 1848;

the Popes of the times – Gregory XVI and Pius IX – struggled vainly to withstand these forces even within the papal states.[12]

The more the Church's leadership struggled to resist the revolutionary insights and values emerging within the Western world the more the Church withdrew from what was taking place in history and in people's lives. At the same time, Rome fostered a form of scholastic philosophy, neo-scholasticism, that provided the Church with a very coherent intellectual framework. Yet this philosophy had one serious disadvantage – namely, it was so self-contained that its supporters saw no need to listen to, and even learn from, other philosophies. The Church as a culture became increasingly closed or inward-looking, defensive and protective of its members, compelled to live in a world considered to be under the direction of evil or subversive forces. Detailed rules and laws were invented just to keep Catholics safe from contact with these agencies, such as Protestants, who were thought to endanger the purity of their faith. The assumption that had existed for centuries – namely, that people had to be changed by religion, not religion changed by them and their cultures – thus became further reinforced throughout the nineteenth century and right up to Vatican II.[13] Pope Pius X in 1907 condemned so-called Modernists within the Church – that is, Catholics who sought to understand and use the new scientific ideas in the service of religion. His condemnation sparked off a tragic witch-hunt craze that stifled creative theological reflection for decades. The Church had the total truth, it was assumed, so it felt it had nothing to learn from the changing world of ideas and technologies. Moroever, the Church was thought to possess and live the 'pure Gospel'. It did not see itself as a culture in its own right with layer upon layer of uncritically accepted Euro-centric customs, aristocratic values and habits.

This negative stance of the Church towards the world and its Euro-centric practices permeated every aspect of ecclesiastical life right through to Vatican II. For example, in 1956 I mentioned to a fellow seminarian that I was to study social sciences in a secular university and he replied: 'What a waste of time! We have nothing to learn from these disciplines. We have social ethics or Catholic sociology and we know exactly how the world should be run by its findings. The empirical sciences have nothing to teach us. We have everything to teach them!' We studied this so-called Catholic sociology and we learnt not that the Church was a pilgrim people, but that we belonged to a *perfect* society. We had all the means for our own salvation and that of the world. The refusal of the world to listen to the Church only confirmed the point that evil resided in the hearts of secular governments and people!

The world's failure to heed the Church's teachings was seen by successive Popes from Pius IX to Pius XII as the cause of much of its suffering and many disasters. The often melancholy statements of these leaders repeatedly highlighted what they thought were the evil effects of technology, democracy and a civilization divorced from the Church.[14] At the start of the Second World War, Pius XII reflected in his first encyclical on the darkness over the world as Nazism, Fascism and Communism began to unleash their destructive powers. These evil political philosophies endangered world peace because the world itself had apostatized from the Church. Doom and gloom was everywhere, except in the Church – understood, of course, primarily as the hierarchical Church, Pope and bishops. It was argued that God was now condemning and punishing the world for its failure to listen to the Vicars of Christ over the past century or more. Later, however, Pius XII became more open in his speeches to the achievements of the world, and became the first Pope publicly to favour democracy over all other forms of government. His theological stance helped to prepare the way for his successor's decision to call the Council.[15]

One day in 1961, while attending an economics seminar at Cambridge University, I was startled to hear the lecturer begin with a comment that went something like this:

> You will be surprised, as I am, to read the letter recently published by Pope John XXIII, Mater et Magistra. This Pope admitting he does not know everything asserts that there are many good and exciting things happening in the world having their source in belief systems radically different from his. His sensitivity to the human issues of change and socio-economic development must be heeded. This is a compassionate and economically incisive document, a highly significant contribution to our understanding of the present world of the rich and poor and the values that must be adhered to, if the division between the two is to be overcome. One does not expect such positive material from the Vatican!

He had reason to be surprised, because with the coming of John XXIII a dramatic paradigm shift in the Church's thinking begins. Catholics must no longer stand back condemning the world's evils and do nothing constructive about them. They, like all peoples, are responsible for the world's problems and they must struggle with those of good will everywhere to foster peace and justice. And not only *may* they, but they *must*, use every human resource available to them in this task: technology, the human sciences, the latest communication skills.

This energizing long overdue approach to the world of change is further elaborated in Pope John's 1963 encyclical *Pacem in Terris*. He details the human rights that demand respect, again reminding Catholics that they must co-operate with all people of good will to build a just society. Gone is the overriding negativity of his predecessors towards the world: 'And since our present age is one of outstanding scientific and technical progress, we cannot enter [secular] organizations and work effectively from within unless we are scientifically competent, technically capable and skilled in the practice of our own particular professions'.[16] He plants a time-bomb within the patriarchal Church with his reference to the rights of women: 'Since women are becoming ever more conscious of their human dignity, they will not tolerate being treated as inanimate objects or mere instruments, but claim, both in domestic and in public life, the rights and duties that befit a human person'.[17]

At the opening of Vatican II Pope John unequivocally condemned the old anti-world paradigm, namely that people are to be changed by the Catholic Church, not the Church by people and cultures in dialogue with Gospel and tradition. He said: 'We are shocked to discover . . . people who . . . see nothing but ruin and calamity; they are in the habit of saying that our age is much worse than past centuries; they behave as though history, which teaches us about life, had nothing to teach them . . .' He disagreed with 'these prophets of doom'. We must recognize the mysterious designs of divine Providence working through people and events – 'even those events which seem to conflict' with the aims of the Church.[18] The Church is not to be outside history or uncritically resist change. It must always be listening to what the Spirit is saying within the hearts of people and the events of history.

Pope John's affirmative thrust is at the heart of the Council's documents. The image of the Church as the people of God points to the radical equality and dignity by reason of their baptism of all members. As Israel struggled to develop itself as God's people in history, so the Church as the pilgrim people of God strives to interact with the world in the hope of reaching the fullness of Christ's Kingdom in the time to come. Until all things are made new in Christ, 'the pilgrim Church, its sacraments and institutions, which pertain to this present time, takes on the appearance of this passing world'.[19]

Thus the Church is imperfect, made up of sinful people groaning for redemption, intimately involved with human history. With the Council we find a timely check to the overstress on the transcendence of God; now, as is so evident in its Constitution on the Church in the Modern World, the emphasis is on the incarnation of Christ and the presence of the Spirit at work within the hearts of all peoples, thus highlighting God's immanence. The more we struggle to preach the Gospel message of faith/justice, the more Christ's incarnation becomes realized within people and society. Discipleship invites us to be one with the poor, the oppressed, the marginalized; authentic belief and action are inseparable realities.

The structures of the pilgrim Church

The primary task is the work that must be done for any group to survive and be true to the purpose for which it was established. The primary task of our imperfect Church, says the Council, is 'to proclaim and to establish among all peoples the kingdom of Christ and of God'.[20] If this mission is to be achieved, the Church, as a pilgrim people, must constantly evaluate its institutional and charismatic structures. Are they hindering or fostering the purpose for which the Church exists?

Institutions (or institutional structures) are the established forms or conditions of procedure, enforced by positive and negative sanctions, characteristic of group life. Institutions are essential for the life of any human group because they provide the stability or order that people need to carry on living, even to be creative. For example, I cannot write this book if I do not have a clearly designated office in which to compose and the institution of a library where I can consult source material. However, institutions can turn into ends rather than means and stifle the creativity of those people questioning the acquired immortality of institutions. These charismatic, innovative persons call institutions to remain true to their primary task and thus open to necessary change. For example, I need people who are far more creative than I am to ask awkward questions like: Are there computer programs better suited to the writing of this book? Is my writing creativity being stifled by too little exercise or my failure to seek better libraries than the ones I now use? These are *awkward* questions, because if I truly listen to them I may have to change my set and comfortable ways of doing things and this does not please me at all!

So also in the Church. The prophetic, responsibly dissenting people in our midst restlessly call the Church to be concerned with its primary risk-involved task of evangelizing cultures right to their very roots.[21] No institution, including the institutional Church, likes taking risks, even those risks necessary for the realization of its primary task, simply because we humans have an in-built fear of the unknown inherent in any change. We are easily corrupted by the enticing certainties of the status quo, even in the Church. Hence the need for charismatic structures alongside institutional structures within the Church – that is, special graces offered by the Holy Spirit to 'the faithful of every rank' for the ongoing refounding of the Church.[22] Karl Rahner contends that charismtic structures belong to the very heart of the Church's life. The Lord, he says, is most directly present and active whenever the Gospel is interacting with the most critical issues of the day – that is, whenever the Church through its prophetic members is at the cutting edge of contemporary cultures and Gospel.[23] Avery Dulles asserts that the Church would 'not be truly Church without . . . the charismatic features, whereby God efficaciously transforms the interiority of concrete persons',[24] and institutional structures.

The institutional structures of the Church can be divided into four categories: doctrines and doctrinal formulations; public worship rituals (e.g. sacraments); structures of government; and the laws and customs that regulate how people should behave. The Council expects all these categories to be constantly evaluated, the measure being what is needed for the primary task of the Church to be realized here and now. Thus questions like the following are to be frequently asked: While the deposit of faith remains unchanged are we able to gain a deeper understanding of this deposit from the lived experience of people? Are there ways of expressing the deposit of faith that better interpret what Christ is saying to us here?[25] Are the structures of the Church's government and laws continuing to foster the Kingdom or are they hindering its realization? Are these structures suffocating the authentic charismatic gifts of its members?[26] The

OPEN	CLOSED
Top official leaders	**Top official leaders**
Integrative/challenging/ enabling	Assume have omniscience/ omnipotence
Encourage feedback to respond to new needs in the light of the group's mission	Control the feedback process to guarantee authority structures can be maintained
Encourage integration of planning and implementation	Discourage interaction between planning and implementation
Decisions for action are hypotheses, open to review by all groups in the light of experience	Decisions for action are final, unless changes are made by top officials
Encourage atmosphere that is goal/mission oriented; challenging, informal	Foster atmosphere that is status-quo oriented; formal
Manage through supportive use of authority, i.e. encourage experimentation, learning from errors, tolerance of ambiguity	Manage through fear, thus discouraging experimentation and ambiguity
Encourage communication at all levels	Communication is one-way: downward

Figure 1.2 Open and closed organizations

Council states that the proper use of the charismatic structures must depend on the approval of those 'who preside over the Church, and to whose special competence it belongs, not indeed to extinguish the Spirit, but to test all things and hold fast to that which is good'.[27] This demands a courageous faith to risk the new, humility, an openness to the Spirit, on the part of the ecclesiastical authorities involved.

When discussing the role of institutional and charismatic structures in the Church, Rahner uses the sociological categories of *open* and *closed* systems or cultures (see Figure 1.2).[28] Thus, if ecclesiastical authorities lack the above spiritual qualities, they will, as Rahner notes, do all in their power to encourage a closed Church system or culture in which authentic dialogue or discernment is impossible. The Church would then become 'an absolute monarchy or totalitarian system'[29] and if that happens it would be impossible for the Church to keep to its primary task of building the Kingdom. Apostolically the Church would stagnate. Officials, instead of listening to the Spirit speaking in the events and aspirations of people, would claim that they alone have the authority and power to decide what the will of God is for the Church, even in matters of little consequence. But any demand for blind and unquestioning obedience can never be a virtue, since it denies the basic human right for people to be heard and involved in whatever pertains to their destiny. It is arrogance to assert that the Spirit works through ecclesiastical authorities *alone*. The inescapable fact is that institutional and charismatic or prophetic structures will not function as the Spirit wishes, unless there are people at all levels of the Church's life striving to foster a spirit of mutuality or interdependence, patience, respect and charity. Only then will the Church be truly an open system or culture as desired and practised by its founder.[30]

Unfortunately, as the summary overview in Figure 1.1 shows, Roman authorities currently are fostering a closed system within the Church. For example, Vatican II in order to counter the overstress on the universal Church gave considerable importance to the role of local and national church structures, but particularly over the last ten years the Roman authorities have been insisting on a highly centralized understanding of the Church. The manner in which bishops are now commonly appointed further illustrates this anti-Council approach.[31] There are energetic efforts to restore the ghetto-like, we-have-all-the-answers and pyramidal structures of the pre-Council Church. At times in papal statements there is a reluctance to accept the meaning of inculturation as developed in the Council and at the time of Paul VI. In the Pope's recent encyclical on mission the 'need to earth the Gospel in the local culture . . . is accepted', writes missiologist Aylward Shorter, 'but strong emphasis is placed on the "purification", "elevation" and "perfection" of the evangelized culture, while little is said about giving the Church, Gospel or Christianity a different cultural expression'.[32] In the inculturation process the Church and cultures become open through dialogue to change. Yet now, despite the many contemporary papal references to the importance of inculturation, the pre-Vatican II assumption that the Church is free of culture or in some way removed from history is being revived. The Church's history is again being seen officially as co-terminous with salvation history; the history of the world is secular and from it we may learn nothing of consequence about how the Spirit is working in the hearts and events of people and their cultures. The two histories are different and salvation for the world must come from the Church as an institution; mission is primarily to serve the Church's institutional needs rather than peoples everywhere regardless of their faith or cultures.

There are isolated complaints about what is happening, for example from various theologians and even some bishops. 'Rome', deplores Walbert Bühlmann, 'currently practices an absolutely unprecedented legalism, hammering on orthodoxy at all cost, church law at all cost. . . . All democratic structures – from local parish councils to the bishops' synod . . . have collapsed like a house of cards.'[33] Cardinal Hume of England is reported to have said in 1985, just before the bishops' synod called to evaluate the impact of Vatican II on the life of the Church, that:

> The process initiated at the Council is far from complete. . . . We still
> lack adequate structures and procedures for the exercise of collegiality

and for the proper consultations of every part of the Church. We need ways to develop the necessary dialogue within the Church, between the Churches and with the world today.[34]

One senses a similar annoyance in the words of Bishop Malone, while president of the National Conference of USA Catholic Bishops, in which he praises episcopal conferences as experiences of collegiality:

> I do not share the view that episcopal conferences ought not to play too large or active a role in the life of the church. Consider the tremendous contribution our conference has made to the public debate on the issue of war and peace or our current grappling with Catholic social teaching and the U.S. economy. How could we have made these and other positive contribution except through our episcopal conference?[35]

Action for refounding the Church: some reflections

At times in the history of the Church the gap between the reality and the ideal is particularly visible and so there develops a growing desire for reform. I believe that particularly at the grassroots of the Church this desire is beginning to emerge, but the problem is to translate this desire into action, since the opposition to refounding according to Vatican II values is strong and well organized. Though more detailed recommendations for action are explained in other chapters of this book, the following are three practical suggestions that may help those interested in the refounding of the Church to get started:

1. Claim your authority as a member of the Church

Take confidence in the fact that *we* are the Church, not just the Pope, the bishops or the sects that aim to rebuild the Church according to the pre-Vatican II model. All of us through baptism legitimately have the right and obligation to call the entire Church to be accountable to the Council's values. We do not need the permission of anyone, but we are called to act with the 'love, joy, peace, patience, kindness, goodness, trustfulness, gentleness and self-control' that Paul speaks of to the Galatians (Gal 5:22). Not to do so is to be untrue to the leadership of Jesus Christ. This is no time to be flinching, fear–gloom-driven members of the Church, though the temptation to be such these days is understandable. What John Paul II says is required in the struggle for justice within the world also applies here: 'there is no justification then for despair or pessimism or inertia. . . . The freedom with which Christ has set us free (cf. Gal 5:1) encourages us to become the servants of all.'[36] And we are further exhorted to assess the Church critically by the imperative of the Bishops' Synod on Justice, 1971: 'While the Church is bound to give witness to justice, she recognizes that anyone who ventures to speak to people about justice must first be just in their eyes. Hence we must undertake an examination of the modes of acting . . . within the Church herself.'[37]

The right and duty to call the Church to be accountable for its actions belong not just to individuals, but to any group committed to preaching the Word of God. Hence Basic Christian Communities in remote parts of South America or the episcopal conference of the United States have the authority to challenge their respective local churches and the universal Church, to be true to their vocation. How refreshing and inspiring it is to see a particular bishops' conference owning its authority by refusing to be submissive to Roman congregations or officials, when the latter act beyond their authority! This is a rare event but it does happen. For example, the bishops' conference in the Philippines resisted efforts coming from the papal nuncio to support the dictator Marcos during the People Power Revolution in 1986.[38] Likewise in the United States. The Pontifical Commission on Religious Life, formed by three American bishops, was mandated by Rome in 1986 to explore the reasons for the decline of religious vocations in the United States. The Commission withstood pressures from Rome to use the study as a way of forcing apostolic religious, especially women religious, to conform to a pre-Vatican II monastic model of religious life.

2. Acknowledge deficiencies in the Church

If there is to be reform or refounding we must admit with honesty, but without bitterness, that deficiencies have existed and continue to do so within the Church. As Catholics we are not particularly comfortable about identifying and acknowledging weaknesses within the Church; instead, we prefer to deny or explain them away and feel that any open criticism is an act of disloyalty.

If we love the Church we cannot afford such misplaced reluctance. It will help to glance at some past defects that for centuries gravely obstructed evangelization. For example, those who dissented from the Church's support for the excesses of the Inquisition, its weak stand against slavery, or the condemnation of Galileo correctly acknowledged the injustices within the Church, though they frequently suffered considerably for their Gospel honesty.[39] The denunciation of dissenters was done with humourless self-righteousness, with so many of the judges firmly believing that God was on their side. By encouraging or assenting to the suppression of human rights they did not see, or did not want to see, that their actions contradicted the basic principles of the Gospels.

Here is another example from the past. A visitor to Asia is confronted by the hard fact that the Church after centuries of evangelization remains in the minds of the people a thoroughly Western or culturally alien organization, but this could have been avoided if the Roman authorities some centuries ago had not condemned in 1742 Matteo Ricci's approach to evangelization in China. Ricci, a Jesuit with extraordinary pastoral insight and cultural sensitivity, had attempted with growing success to enter into a dialogue with Chinese culture. He dissented from the contemporary view that to teach the faith one also had to impose on people European customs and attitudes. For example, Ricci and his companions had used Chinese words to express Christian ideas and they also had given permission to their converts to peform, under certain conditions, the rites in honour of Confucius and their ancestors. They were condemned by Roman authorities for encouraging what the latter wrongly thought was idolatry. In reality, this meant that the Jesuits had refused to impose on the Chinese the faith mixed with European cultural values and customs. The denunciation of Ricci signified that the lesson of the hard-won victory at the Council of Jerusalem in the time of St Paul favouring inculturation had been forgotten. The judgement passed against Ricci's actions was revoked by Pius XII in 1939, but this was far too late to undo the harm done to the Church's missionary thrust in Asia and elsewhere![40]

Rome's treatment of religious women over the centuries is one further example of what happens when administrative officials do not acknowledge early enough their mistakes or deficiencies in judgement. St Clare, a close companion of St Francis of Assisi, in the early thirteenth century sought to develop a directly apostolic group of women, but very quickly monasticization was forced on the movement. This pattern was to be repeated over and over again in subsequent centuries: the flexibility allowed to apostolic congregations of men, such as the Jesuits, was not to be permitted for women. Women tried with minimal success to change this ecclesiastical policy. Angela Merici formed the Ursulines in 1535 as a community dedicated directly to the apostolic life. They were to take the vow of chastity, teach but live at home with their families; after initial approval the Ursulines lost the apostolic flexibility of their lifestyle and were confined to the restricting structures of the cloister. Mary Ward in the seventeenth century also attempted to establish the Institute of the Blessed Virgin Mary as an apostolic congregation, but her ideas were condemned and she was branded as a 'heretic, schismatic and rebel to the Holy Church' and imprisoned by ecclesiastical authorities for a period of time.[41] It was only in the nineteenth century that Rome finally acknowledged that there could be active congregations of religious 'sisters', as distinct from contemplative 'nuns', but the former still had imposed on them many restrictions of the cloister. This policy continued until the reforms of Vatican II became effective.[42]

In order to uncover the deficiencies in the Church *today* we need one foot solidly in the theology of Vatican II and the other in the findings of historical research; armed with this knowledge we are then able to critique what is happening. Recall that one of the fundamental emphases in the Council is the importance of consultation in decision-making at all levels of the Church. Yet there is ample evidence that, for example in the choice of bishops, Rome commonly decides matters without adequate consultation. In support of this selection system it is often said that 'the Church is not a democracy – it has never been and will never be one'; hence Rome can justifiably ignore the values of participative or consultative leadership. Not only is this contrary to the spirit of the Council, but it also goes against the custom of a significant period of history. Historian Leonard Swidler points out that basically the choice of bishops by clergy and people remained effective until the twelfth century. John Carroll, the first bishop of the United States, was chosen with Rome's approval by at least all the priests of the country. As late as the beginning of the twentieth century, Swidler notes, less than half of the world's bishops were directly chosen by the Pope.[43] Thus sweeping comments like 'the Church is not a democracy' should not dissuade us from a rigorous evaluation of Rome's contemporary administrative methods or of how individual bishops go about decision-making.

3. Naturing one's faith in prayer

We cannot acknowledge the administrative mistakes of the Church's past and present and still remain loving, tolerant and zealous for the Church as Christ and St Paul did (cf. Eph 5:25; 2 Cor 11:28), if we are not actively committed to the prayerful walking with the Lord. Without prayer we become bitter and self-righteous because we fail to realize that, like the Church, we also are sinners and powerless to do good without the saving grace of the Spirit. We can commit ourselves to evangelize the Church only if we first admit to our own need of ongoing conversion and evangelization. We are required, and it ultimately can only happen through prayer, 'to listen unceasingly to what [we] must believe, to [our] reasons for hoping'.[44] Refounding the Church is a journey into the paschal mystery for mission, requiring that we walk at times in considerable faith darkness and ambiguity. It is impossible to begin or continue this journey if we are not in constant touch with the presence of the Lord within our hearts and the Church itself. Refounding is an awesome task. If we are not humanly frightened by the challenge and the risks of marginalization it inevitably involves, then there is something quite wrong with us! In the garden of Gethsemane Jesus Christ was shaking with fear as he contemplated what the founding of the Church would mean for him (cf. Mk 14:32–42). He could continue his journey to Calvary only after acknowledging in the presence of God the Creator his own powerlessness: 'And he began to feel terror and anguish. . . . And going on a little further he threw himself on the ground and prayed that, if it were possible, this hour might pass him by . . .' (Mk 14:34–35).

Summary

The refounding of the Church, as commanded by Vatican II, was bound to be a messy and a thoroughly painful business, though at the Council's euphoric ending few would have imagined this would be the case. Nor was it envisaged that we would two decades later be caught in a powerful restorationist thrust led from the very centre of the Church itself. The Council called us to bridge the gap between faith and daily life, but to do this it recognized the need for the Church to be an open body, ever listening to the hopes and anxieties of the world. If we do not listen or try hard to understand the world in which we live, it said, how could we offer people the Good News in ways that could touch their yearning for meaning?

But the Church is again becoming a closed body, unwilling to listen. Key values like the theological importance of local churches, collegiality and inculturation are *in practice* being effectively downplayed. All this is in quite vivid contrast to many inspiring documents from Rome on the need for the whole Church to respond to the new missionary exigencies. 'Solutions', says Pope John Paul II, 'to [these] pressing problems must be studied, discussed and worked out with the involvement of all.'[45] On the one hand we are told that we must be pastorally collegial, but on the other hand the Church's structures are reverting to the pastorally inhibiting pre-Vatican II hierarchical–vertical form. We are being given contradictory signals. Little wonder that the missionary zeal within the Church has slowed down, because a closed organization discourages the apostolic creativity essential to the refounding process.

Historian Thomas Bokenkotter concisely summarizes the fundamental cause of the contemporary crisis in the Church; it is the tension of letting go the long-held classicist view of the Church in favour of the historically conscious stance. The former view sees the Church as moving through the centuries 'more or less unaffected by history'. The second approach, he says, 'acknowledges how much institutions, governing precepts, and basic ideas about religion and morality are shaped by history and therefore how relative they are'.[46] Vatican II sought to counter the excesses of the classicist view by emphasizing the values of the second position, but restorationists uncompromisingly seek to return the Church to the classicist mentality.

Notes

1. A. Dulles, *A Church to Believe in: Discipleship and the Dynamics of Freedom* (New York: Crossroad, 1992), p. 3.
2. John Paul II, Encyclical Letter *Mission of the Redeemer* (Boston: St Paul Books, 1991), p. 10.

3. See W. Brueggemann, *Hope Within History* (Atlanta: John Knox, 1987), pp. 58ff.
4. W. Bühlmann, *With Eyes to See: Church and World in the Third Millennium* (Maryknoll, NY: Orbis Books, 1990), p. 148; see also relevant comments by R. P. McBrien, 'The Church (Lumen Gentium)' in A. Hastings (ed.), *Modern Catholicism: Vatican II and After* (London: SPCK, 1991), p. 91 and *passim*; P. Hebblethwaite, 'Changing Vatican Policies 1965–85: Peter's Primacy and the Reality of Local Churches' in T. M. Gannon (ed.), *World Catholicism in Transition* (New York: Macmillan, 1988), pp. 36–53; P. Lernoux, *The People of God: The Struggle for World Catholicism* (New York: Penguin, 1989), pp. 206–57 and *passim*.
5. *Southern Cross* (14 June 1992), p. 10. For reference to legitimate diversity in expressing the faith locally, see 'Decree on the Missionary Activity of the Church' in W. Abbott (ed.), *The Documents of Vatican II* (London: Geoffrey Chapman, 1966), pp. 612f.
6. T. S. Kuhn, *The Structure of Scientific Revolutions* (2nd edn; Chicago: University of Chicago Press, 1970), p. 175. See also G. A. Arbuckle, *Earthing the Gospel: An Inculturation Handbook for Pastoral Workers* (London: Geoffrey Chapman/Maryknoll, NY: Orbis Books, 1990), p. 44.
7. See 'Dogmatic Constitution on the Church': Abbott, op. cit., p. 24.
8. 'Decree on Ecumenism': Abbott, op. cit., p. 350.
9. 'Pastoral Constitution on the Church in the Modern World': Abbott, op. cit., pp. 199f.
10. See Arbuckle, op. cit., pp. 2–25.
11. Ibid., pp. 208–20.
12. See G. A. McCool, *Catholic Theology in the Nineteenth Century* (New York: Seabury Press, 1977), pp. 23–7.
13. See J. W. O'Malley, 'Reform, Historical Consciousness, and Vatican II's Aggiornamento', *Theological Studies*, vol. 32, no. 4 (1971), p. 591 and *passim*.
14. See E. E. Y. Hales, *Pope John and His Revolution* (London: Eyre & Spottiswoode, 1965), p. 34.
15. See D. Dorr, *Option for the Poor: A Hundred Years of Vatican Social Teaching* (Maryknoll, NY: Orbis Books, 1983), pp. 76–9; see also helpful overview by C. E. Curran, 'A Century of Catholic Teaching', *Theology Today*, vol. XLVIII, no. 2 (July 1991), pp. 154–69.
16. See J. Gremillion, *The Gospel of Peace and Justice: Catholic Social Teaching Since Pope John* (Maryknoll, NY: Orbis Books, 1976), p. 223, para. 148.
17. Ibid., p. 209.
18. John XXIII, opening speech to the Council: Abbott, op. cit., p. 712.
19. 'Dogmatic Constitution on the Church': Abbott, op. cit., p. 79.
20. Ibid., p. 18.
21. See Paul VI, Apostolic Letter *Evangelization in the Modern World* (Sydney: St Paul Publications, 1982), pp. 25, 67f.
22. See 'Decree on Ecumenism': Abbott, op. cit., p. 350.
23. See K. Rahner, *Theological Investigations*, vol. 12 (New York: Seabury Press/London: Darton, Longman and Todd, 1974), p. 83.
24. Dulles, op. cit., p. 31.
25. See N. Lasch, *Change in Focus: A Study of Doctrinal Change and Continuity* (London: Sheed & Ward, 1973), pp. 59–154 and *passim*.
26. See J. M. Huels, 'The Role of Canon Law in Light of Lumen Gentium' in J. K. Mallett (ed.), *The Ministry of Governance* (Washington, DC: Canon Law Society of America, 1986), pp. 98–120.
27. 'Dogmatic Constitution on the Church': Abbott, op. cit., p. 30.
28. See O. G. Mink, J. M. Shultz and B. P. Mink, *Developing and Managing Open Organizations* (Santa Barbara: Organization and Human Resource Development Associates, 1979), pp. 3–19.

29. Rahner, op. cit., p. 89.
30. Ibid., pp. 94–7; also Rahner, *Free Speech in the Church* (London: Sheed & Ward, 1959), *passim*.
31. See relevant articles by Scrutator in *The Tablet* (London) (21 September 1991), pp. 1142f.; (5 October 1991), pp. 1201f.; also the comment by the Episcopal Conference of England and Wales in their report to the 1985 Bishops' Synod, 'Suggestions', para. v in *The Tablet* (3 August 1985), p. 814.
32. *The Tablet* (9 February 1991), p. 179; see also relevant comments on Rome's preparation for the African Synod by A. Shorter, *The African Synod: A Personal Response to the Outline Document* (Nairobi: St Paul Publications, 1991), *passim*.
33. Bühlmann, op. cit., pp. 148f.
34. Cited by J. Kerkhofs, *Vatican II: Twenty Years On* (Brussels: Pro Mundi Vita, 1985), bulletin no. 102, p. 50; also see Report of the Episcopal Conference of England and Wales, op. cit., 'Reflections', para. iv, p. 816.
35. *Origins*, vol. 15, no. 7 (1985), p. 101; also Bishops' Conference of England and Wales, op. cit., 'Difficulties and Failures', para. iv, p. 814: 'There are signs of a lessening of the involvement and real responsibility of members of bishops' conferences in the membership and consultancy of the organisms of the Holy See. This weakens an important expression of collegiality which flowed from the teachings of the council.'
36. John Paul II, Encyclical Letter *Social Concerns* (Vatican: Vatican Press, 1988), p. 34.
37. See Gremillion, op. cit., p. 522.
38. See Paul Lernoux, op. cit. (note 4 above), pp. 47–9.
39. See S. Callahan, 'Conscience Reconsidered', *America*, vol. 155, no. 12 (1 November 1986), pp. 251–3.
40. See Arbuckle, op. cit., p. 12.
41. For a history of Mary Ward and the radicality of her vision, see *The Way Supplement*, no. 53 (1985), *passim*.
42. See T. P. Rausch, *Radical Christian Communities* (Collegeville, MN: Liturgical Press, 1990), pp. 79–81, 93–5.
43. See L. Swidler, 'Democracy, Dissent, and Dialogue' in H. Küng and L. Swidler (eds), *The Church in Anguish* (San Francisco: Harper & Row, 1986), p. 310; see also G. B. Wilson, '"The Church Isn't a Democracy" – Meaning?', *America*, vol. 163, no. 7 (22 September 1990), pp. 157–9, and P. Kaufman, *Why You Can Disagree and Remain a Faithful Catholic* (New York: Crossroad, 1991), pp. 117–62.
44. Paul VI, op. cit., p. 20.
45. John Paul II, Encyclical Letter *Mission of the Redeemer*, op. cit., p. 54.
46. T. Bokenkotter, *A Concise History of the Catholic Church* (New York: Doubleday, 1990), p. 401.

2 The Church in chaos: an inevitable experience

As soon as symbolic action is denied . . . the flood-gates of confusion are opened.

(M. Douglas)[1]

No large institution will overnight transform its paradigm into something entirely different . . . especially not an institution so deeply embedded in human culture as the Roman Catholic Church.

(J. W. O'Malley)[2]

This chapter explains:
- the meaning of culture and its constituent aspects: symbol, myth and ritual;
- the human pain and confusion that results from the sudden disintegration of a culture;
- how the mythology of the Catholic culture changed radically with Vatican II, causing inevitable chaos;
- the symptoms of the ageing culture of the Church today;
- why sect-like fundamentalist movements within the Church are so powerful.

Sociologist Peter Berger pictured American 'culture Protestantism' in 1961 as being 'secure, well-established, and generally self-satisfied'. But by 1977 this culture was experiencing a widespread demoralization with expressions 'ranging from masochistic self-laceration to hysterical defensiveness'.[3] So also Roman Catholics. Once 'sitting pretty on their Rock of Peter', they are now rushing to find some 'plausible lifeboats with the rest of us'.[4] Berger is correct. The 'Catholic culture' crashed in the late 1960s and early 1970s beyond anything that could have ever been imagined back in 1961. All the securities and boundaries that had identified Catholics collapsed, and like their former foes they began to discover what chaos is like. The struggle for new or restored cultural identities of Catholics continues, even to the extent of many joining new sects or cults within or outside the institutional Church. Meanwhile the chaos continues apace, a source of immense depression to some and hope to others.

In the previous chapter I outlined according to theological and historical perspectives the tensions within the Church between those wishing for the return of the Counter-Reformation façade and those yearning to refound the Church according to Vatican II values. In this chapter I draw on the insights of cultural anthropology to explain at greater depth some causes of the contemporary cultural chaos and polarization within the Church. The sources of the breakdown of the traditional Catholic culture are many and complex – for example, by the early 1960s many Catholics in the West were no longer poor and uneducated migrants. Now they were well informed and increasingly in the middle-income bracket; inevitably a growing number of these Catholics were becoming ill-at-ease with a Church encouraging undue dependency on clerical institutions and frowning on democratic principles and scientific advances. However, in this book I concentrate particularly on the way in which Vatican II itself contributed to the present chaos. The Council's values helped to undermine the creation mythology of a vigorously strong church culture and chaos was a logical consequence. In the light of this analysis it will be seen that the contemporary restorationist emphasis in Rome is understandable, even predictable, but sadly unfortunate.

Understanding culture and mythology

Only those people who assume that the Church is a pure spirit can claim that it does not form a culture. Henri de Lubac supports this: 'Like all human institutions, the Church has her exterior façade, her temporal aspect, often ponderous enough – chancelleries, code of law, courts. There is certainly nothing "nebulous and disembodied" about her – far from it.' As he says, it is no 'misty entity'.[5] Every lasting human venture must embody itself in recognizable symbols and institutional structures and Catholics are no exception. So we can speak of the living culture of the Church in this or that parish or country or at the international level. Of course people will be committed to this culture in varying degrees. For some the culture will impact on their lives in very detailed ways, for others it will be little or barely at all.

By culture I mean a pervasive 'pattern of meanings embodied in symbols, a system of . . . conceptions expressed in symbolic forms by means of which [people] communicate, perpetuate, and develop . . . attitudes toward life'.[6] These symbolic forms or patterns of interaction operate most powerfully at the level of the *unconscious*, giving us that all-important sense of experienced meaning and order. 'The cultural unconscious', says anthropologist Edward Hall, 'like Freud's unconscious, not only controls our actions but can be grasped only through difficult and challenging analyses.'[7] Thus for most of our lives we are rarely aware of the degree to which culture powerfully influences our thoughts, emotions and actions.[8]

All cultures (or subcultures) contain three elements: symbols, myths and rituals. A *symbol* is any reality that by its very dynamism or power leads to (i.e. makes one think about, imagine, get into contact with, or reach out to) another deeper (and often mysterious) reality through a sharing in the dynamism that the symbol itself offers (and not by merely verbal or additional explanations).[9] A symbol has two particular qualities of meaning and emotion. The meaning dimension conveys a message about something; it causes me to react with negative or positive feelings. The photograph of my mother makes her real to me and I experience sadness because she is no longer alive. *Myths* (and mythology which is a network of interrelated myths) are symbols in narrative form – for example, the creation stories in the Book of Genesis. They are stories or traditions that claim to reveal imaginatively or symbolically a fundamental truth about the world and human life; ordinary or purely scientific language cannot convey the power of the truth that is regarded as authoritative by those who accept it. *Rituals* are the visible acting out of the myths and they are as many and as various as human needs.[10]

But more about myths. They speak primarily to the hearts and feelings of people, even though there is also a cognitive or intellectual dimension present. Therefore, because myths relate especially to the heart we are never able to exhaust their richness of meaning. The more we ponder myths the more new insights are revealed to us. They inspire us to extend ourselves beyond what we thought were the limits of our resources, as is the case for example in nationalism. Through myths we know that we fit into a particular part of the world and that there are ways we must organize our lives to avoid falling into the frightening state of chaos. Of the many types of mythology, creation myths are of particular importance to us in this book. Creation myths speak about the first causes; in them people express their primary understanding of humankind, the world or the particular part of it in which they live.

By way of example, the Exodus story tells the Israelites how they were formed and for what purpose. And like all creation myths, the more frequently the Israelites recount the myth the more they become aware of its profound meaning and demands on them. In the Psalms, for instance, the poets reflect on the times they themselves and their people fell into the chaos of paganism or exile and the ways in which Yahweh responded creatively and compassionately to their pleas for forgiveness. The retelling of familiar myths like the Israelites' founding story energizes people, reaffirming their identity. Myths, like the symbols that form them, are storehouses of memory, linking people to the past and providing them with the identity and drive to face an uncertain future. Myths also give legitimacy to a culture's economic, social, political and legal structures. Hence, demolish a group's creation mythology and equivalently they are destroyed as a people. No wonder the Israelites in exile felt so utterly lost, for their three pivotal institutions – the temple, Jerusalem and the kingship, that signified for them their election by Yahweh as the chosen people – had been destroyed: 'By the rivers of Babylon we sat and wept at the memory of Zion' (Ps 137:1).

A remarkable quality of both symbols and myths is that they contain within themselves polar opposite meanings. The colour white cannot really be described without reference to its opposite black. So in the symbol of the colour white there is contained also the symbol of black; one connotes the other. Thus the founding myth of the United States contains several sets of polar opposites: the dignity of the individual and his/her freedom, and on the other pole the rights of the community over individuals. On the organizational side there are the rights of sovereign states over against the rights of the central government. However, creation myths do not spell out how their polar opposites are to be balanced in reality. Thus there is a built-in ambiguity or vagueness in all creation mythology that inevitably leads to tensions. Factions can form around both polar opposites in the mythology, one faction claiming that it has the correct understanding of the mythology and demanding respect for their position; the faction around the other polar opposite can do the same. In practice, one pole tends to dominate to the detriment of its opposite. This causes ideological polarization within a group calling forth bitterness, even at times violence. Such is the case in the United States when the rights of the individual become so emphasized that community rights are repeatedly neglected. Thus, for instance, the individual has an unqualified right to own guns despite the tragic consequences for the community.[11] A similar distortion exists in the secularized version of the Genesis creation story; liberal capitalism stresses the rights of the individual to an extreme degree over those of the community, and the opposite is the case in Marxism.

To avoid the negative effects of a mythology's polar opposites and to permit all parties to live in peace, it is necessary for people frequently to recall what the creation story was designed to achieve. For the contrary demands of the polar opposites to be kept in some balance, considerable wisdom, trust and a spirit of discernment (or at least an openness to bargaining or negotiation) are required on the part of the parties involved. If not, the group will tear itself apart. It is an ongoing struggle for people to maintain the balance between the polar opposites of a mythology because some ambiguity or vagueness always remains.

The Church: tensions within its creation mythology

Vatican II radically affected the Church's contemporary expression of its creation mythology in two ways and the result had to be the confusion or malaise of chaos. First, it sought to reintroduce a much-needed *balance* within the mythology; for example, the principle of collegiality was highlighted in order to counter the centuries-long over-emphasis on its polar opposite, namely papal authority. The documents are filled with ambiguities and tensions, resulting from the reintroduction of the polar opposites of key myths within the creation mythology. Gone are the many stated certainties of the pre-Vatican II apologetics constructed on the assumption that theological polar opposites did not exist. Ponder some of the ambiguities contained within the documents:

> The Church is an institution under the leadership of the bishops; *but* it is also the People of God who as pilgrims are not concerned about rank.
>
> The Church is universal, *but* it is to be incarnated within local churches to reflect their diversities of culture.
>
> The Catholic Church was established by Christ for the salvation of the world, *but* Christians of other Churches also belong to the Church of Christ and can be saved through their traditions.
>
> Heaven is our final destiny, *but* for our salvation we must struggle for faith/justice in this world.
>
> The Word of the Lord is to be found in the Bible, *but* the meaning of what is said in the Bible must be clarified by the Church.
>
> Priesthood is a sacrament and ministry established by Christ, *but* all who are baptized are priests.
>
> The aim of liturgy is to help us adore God our Creator, *but* it must reflect the needs and customs of different peoples and cultures.
>
> Religious are consecrated to the Lord by vows and are to witness to the qualities of the Kingdom to come and need some distance from the world, *but* they must be in the world as prophetic figures.

Nowhere in the documents does the Council spell out precisely *how* these polar opposites are to be balanced in real life, and in fact it simply could not do so. Rather, it challenged Catholics to struggle in faith to develop a *living balance* between the opposites. Ultimately this balance can be achieved over time only if all sides interiorize the vision of the Church as Christ's Mystical Body given us by St Paul:

> There are many different gifts, but it is always the same Spirit. . . . There are many different forms of activity, but in everybody it is the same God who is at work in them all. The particular manifestation of the Spirit granted to each one is to be used for the general good. . . . For as with the human body which is a unity although it has many parts . . . so it is with Christ. . . . As it is, the parts are many but the body is one. The eye cannot say to the hand, 'I have no need of you,'. . . . Now Christ's body is yourselves, each of you with a part to play in the whole.
>
> (1 Cor 12:4, 6, 12, 20, 21, 27)

For example, people/structures representing the local and universal Churches will work together *only* if they recognize that they must pursue a common mission or task – Christ's mission to the world. This does not mean abdicating the gifts and authority given them by the Lord; in fact, as Paul so eloquently describes, the Church cannot be truly itself if any structure claims it can function without structures representing the polar opposites in the Church's mythology. Nor can they work together constructively unless each is accountable to the other and to the whole. Thus the Council established the synod of bishops and episcopal conferences to model to the rest of the Church how Rome and the bishops must be accountable to one another for the sake of mission. Other structures of accountability were to be formed at every level of the Church whenever the needs of mission demanded (e.g. parish councils).

However, structures of accountability for mission are useless if people are not attitudinally willing to talk to one another; dialogue means being open to other people's views, even to the extent of being changed by them if the common good requires. A quick review of the governmental system within the United States built on the myth of checks and balances illustrates how aberrations emerge once people are unwilling to use structures of dialogue and accountability. The Watergate scandal, and more recently the Irangate scandal, developed because the presidential or executive powers sought to bypass the legislative wing, acting on the assumption that they did not have to be publicly accountable for their actions to anyone. For many years, the political crises have de-energized the nation.

Historically, of course, the Council's call to foster through dialogue a living balance between the mythological opposites within the documents has all too rarely been heard and owned. Following the Council, people opted with growing emotional intensity for one pole or the other in the myths. For example, one group would say, 'The Council says that the Church is universal and this must be respected above everything else!' Another would say, 'The particular churches must take precedence because that is what the Council says!' Theological, pastoral and liturgical controversies rapidly emerged, and especially in the early years after the Council protagonists were able to grab the media headlines adding fuel to the already existing tensions between opposing groups. Today, the restorationist movement with its sect-like and fundamentalist qualities is in the ascendancy, as is evident, for example, in the undermining of the powers of the synod of bishops and episcopal conferences. Such reactions have generated an atmosphere in which opposing sides do not trust one another and the situation continues to deteriorate. Apostolic energy throughout the Church, which should be directed outwards, is being drained away simply because Rome assumes accountability on its part is unnecessary and undesirable.

The second quality of the documents that intensified the chaos was the Council's decision, in contrast to major previous Councils, not to give a sharp focus at any stage to its deliberations. 'Nothing', writes John O'Malley, 'is more characteristic of Vatican II than the breadth of its concerns, never neatly packaged into a central issue.'[12] Fundamentally the Council said 'take the Good News out to the world, but listen to its needs and be prepared to learn and be changed by it'! It could not tell us how to respond to this imperative pastorally, just as it could not spell out how to reconcile the polar opposites in the myths listed above.

As a theologian I am grateful for the Council's documents and regret that the Council was not called earlier, but as an anthropologist I believe the Council was naïve about the cultural effects on Catholics of its decisions. It failed to remind Catholics that the implementation of the Council's thrusts would be a really messy, painful or grief-evoking process. The fact is that Vatican II radically altered the mythic structure of the Church and no such change is possible without being catastrophic for the people involved. For centuries Catholics were treated like dependent children for they were told by a clerical leadership exactly how to win salvation by obeying a list of detailed rules or 'how-to's. Suddenly the Council says Catholics are to stand on their own feet and make decisions for themselves in the light of the needs of the world, the Gospel and Church teaching. If bishops at the Council had been more open to the social sciences they would have been more sensitive to, and better prepared for, the explosive cultural implications of their documents on their return to their dioceses. Cultures, and especially the long-established culture of the pre-Vatican II Church, do not change smoothly simply because a document or authoritarian leaders say they should. The resulting turmoil should have been expected and better catechesis prepared to explain the inevitable chaotic, yet potentially creative, consequences of the Council's decisions. The Council fathers could have saved themselves a good deal of trouble if they had taken to heart the advice of that shrewd political observer of change, Niccolò Machiavelli (1469–1526), in *The Prince*: 'It must be considered that there is nothing more difficult to carry out, nor more doubtful of success, nor more dangerous to handle, than to initiate a new order of things'.

In fairness to the Council fathers, they were but men of their times and we moderns (especially from the West) are rarely attuned to appreciate the devastating nature of radical mythological changes. We are accustomed to seeing entire landscapes being destroyed and redeveloped over a short time. In our naïve appreciation of the power of technology, we assume that the same destruction and redevelopment can take place within cultures. We assume that symbolic landscapes of peoples can be destroyed, the familiar sights, sounds and routines in which peoples are nurtured can be obliterated overnight without particularly negative results for them.

This is simply not so. Symbols, myths and rituals are not replaced as quickly or easily as buildings or landscapes or mass-produced as neatly as automobiles or toothbrushes. The uprooting of the inner framework of cultures, even when there is conscious and intellectual assent to what is happening, destroys the stable sense of belonging and people's individuality. They are bound to experience moments of intense loss. Take the example of the civil rights movement in the United States in the 1960s. Many white Americans agreed wholeheartedly in principle to extend civil rights to blacks and other minority groups. However, when the legal changes required that they *themselves* attitudinally and behaviourally alter their long-lived, white-centred interpretation of the founding story, they experienced all kinds of personal and class chaos, as the following comment by a former white liberal illustrates: 'I fully believe blacks should have civil rights, but do they really need to buy houses in my street!' Remember a key fact in this analysis: myths relate to the heart. We can change our ideas and make all kinds of rational plans with ease, but dramatic change in the mythic structure of a people is a chaotic experience for them, since the mythic structure is in the last analysis the way people impose a felt order or meaning on their world and hold back anxiety-creating chaos.[13]

Life-cycles of cultures: application to the Church

Cultures of a country or of organizations have life-cycles just as living organisms do, and they must pass through the normal problems accompanying each stage. They learn to cope with these difficulties or they foster all kinds of abnormal 'diseases' that prevent growth. Thus we even speak of neurotic or sick cultures. As we have seen, culture is truly a hidden language,[14] inasmuch as we are so often unaware of the power of symbols, myths and rituals in our lives. Without our quite knowing what is happening, this hidden language is like an invisible hand influencing in subtle and complex ways how we frame reality and make decisions, reject or accept forms of leadership. When a culture becomes neurotic or sick we unwittingly lose control over reality; the culture, with its infrastructure of symbols, myths and rituals, ceases to be our servant and perniciously traps us in destructive ways.[15]

Because culture is such a perplexing and powerful phenomenon and incomprehensible in its totality, social scientists, as was explained in the previous chapter, develop theoretical scaffoldings or models that highlight particular emphases. The following two models provide a variety of insights into the change process of cultures and help us to understand better the contemporary movements in the Church.

Model 1: Into chaos – Vatican II and revitalization

We can look at change as a series of stages (see Figure 2.1). A culture in which the pivotal identity symbols and mythology are undermined or swept aside by powerful internal and/or external cultural forces normally passes through four major stages of 'adjustment' prior to achieving a new level of integration. I say 'normally because it is possible for cultures to move back through the stages or even to become locked in on one stage; movement forward is not in any sense inevitable. Often a particular culture will have symptoms of all four stages at the same time, but one stage will tend to dominate at a particular time. If the last stage of integration is reached people will have agreed to and developed symbols, mythology and rituals that are in touch

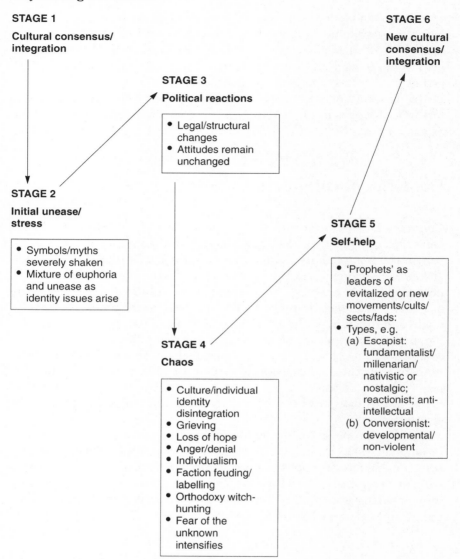

STAGE 1

Cultural consensus/integration

STAGE 3

Political reactions

- Legal/structural changes
- Attitudes remain unchanged

STAGE 6

New cultural consensus/integration

STAGE 2

Initial unease/stress

- Symbols/myths severely shaken
- Mixture of euphoria and unease as identity issues arise

STAGE 4

Chaos

- Culture/individual identity disintegration
- Grieving
- Loss of hope
- Anger/denial
- Individualism
- Faction feuding/labelling
- Orthodoxy witch-hunting
- Fear of the unknown intensifies

STAGE 5

Self-help

- 'Prophets' as leaders of revitalized or new movements/cults/sects/fads:
- Types, e.g.
  (a) Escapist: fundamentalist/millenarian/nativistic or nostalgic; reactionist; anti-intellectual
  (b) Conversionist: developmental/non-violent

Figure 2.1 Cultural breakdown and transformation

with the real world. No longer are they overwhelmed with widespread polarizations and chaos in the midst of a threatening world. In summary, integration here means a system of values and a set of behaviour patterns that are at once imposed with all the authority of evidence on the conscious or unconscious of all the members of a community or culture, and which ensure peaceful coexistence between individuals and groups.[16]

The stages of the model

In stage 1 of the model the status quo is generally accepted by people, but in stage 2 internal or external forces threaten to break up the group's mythological consensus. Some people may initially enjoy the changes, while others begin to fear for their cultural and personal identity/security. As unease or stress increases there is a move to freeze the changes in legislative action (stage 3). It is felt that legislation will contain or stop the anxiety-evoking changes, but there are others who believe that more legislation will rapidly promote in-depth change. Both views fail to understand that legislation by itself will not alter anything, because along with structural change there must go the more difficult attitudinal conversion or adjustment. This is why the fourth, or chaos, stage emerges. People become disillusioned when legislation fails to fulfil their hopes and all the cultural and personal disintegration symptoms of chaos develop – for example, anger; rage; a sense of drifting without purpose or 'lostness'; depression; paralysis, or the go-it-alone efforts of the individualists; witch-hunting in order to blame individuals for the chaos; even denial that there are problems at all. In the midst of chaos, people, as individuals and/or as groups or cultures, grieve the loss of the familiar; they unsuccessfully stumble painfully and blindly to find reference points for a new identity or the restoration of the old.[17] We popularly call the resulting personal and group upheaval *culture shock*, yet the very naming of the 'disease' can mock the enormity of the human tragedy involved.

Paradoxically, chaos (if rightly used) can be the catalyst for enormous personal and group growth. Chaos provides us with a liminal space in which old familiar securities have gone and we can ask ourselves questions about the meaning of life and the authentic sources of human identity.

Recently, after serious heart surgery, I experienced a sadness or depression that generally follows such operations. While I had been a frequent visitor to Australia where the surgery was carried out, I developed a desperate yearning to return to my home country of New Zealand. I wanted to touch the trees so familiar to me in my youth, to see the sea and hills so distinctively New Zealand. Despite the warmth and support of my Australian friends, I felt an inner pain, a desperate loneliness that nothing seemed able to assuage. God appeared to have left me. If I was to be entirely healed – body and soul – I needed as soon as possible to return to my cultural spiritual/mythic roots. If anyone had said to me before the operation that this was how I would feel, I would have laughed at them. I would have said: 'I am an international person. I feel at home wherever I work!' Not true, I found. In the midst of my powerlessness I had to ask myself some serious questions about my relationship with God, the impact of my culture-of-origin on my life, and relive some scenes of my early life in which God had particularly revealed his love for me in the midst of darkness. The experience was energizing and creative in ways that would not have occurred if my secure world had not earlier fallen apart; I felt, as though for the first time, what it means to walk in the darkness of faith – waiting, listening, hoping, risking the unknown. The poet John Keats correctly believed that the foundation for creativity is 'negative capability . . . when a [person] is capable of being in uncertainties, mysteries, doubts, without any irritable reaching after fact and reason'.[18] St John of the Cross would have agreed with this insight.

Not everyone uses chaos as a catalyst for growth; some remain overwhelmed and paralysed by its confusion. However, stage 5 sets out two significant options open to those who recognize that nothing can be done about the chaos unless *they* are prepared to act themselves. There is the conversionist option, the one I was able to take after my heart surgery. Change is understood to be slow and at times filled with uncertainty, demanding tolerance, patience or an on-going struggle for inner and outer conversion and an openness to alternative or imaginative ways of doing things. The other significant option in this stage is to attempt anxiously to escape the frustration of chaos, by retreating as individuals or as groups into a comforting world of unreality, building a wall of intolerance around them and staying there; they remain rigid, see the world in black and white terms, and are deeply fearful of the new. The culture they form is neurotic, out of touch with reality. In this atmosphere all kinds of sects, cults and fads erupt such as were evident during the enormous cultural upheaval within the Western world of the late 1960s and early 1970s.

Sects are distinguished by various qualities: their leaders are gifted with ability to propose convincing, simplistic alternative ways of doing things; elitist and intolerant of diversity expressed in moral and/or physical violence against dissenters; inward-looking, hostile or indifferent to the contemporary secular world; beliefs at times are millenarian.[19] Millenarian or messianic movements, which have flourished within Christianity especially in times of social or religious turmoil, believe that change can be radical through the removal by divine intervention of all that disturbs the status quo; often this involves, as a prerequisite of one's authenticity or loyalty, the visible destruction of property or, in extreme situations, the marginalization or death of those opposing the movements.[20]

During the Expressive Cultural Revolution of the 1960s and 1970s two particular types of sects emerged: self-religions or inner-directed movements (e.g. encounter, therapeutic and rebirthing groups, the New Age) that offer ways for people to feel good within themselves. The second type of sect (sometimes popularly called 'the cults') embrace movements (e.g. the Unification Church or Moonies) that are highly authoritarian or have a 'this is the way it is' approach. Here the stress on individual identity and self-direction gives way to the dominance of the group; the individual's sense of belonging will come not so much from internal self-discipline, but from submission to the insistent demands of the group. Both groups of movements offer their followers reassurance within a chaotic world. Cults are a milder form of sect; fads are typified by the rapid, sudden and ephemeral collective adoption of novel behaviour that affects only superficial or trivial areas of life.

Fundamentalism can be a mark of these retreatist or reactionary movements. Reflecting on fundamentalist organizations within the world's mainline religions, Patrick Arnold defines fundamentalism as 'an aggressive and marginalized religious movement which, in reaction to the perceived threat of modernity, seeks to return its home religion and nation to traditional orthodox principles, values, and texts through the co-option of the central executive and legislative power of both the religion itself and the modern national state'.[21] James Hunter says that 'all fundamentalist sects share the deep and worrisome sense that history has gone awry. What "went wrong" with history is modernity in its various guises. The calling of the fundamentalist, therefore, is to make history right again.'[22] Hunter calls fundamentalism a form of 'organized anger'.[23] The contemporary fundamentalism within Islam aptly illustrates this definition. John Coleman highlights the way in which fundamentalists are ambiguous about modernity: 'Unlike world-rejecting sects and cults, fundamentalists seek to live in modernity (and influence its direction) but not be part of it'.[24]

The cultural breakdown model helps to illustrate the factors involved in the dramatic collapse of Soviet Communism.[25] Under Lenin and Stalin there was a revolution to impose on millions of people an authoritarian, rigid, self-contained, highly structured, secularized millenarian culture. Orthodoxy witch-hunts and the fear of punishment for people daring to transgress the demands of the totalitarian system were aimed at rigorously controlling the system. Mikhail Gorbachev offered dramatic changes through perestroika and glasnost, the freeing up of the Communist world. Communism had to be updated. So he articulated a radically different mythology upon which the Soviet Union's culture should be built: free elections, reduction of armaments and military strength, free press, freedom of worship, the right of trade unions to bargain collectively, an ultimate vision of a free-market economy.

Gorbachev's years fostered remarkable political flexibility, but economic and social chaos rapidly emerged; this was not at all surprising in view of the rigidity of the old Communist mythology. Legislation alone would not effect the desired freedom and socio-economic advances. The bureaucratic party elite became rapidly aware of the security, power and benefits they had to give up if the reforms were to succeed. This was too fearful an option for them, so they sought to stop the Gorbachev-led revolution in every way possible – by scapegoating reformers as traitors to the Communist cause and finally by attempting a coup to overthrow Gorbachev. The elite, under the direction of the coup leaders, like all good fundamentalists, claimed to be the only authentic keepers and interpreters of the Communist mythology. They professed that they were in favour of the reform movement but were anxious for the people about the harsh excesses of the chaos; once law and order had been re-established together with all the former 'protective' systems, the Soviet state would be set once more to achieve the Communist ideal way of life.

The insight of Alexis de Tocqueville is relevant here. Reflecting on the power of revolutionary forces, he said that dissatisfaction becomes increasingly evident whenever the conditions that give rise to it cease to be seen as inevitable and the possibility for correcting them arises. In these circumstances the momentum for change cannot be slowed down, even though some of the changes being introduced in the outpouring of enthusiasm may not be the most prudent.[26] For some seven decades the lid had been firmly kept on Soviet society by a ruthless authoritarian elite, but once it became clear that under Gorbachev an alternative system was possible then there was no stopping the onrush of political enthusiasm. The break-up of the Soviet Union into nation states could not be halted. The coup ultimately failed because its leaders could no longer be taken seriously; no matter what the chaos, these coup planners belonged to a former age and the people no longer feared them.

Application of the model to the Church

This example of what happened to the Soviet Union clarifies to some extent what has taken place within the Church since Vatican II. The patterns of change, chaos and revitalization efforts follow the stages set out in Figure 2.1 in both the Soviet Union and the Church. Both organizations had become over the years highly centralized and authoritarian, with no diversity or questioning of the centre allowed. The Gorbachev of the Church is John XXIII, the party conference of 1988 at which Gorbachev presented his vision is the Vatican II for the Church. Both men initiated a revolution, though some initial preparations were done through principled dissenters in both systems. For example, in the Church there were Henri de Lubac, Teilhard de Chardin, John Courtney Murray and Yves Congar, but like their Soviet counterparts they had been marginalized or silenced, though their influence would eventually be powerful within Vatican II itself. Like Gorbachev, John XXIII challenged the Church with a sweeping vision, the consequences of which, or the methods to realize it, he was unable to spell out in any detail. Nor could Vatican II. Both leaders struggled to open their respective cultures to worlds of extreme complexity economically, politically and socially. At the time of the Council the world was in a particularly tumultuous phase, the period we call the Expressive Cultural Revolution in which every basic value in the Western world was being challenged or turned upside-down.[27] John XXIII also faced growing opposition from within the Church's bureaucratic elite just as Gorbachev did within his party structure. One significant difference must be mentioned; John XXIII aimed to *refound* the Church according to a purified mythology, but Gorbachev sought rather to *found* for the first time a Soviet Union based on a mythology fundamentally opposed to that established by his predecessors. After the coup attempt Gorbachev finally had to admit he could not change the nation through the Communist party system for the latter's mythology was totally foreign to the axioms of open government and democracy.

Figure 2.2 summarizes what has occurred within the Church since Vatican II. Recall that the dominant symbol of the church culture in the pre-Vatican II world was a fortress, the perfect society, built and constantly

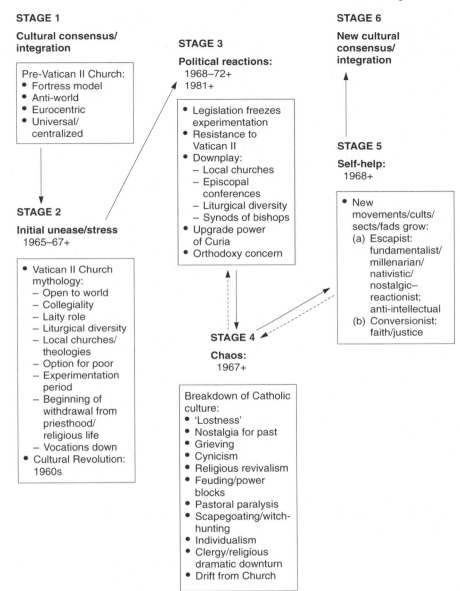

STAGE 1

Cultural consensus/ integration

Pre-Vatican II Church:
• Fortress model
• Anti-world
• Eurocentric
• Universal/ centralized

STAGE 2

Initial unease/stress
1965–67+

• Vatican II Church mythology:
  – Open to world
  – Collegiality
  – Laity role
  – Liturgical diversity
  – Local churches/ theologies
  – Option for poor
  – Experimentation period
  – Beginning of withdrawal from priesthood/ religious life
  – Vocations down
• Cultural Revolution: 1960s

STAGE 3

Political reactions:
1968–72+
1981+

• Legislation freezes experimentation
• Resistance to Vatican II
• Downplay:
  – Local churches
  – Episcopal conferences
  – Liturgical diversity
  – Synods of bishops
• Upgrade power of Curia
• Orthodoxy concern

STAGE 4

Chaos:
1967+

Breakdown of Catholic culture:
• 'Lostness'
• Nostalgia for past
• Grieving
• Cynicism
• Religious revivalism
• Feuding/power blocks
• Pastoral paralysis
• Scapegoating/witch-hunting
• Individualism
• Clergy/religious dramatic downturn
• Drift from Church

STAGE 6

New cultural consensus/ integration

STAGE 5

Self-help:
1968+

• New movements/cults/ sects/fads grow:
  (a) Escapist: fundamentalist/ millenarian/ nativistic/ nostalgic– reactionist; anti-intellectual
  (b) Conversionist: faith/justice

Figure 2.2 Reactions to Vatican II

reinforced to withstand the attacks of the enemies: Protestants, heretics and the evils of the Enlightenment. The boundaries of the fortress were sharply marked out and effectively patrolled lest people attempted to break in or out (that is, stage 1: cultural consensus/integration). Pope John, first by his example and then by words, challenged the familiar mythology of the fortress Church; people began to feel that alternative ways of doing things in the Church might now be possible and the Council legitimized this feeling of growing openness.

For example, the principle of collegiality runs like a thread through the Council documents at the level of the universal Church (through synods and episcopal conferences), and in the dioceses (priests' and parish councils). Individual bishops are no longer to be mere lieutenants of the Pope, but leaders in their own right. Pastors are to give greater recognition to the gifts of believers and seek their co-operation.[28] Considerable euphoria erupted among those who had long felt the need for a mythological balance to the excesses of the Roman centralized authoritarian culture, but at the same time a sense of unease began to surface at various levels. First, there were those who, while accepting the new balance in theory, were left wondering just how it was to be implemented. Others did not agree with the collegiality thrust at all and were out to stop it both during and after the Council.[29]

Following the Council, Rome issued various directives to guide the implementation of the conciliar documents; people hoped these regulations would enshrine for ever the restored mythology or at last put a stop to the malaise developing within the Church. Under John Paul II the latter aim predominates, but in favour of pre-Vatican II values. For example, the role of episcopal conferences and the bishops' synods and the collegial development of particular local churches have been significantly restricted. The revised Code of Canon Law was promulgated in 1983 and, as Ladislas Örsy notes, it 'offers little or no help for [the] evolution' (of particular churches) 'and we are all the poorer for it'.[30] The Code stresses the 'power to govern' and restricts this to those with orders, so that lay men and women do not share this power but must co-operate with the ordained. Here was a chance to move the Church forward and the Code did not do so, because historically lay people have at times exercised the power to govern and 'did participate in important decision-making processes, including synods and Council'.[31]

The chaos of stage 4 within the Church started about 1967 and continues to this day, but the period of greatest publicly expressed turmoil continued from roughly 1967 through to about 1972 exacerbated by the reactions to Paul VI's document *Humanae Vitae* of 1968. As mentioned in the introduction to this chapter, Berger's description of what happened is correct – the chaos expressed itself in ways 'ranging from masochistic self-laceration to hysterical defensiveness'. As an anthropologist, however, I need to repeat a fundamental point of this book: interfere with a culture's creation mythology – even for the noblest of reasons – and chaos results. Rapid culture change is not an abstract concept, but a high order of human drama in which most people feel uprooted, lost, disillusioned, angry. Vatican II had to be. The tragedy is that it was too long delayed, thus allowing the Catholic culture to become increasingly rigid and removed from reality. When change became possible through the Council, the explosion of expectations and anxiety-created counter-reactions startled all with its intensity and ferocity. If de Tocqueville had been living at the time, he might well have said: 'Did I not tell you it would happen this way!' The open polarizations and feuding, the name-calling, the often sensational ways in which priests and religious left their posts made millions of Catholics aware that Vatican II was not an abstract concept, but a human drama affecting the hearts and lives of all. It was not a time for cool, rational argument; people were grappling at the heart level with basic identity issues.[32]

Shortly after the Council's closing, signs characteristic of stage 5 began to emerge, for example various adjustment movements, cults and sects. Elsewhere I have analysed the combined influence on Catholics of Vatican II and the Expressive Cultural Revolution of the late 1960s.[33] Sufficient to note here that the world towards which the Church was opening its windows was in an unusually intense cultural upheaval; no value, custom or institution remained unaffected. The year 1968 marked the revitalization of old sects/cults or the formation of new ones, and many Catholics, especially younger members, turned to them for the identity and security they so needed. Examples are the Unification Church (Moonies), Hare Krishna, Zen and Ananda Marga. In general, among Catholics remaining within the Church we can distinguish two broad types of such groupings: people or grassroots movements and authority-led organizations, though sometimes these overlap and support one another. Both types are either escapist or conversionist.

I use the term 'escapist' to stress the point that movements of this type insulate their followers from the anxiety-evoking complex challenges of the Council by offering simplistic answers and instant identity/security systems. Theirs is a world of clear-cut contrasts: God/Satan, Christ/Anti-Christ, Christians/'secular humanists'.

The 1960s' Expressive Cultural Revolution was considered a most powerful example of 'satanic secular humanism'. On the one hand, it supported increased aid for the poor, civil rights, the rejection of the capitalist system, and anti-war rallies, and on the other hand, the relaxation of the existing anti-abortion and anti-pornography laws. People would point to the insidious impact of the revolution's secular humanism in such documents as *The Church in the Modern World* (Vat II), the encyclical *Populorum Progressio* (1967) by Paul VI, and *Justice in the World* by the Synod of Bishops (1971). If the Church continued to become involved in the support of social justice, it was said, where would it all end! The Church must withdraw immediately from its dangerous movement into the world. Thus sects like Catholics United for the Faith (CUF) were formed to defend the Church against the 'evils of secular humanism' or the 'liberalizing excesses that Vatican II' inspired; the Latin Mass movement gave some Catholics the nostalgic support they craved, and some eventually moved out of the Church to join the Lefebvre sect. A wide variety of cults developed around supposed apparitions of the Mother of God – for example, at Garabandal in Spain and Bayside, New York – and commonly their message was the same: the need to return to traditional practices of the Catholic faith; the world is basically evil; threats of imminent divine chastisement if the revelations are not listened to.[34] In brief, the message was: return to the pre-Vatican II Church or face the consequences! The Catholic Charismatic Renewal Movement developed from within North America in 1967 and became one of the major movements of the 1970s. However, it often fostered sect-like qualities contrary to Vatican II values – for example, opposition to commitments to social justice, elitism, fundamentalism with regard to the interpretation of the Scriptures and authoritarian male leadership.[35]

There are other movements of grassroots origins with retreatist, sect-like qualities that have subsequently become particularly supported by Rome. Opus Dei, made up of members of the hierarchy, priests and influential lay people, was founded in Madrid in 1928 by the controversial and recently beatified Escrivá de Balaguer. This movement has been described by Andrew Greeley as a 'devious, antidemocratic, reactionary, semi-fascist institution, desperately hungry for absolute power in the church. It ought to be forced either to come out into the open or be suppressed.'[36] Many would agree. The movement is decidedly anti-Vatican II, not simply because it has retained a Latin liturgy and various pious practices of a former age, but especially since it gives uncritical and powerful support to right-wing political groups in Latin America and to capitalistic structures in the West. Liberation theology or involvement in social justice issues and the development of Basic Christian Communities are seen by it as undermining the authority of the Church and the message of Christ. Despite this, the Pope has publicly and frequently supported the movement and in 1982 declared it the first personal prelature, thus giving it considerable independence from diocesan control and accountability.

A less secretive and papally supported movement is the Comunione e Liberazione of Italian origin, but like Opus Dei it is openly hostile to Vatican II theology.[37] Similarly antagonistic to the Council's mythology is the Neo-Catechumenate. Founded in Spain, it has similar qualities to the above organizations: theologically fundamentalist, an emphasis on an interiorized piety without commitment to social activism, authoritarian, secretive, elitist. When the movement is allowed into parishes it demands to be independent of parochial authorities and responsibilities. Inculturation is anathema to the movement's members for they allow no adaptation to local conditions or cultures; hence liturgies, including the hymns, are designed in Europe and imposed on their followers throughout the world with no alterations permitted. Despite these negative qualities, John Paul II published a letter on 30 August 1990 in praise of the movement 'as an itinerary of Catholic formation, valid for our society and for our times. It is therefore my desire, that the Brothers in the Episcopate – together with their presbyters – value and support this work for the new evangelization . . .' In practice, this papal support is giving the movement something of the exemption from diocesan control that Opus Dei has been officially assigned.

Fundamentalism is a quality found in all the above grassroots movements. Self-righteously, they take upon themselves the duty to smell out anything they consider unorthodox and then with harshness condemn the wayward. They are highly selective about what is at the heart of the Church's teaching, conveniently overlooking the social documents and concentrating instead on matters of lesser importance, for example liturgical rubrics, or on issues of private sexuality. At times Catholic fundamentalists are estimable leaders in the anti-abortion campaign, but wider issues of social justice are overlooked and anyone involved in them is apt to be branded as a 'reckless liberal'. Their assumption is that history must be put right and the Church rescued from the 'dangerous modernists' and returned to its 'golden pre-Vatican II era'.[38] They actively look to Rome to use its coercive power 'to put the Church right'. And Rome responds positively. At first sight these new movements appear to be thoroughly concerned about the need to preach the Gospel creatively to a changing world – for example, Opus Dei urges its followers to be active citizens. However, their vision of what they want the world to be is that of the patriarchal pre-Vatican II Church. Theologian Joe Holland perceptively comments that the

> new wave of postmodern lay communities are tempted to pursue a cultural strategy of classical restoration, rather than of postmodern regeneration. Such a strategy would . . . restore exclusively the classical transcendent and hierarchical disclosure of the masculine face of God . . . [It] would attempt to reassert patriarchy . . . as an authoritarian means of combating the disintegrating crisis of late modern culture . . . [and] approach society predominately in fear and resentment rather than in compassion and healing.[39]

Rome not only openly supports many of these fundamentalist-oriented organizations, but itself appoints people such as anti-Council bishops who then initiate movements with fundamentalist qualities. Paradoxically, at the same time the Pope has published some social encyclicals, for example *Sollicitudo Rei Socialis* (1987), that radically critique society according to Vatican II values of justice which fundamentalist bishops and Catholics immediately overlook. Rome invariably ignores complaints about what is happening.[40]

Fundamentalism is not a disease of the right alone, because it also exists among people who intolerantly condemn anything of the *past* as evil or contrary to Vatican II values. Like all fundamentalists, there is a destructive violence behind this intolerance – either one is for the movement or one is not, there are no grey areas. To prove one's loyalty, therefore, one must destroy ideas or ways of acting that may give the impression that one is compromising. If there is any compromise, then the desired security would not eventuate. This is the naïvety of millenarianism, as Thomas Merton reported in 1968, to be found among Catholics who repudiate everything of the pre-Vatican II Church. They are as dangerous to truth and freedom as those seeking to destroy everything that is new in the Church.[41] This uncritically accepted anti-traditionalism has caused untold harm to Catholics when it has resulted in, for example, the insensitive destruction of popular religiosity in its many forms. With intolerant fervour, pastoral agents helped to undermine the faith of people by scorning their pious devotion to the Mother of God and patron saints, failing to see that millions desire to express their faith in the Lord through concrete symbols and actions. Popular religiosity is a way of life and to undermine it without due cause is to leave people in a cultural–religious vacuum, a prey to all kinds of fundamentalist sects.[42]

Conversionist groupings within the Church embrace a wide variety of communities or movements that have sprung up inspired by the Council's urging to take a radical stand for Gospel values in the world. For example, there are forms of parish updating like RENEW and the revitalized Ignatian spiritual exercises to give life and vigour to the apostolic life of laity, religious and priests. The Basic Christian Communities (BCCs) of South America and Asia are essentially lay movements in which small groups of generally poor people meet to reflect on the Bible, pray and work for justice.[43] Unlike the escapist movements, these gatherings recognize that life is a journey of faith in and through darkness: 'Now we see only reflections in a mirror, mere riddles, but then we shall be seeing face to face. Now, I can know only imperfectly; but then I shall know just as fully as I am myself known' (1 Cor 13:12). BCCs understand that the world is complex, demanding of people mutual support and discernment in order to discover how to live the Gospel in a rapidly changing society. And no one can escape the commitment to struggle for justice in *this* world as it is integral to the life of the Christ, a symbol of 'the new heavens and new earth' yet to come 'where uprightness will be at home' (2 Pet 3:13).

What particular lesson can we draw from this model of analysis? Our inability to tolerate ambiguity when confronted by complicated issues and problems makes us vulnerable to anything that offers instant relief. We fear chaos. We want instant assurance that we have the total truth right now, not tomorrow! This is the sure road to fundamentalism within the Church. Sooner or later, however, each of us must accept the fact that the way to relate the Gospel to the changing world demands a constant searching. In the refounding process pastoral order begins in chaos and we can never say in this post-Vatican II world that we are ever fully out of it. As William Blake wrote: 'without contraries, there is no progression' (*The Marriage of Heaven and Hell*). Recall also the conversion story of the apostle Thomas. At first he acted like a fundamentalist when he demanded as a condition of his belief that he 'see the holes that the nails made in [Christ's] hands' (Jn 20:25). When Jesus appeared later, Thomas had his condition fulfilled, but he was then rebuked for his insistence on human rather than faith certitude: 'You believe because you can see me. Blessed are those who have not seen and yet believe' (Jn 20:29).

The following model now looks at the restorationist trend from a somewhat different perspective; we are able to see a little more sharply the way leadership can negatively or positively influence an entire organization.

Model 2: The Church – from a 'growing' to an 'ageing' culture

Ichak Adizes distinguishes two variables in his method of evaluating cultures of groups: flexibility and controllability.[44] *Growing* or *youthful* cultures encourage considerable flexibility; since they have not yet become set in their ways there is a readiness to take on new ventures. The lessons of tradition are respected, but it is not the sole or primary factor influencing decision-making. *Ageing* cultures, however, have lost flexibility and have developed principles of control or powerful traditions that obstruct adaptability or creativity in the face of changing conditions. Most commonly, youthful cultures become ageing ones; we grow weary of having to live in an unpredictable world of experimentation and the on-going change that this involves. We fall victim to the comforting predictability of an orderly life with its network of status, power and prestige positions. Youthful experimentation is less and less attractive to us, so all kinds of resistance mechanisms at the level of the culture unconscious emerge and discourage change. We then assume all is going well and significant improvements are no longer necessary or even desirable; there is nothing to be learnt from the experience of others. This self-conscious assumption of perfection is termed the 'utopian flaw' and, if left unchallenged, it is the sure recipe for disaster and the eventual death of the group, as the following case study shows.[45]

Case study: The utopian flaw paralyses a congregation

In the early 1970s a survey was conducted of a province of a religious congregation which was then heavily committed to private education. Its schools had been established over several decades through the inventiveness, hard work and sacrifices of teachers and parents. However, at the time of the survey, signs of the ageing culture were clear. Despite the fact that most congregational teachers were poorly trained as educators by government standards, a high percentage of respondents felt that they had little to learn from government-run schools about teaching methods and management planning. One respondent summed up the general feeling: 'Our schools have a quality about them that is the envy of the state system of education. Really we have nothing to learn from them.'

In fact by 1990 the culture of the religious schools had become so aged that it lacked the inner vitality to recognize, and respond to, the fact that the congregation could no longer supply teachers since recruitment had fallen off so dramatically. Many teachers continued to believe that the congregation faced no significant problem at all in its schools. In the late 1980s several devoted teachers in the congregation attempted to challenge their colleagues within the schools with the facts, but they were branded as being 'anti Catholic education' and 'radicals'. Eventually the congregation had to withdraw from most of their schools without leaving any significant infrastructure to guarantee some kind of on-going congregational presence.

The primary task of the officially appointed leadership of a group involves acknowledging and then acting to stop the ageing process. Sensitive leaders will normally aim to achieve the correct balance between the polar opposites of control/tradition – flexibility/innovation. Where this balance is occurring we can speak of an organization having a *prime* culture. Ultimately, if leadership fails to foster the appropriate equilibrium, then pathology will emerge and lead to the disintegration of the organizational culture. The ageing culture would have so lost touch with reality that revitalization is impossible. St Paul and others see this danger by acknowledging that the early Church has become so comfortable with the settled ways of its already ageing culture that non-Jews are being forced to accept Jewish customs as a precondition for becoming Christian. So Paul and Peter draw on their leadership authority and forthrightly summon the Church to admit that its early apostolic dynamism has faded: 'Why do you put God to the test now by imposing on the disciples the very burden that neither our ancestors nor we ourselves were strong enough to support?' (Acts 15:10). They succeed, and the Church enters again into a new missionary Pentecost; it is saved from becoming an irrelevant and dying sect. In the above case study of the religious schools, the province's congregational leader refused to accept the findings of the survey that warned of what would happen to the province's involvement in education if the denial in the congregational culture remained unchallenged. In so doing, he refused to claim his rightful authority to lead.

Growing and ageing organizational cultures are similar in many ways to organic and mechanistic cultures of organizations as described by T. Burns and G. Stalker (see summary in Figure 2.3).[46] Within *organic* cultures there are few rules and regulations; the emphasis is on innovation, creativity and evaluative feedback in order that the organization may keep responding adequately to a changing world. The leadership fosters in organic cultures a participative and transformative atmosphere in which people feel they can create and be supported by others in the group. Decision-making is primarily *proactive* rather than *reactive* or crisis solving. That is, organic administrations consist of 'anticipative people'; as they see changes are about to happen they plan ways to adapt to them, recognizing the need to create and control change rather than being its passive agent.

In *mechanistic* cultures, on the other hand, the tasks of the organization are considered predictable or unchanging; the leadership's role is to ensure

	CULTURES	
	Growing/organic culture	**Ageing/mechanistic culture**
Vision	Clearly articulated; outward/change oriented	Clearly articulated; inward/status-quo oriented
Risk	Prepared to accept ambiguity as integral to risk-taking	Fearful of ambiguity
Mission	Priority over maintenance of status quo	Status quo has priority
Structures	For growth	For status quo
Creativity	Vigorously encouraged	Vigorously discouraged; priorities given to tradition
Evaluation	Emphasis on reality testing to assess effectiveness	Reality testing not needed
Rules	Constantly checked lest they obstruct creativity	Multiplied to maintain status quo
Leaders	Not primarily administrators; concern: creating, articulating a vision and strategizing for action/evaluation	Primarily administrators; priority given to detailed planning/status quo
Conflict resolution	Through negotiation/ dialogue	Through suppression/ coercion

Figure 2.3

that these long-established and neatly set-out rules of operation are being followed. Creativity is unnecessary and to be discouraged because it threatens a predictable way of acting. Such cultures are totally unsuited for a world in change. Before Vatican II the Church had become a mechanistic culture, the very culture that Paul and Peter told the Council of Jerusalem was alien to Christ's missionary message. This mechanistic culture affected all levels of Church life. For example, I once reviewed the provincial chapter decrees of an apostolic male congregation from 1894 to 1956. Never at any point was there reference to the need for pastoral creativity; instead, the emphasis was on control through the maintenance of detailed disciplinary rules. In the decrees of the chapter of 1900, phrases like 'the present Chapter reasserts the prohibition against' are commonplace and repeated in all subsequent chapters.

Both culture types will need leaders of vision, but there will be a fundamental difference in the nature of visions. While one leader will call the culture to be outward and proactive in the face of new challenges, as Paul and Peter did at the Council of Jerusalem, the other leader will call for the maintenance of the status quo, as did Pius IX and his successors up to

Vatican II; both will articulate the vision frequently and clearly in order to be effective.[47]

Application of the model to the contemporary Church

Pope John XXIII's revolutionary intuition has already been referred to – namely, that the Church desperately needed to be brought up to date and be made effective as a dynamic evangelizing force within the contemporary world. This insight led to the decision to call the Council and it pervaded every document that emerged from its deliberations. He impressed on the assembly the need to listen to the world and to respond with understanding and mercy, not with condemnations characteristic of previous such gatherings.[48] Like all great charismatic leaders, this Pope impressed people with his inspirational vision, but he died before he could lead the Church through the practical implications of the Council. The Council's overall thrust was that a new youthful, growth-oriented culture should emerge throughout the Church aided by appropriate structures, but it was unable to spell out in detail what they should be except in two significant cases: the synod of bishops and episcopal conferences.

While it can be difficult to initiate a revolution in ideas and structures, it is far more challenging to guide the process of change. Even though many would think Paul VI's reiteration of traditional teaching on birth control in *Humanae Vitae* (1968) was disastrous, many would still agree that Paul VI genuinely sought to encourage the Church to become a growth/evangelization-oriented culture. Significant groups sought to halt the process and return the Church to the pre-Vatican II ageing/mechanistic culture. For example, in 1972 he was pressured by some, including Cardinal Wojtyła, the future John Paul II, to make the theme of the 1974 synod of bishops 'respect for the magisterium and orthodoxy'. Theologians, they felt, should be sharply reminded that they must be without question subject to the magisterium. Paul VI resisted this move and decided instead to take evangelization as the theme of the synod.[49] Eventually in 1975 he published the most outward-looking document on evangelization since Vatican II: *Evangelii Nuntiandi*. Though he criticized many experiments in liturgy and refused to face issues like the ordination of women and of married men, he did not use any dramatic disciplinary directives. He showed particular concern for the poor in the Third World, both in his writings and travels, deliberately fostering interest in the emerging theology of inculturation. In short, I judge that overall Paul VI remained true to the youthful openness of Vatican II theology, despite the enormous reactionary forces allied against him.

John Paul II is also a man of vision, but, unlike his predecessor Paul VI, he is particularly clear about the structures and strategies needed for his vision to be realized. He was determined from the beginning of his pontificate in 1978 to end the confusion catalysed by the Council; from an outward-oriented culture he would seek to move the Church back to a culture that has its boundaries clearly defined and fully under control – that is, from a growth-oriented/organic culture to an ageing/mechanistic one. As a Pole he saw the Western world grown morally and religiously soft and he would sternly challenge it to resist materialistic and secularistic values.[50] There is even a touch of messianism to his thought and action. The intensity of the sufferings of the Polish people and the consequent depth of their faith convince him that they are the model for the entire Church, especially in the West. On a recent visit to Poland he said publicly that 'We do not have to become a part of Europe, we created it. We created it, incurring greater hardships than those who are credited with, or who credit themselves with, being the keepers of the European spirit.'[51] The Church in Poland has a mission to re-evangelize Europe and to be an example to the entire world of faithfulness to the Gospel in the midst of persecution, the decadence of Western materialism and secularism.

The Pope is zealous and tireless in his efforts to preach the Word. Yet his image of the Church is hierarchically vertical or pyramidal according to the pre-Vatican II model. On the one hand, therefore, he can exhort Catholics to be bold in preaching the Gospel,[52] but it is to be a boldness *within* the rule-oriented structures of a mechanistic culture. The atmosphere of negativity[53] that he complains of is a result mainly of this over-stress on the dated model of the Church. Apostolic boldness directed at secularism and the demands of re-evangelization are impossible within a Church where people are fearful of being reported to bishops and the Roman curia for daring to devise refounding pastoral strategies. Everything is against such pastoral boldness developing and being sustained.

As mentioned in Chapter 1, the Pope frequently speaks of the need for inculturation – that is, 'the synthesis between culture and faith is not just a demand of culture, but also of faith'. For him, 'a faith which does not become culture is a faith which has not been fully received, not thoroughly thought through, not fully lived out'.[54] However, his emphasis in practice is to foster a mechanistic church culture that effectively inhibits grassroots freedom within local churches for incarnating the Gospel. I agree with Aylward Shorter's assessment: 'One feels that he [the Pope] appreciates the synthesis in the historic cultures of Christian Europe, and fears for their future, while at the same time hesitating to risk the deposit of faith in a dialogue with the cultures of the non-Christian Third World'.[55]

The Pope's appointment of Cardinal Ratzinger as prefect of the Congregation for the Doctrine of the Faith in early 1982 caused concern to evangelizers committed to a culture of openness and apostolic boldness within the Church. A reading of the cardinal's evaluation of the post-Vatican II Church published in 1985 does nothing to dispel this concern.[56] Even allowing for obvious excesses following the Council, the emotive and condemnatory expressions he uses of the post-conciliar years are disturbing (e.g. a period of 'self-destruction', 'discouragement' and 'decadence').[57] The model of the Church as 'the people of God' causes him anxiety,[58] as also the prominence being given to the teaching role of episcopal conferences. He highlights the relevance of the necessity of excommunication as a way ultimately to control theologians or others threatening the purity of the Church's teaching.[59] Overall, there is a negativity and an undisguised fear of the new throughout the book; nothing is said about the need to interact positively with the world or the role of prophetic persons who risk the new for the building of the Kingdom. It is a depressing book.

Vatican II highlighted the need for us to look at authority as service exercised through subsidiarity and co-responsibility. This means that all structures in the Church must be frequently assessed for their effectiveness in the exercise of an authority understood as functional and diffused among the people of God. Where necessary, new structures must be established. When the new Code was promulgated in January 1983 one expected to find these guidelines clearly respected and fostered, but overall the hierarchical structures have been further enhanced to the detriment of collegiality. As one canonist writes: 'If one simply reads the new code precisely, one recognizes behind the pleasant-sounding formulations a papal "emergency powers law" for the universal church. How can collegiality between people and bishops continue to develop in such a framework?'[60] Sister Marie Augusta Neal, a widely celebrated sociologist of religion, writes with deep concern about the restrictions – for example, the way in which authority/obedience is to be exercised – that the new Code places on religious who belong to the charismatic structures of the Church:

> Many Catholic sisters face a serious dilemma of obedience in the 1980s and will continue to do so in the 1990s. This dilemma takes the form of a conflict between honoring Vatican Council mandates to prophetic ministry and resuming the traditional form of the vow of obedience in the practice of submission to the will of a specific person in a position of authority.[61]

She rightly complains that despite the years of experimentation and lived experience of collegial governance and shared authority within many congregations, the new Code reaffirms the traditional assumption that the decision-making power of one person as administrator and ultimate authority is the only form possible and therefore to be followed. Sandra Schneiders, also an acute observer of trends in religious life, argues that all Vatican documents on religious life since 1969 have 'witnessed to a gradual but steady retrenchment of even the moderate openness of the Council'.[62]

The particular structures established by Vatican II to express collegiality and openness for mission are the episcopal conferences and the bishops' synod.[63] Both structures were taken up with considerable enthusiasm, but their initiatives and effectiveness have weakened as the centre has increased its control over them. Control began over the episcopal conferences with the Extraordinary Synod of 1969 which had been convoked to deal with the reactions to *Humanae Vitae*. Comments from various conferences on the document had not been uniform, so the present Pope, as Cardinal

Wojtyła, warned against the dangers of 'nationalism', which 'always and everywhere is and will be most dangerous to the unity, faith and charity of the Church'.[64] This view prevailed. For example, the new Code concretizes the weakened status of the conferences. It speaks about the collaborative rights of the episcopal conferences in about ninety places, but on careful evaluation it is clear that allowances made for decentralization are outweighed by the emphasis given to the role of Rome. The function of the conferences is frequently seen to be of limited importance compared to that of individual bishops; secondly, the approval of the Holy See for their decrees and resolutions is needed.[65]

However, many bishops maintain that the conferences are able to have a far greater pastoral impact than a bishop acting alone. Archbishop (later Cardinal) James Hickey of Washington, DC, commented in 1982 that 'Our collective exercise of the teaching office is necessary to answer specific challenges that arise for us from the collective life of the nation'.[66] In their report for the 1985 bishops' synod, the bishops of England and Wales are reacting to Roman centralism when they assert that 'The role of the . . . bishops' conference in protecting both diversity and unity inevitably brings tension, but this can be seen as a creative aspect of the life of the Church and not to be resolved by recourse to uniformity of practice'.[67] The report complains that their conference has to refer to Rome matters that should be within its own competency, for example 'recognition of particular laws'.[68]

The Roman bishops' synods, the second significant structure established by the Council, are to act 'in the name of the entire Catholic episcopate' and they will 'demonstrate that all the bishops in hierarchical communion share in the responsibility for the universal church'.[69] This structure, which could have been a powerful force to call all sections of the Church to be accountable, including the Roman curia itself, has been reduced to a simple advisory group that basically approves of what has been previously decided by Rome itself. Again the English and Welsh bishops complain about the lessened status of the bishops' synod: 'The Synod of Bishops should be seen as a more effective expression of collegiality and its processes revised in the light of experience. The original purposes of the synod included "facilitating agreement on central points of doctrine and on methods of procedure in the life of the Church".'[70]

At the 1991 synod on priestly formation a number of bishops publicly spoke about the urgency to review the celibacy law as a precondition for ordination. They spoke movingly about the lack of priests in their dioceses, for example in South America, but the issue was quietly and effectively pushed aside by the synod's moderators – scarcely an example of dialogue for mission or of 'facilitating agreement on . . . methods of procedure in the life of the Church'! The fact is that the Church will require by the end of the century over seventy thousand priests but there will be available only about a third of this number; approximately half of them will be aged 55 or over with only an eighth aged 34 or younger.[71] There is every possibility within a few years that some dioceses in the world will have no priests whatsoever. What has the theological priority: eucharistic communities or a celibate clergy? Yet Rome refuses to allow open discussion and debate about the possibility of married and/or women priests. This is the negation of the dialogue and accountability demanded by Vatican II.

Summary

Many forces helped cause the disintegration of the traditional Catholic culture, but Vatican II was undoubtedly the most significant long-term factor. For centuries the Church had become an inward-looking culture: anti-world, defensive, personal piety-based, highly stratified and rule-oriented. But the Council articulated a mythology challenging the existing culture to its very roots and the reactions to this within the Church are similar to those found within cultures everywhere when they experience sudden disintegration. The reality is, and the Church is no exception, that cultures or organizations in transition are not a pretty sight; the atmosphere becomes thick with confusion, tensions, polarizations, scapegoating and low morale.

The Council's call to refound the Church means not an escape from the world, but the development of creative pastoral schemes to relate the Gospel to the issues of today. This requires a high tolerance of ambiguity with chaos as we grapple with the pastoral implications of Vatican II's mythology. Many in the Church find the ambiguity and patience too much to take and they yearn for simplistic answers and the return to the order of the pre-Vatican II Church. Sect or fundamentalist movements, such as Opus Dei and the Neo-Catechumenate, provide their followers with a refuge from a fear-evoking world and a reason not to be involved in the struggle for justice. Rome sympathetically and actively supports both this yearning and fundamentalist groups, and is leading the Church back to the dependent, highly structured and hierarchically oriented culture of the pre-Council era.

Unlike Pope John XXIII, the present Pope saw the purpose of the Council as primarily defensive or as an opportunity to protect doctrinal orthodoxy, not as a springboard for a revitalized mission to the world.[72] So today we are encountering the wide-ranging effects of his interpretation of the Council's purpose, such as the weakening of collegiality, the return to a clericalism, an anti-world ideology, and the support of anti-Council fundamentalist movements. If the process continues the Church will become more and more a sect-like organization, a refuge for frightened defensive people, with a message that is increasingly irrelevant to a world crying out for the meaning to be found in the message of the Lord. A sect that does not 'bear fruit in love of one's neighbor and in justice directed toward the life of the world is worth nothing', rightly declares Bernard Häring.[73] Restorationists would be wise to heed this warning.

The next chapter analyses the factors that are causing the contemporary vigorous insistence on orthodoxy and secrecy within the Church; both are symptoms of the anti-Council movement encouraged from the top.

Notes

1. M. Douglas, *Natural Symbols: Explorations in Cosmology* (New York: Pantheon Books, 1970), p. 38.
2. J. W. O'Malley, 'Developments, Reforms, and Two Great Reformations: Toward a Historical Assessment of Vatican II', *Theological Studies*, vol. 44, no. 3 (1983), p. 406.
3. P. Berger, *Facing up to Modernity* (Harmondsworth: Penguin, 1977), pp. 227f.
4. Ibid., p. 228.
5. H. de Lubac, *The Splendour of the Church*, trans. M. Mason (London: Sheed & Ward, 1956), p. 114.
6. C. Geertz, *The Interpretations of Cultures* (New York: Basic Books, 1973), p. 89.
7. E. Hall, *Beyond Culture* (Garden City, NY: Anchor Books, 1977), p. 43.
8. See helpful insights of E. H. Schein, *Organizational Culture and Leadership* (San Francisco: Jossey-Bass, 1987), *passim*.
9. For a fuller explanation of symbol, myth and ritual, see G. A. Arbuckle, *Earthing the Gospel: An Inculturation Handbook for Pastoral Workers* (London: Geoffrey Chapman / Maryknoll, NY: Orbis Books, 1990), pp. 26–43. I am especially grateful to Adolfo Nicolas for the definition of symbol as given here.
10. See overview of W. G. Dotty, *Mythology: The Study of Myths and Rituals* (Tuscaloosa, AL: University of Alabama Press, 1986), *passim*.
11. See R. N. Bellah *et al.* for an analysis of the tensions between the polar opposites in the American founding story: *Habits of the Heart: Individualism and Commitment in American Life* (San Francisco: Harper & Row, 1985), *passim*.
12. O'Malley, op. cit., p. 395. Also see relevant insights of O'Malley, 'Reform, Historical Consciousness and Vatican II's Aggiornamento', *Theological Studies*, vol. 32, no. 4 (1971), pp. 573–601.
13. See Arbuckle, op. cit., pp. 167–86.
14. See E. Hall, *The Silent Language* (New York: Doubleday, 1959), *passim*.
15. See M. F. Kets de Vries and D. Miller, *The Neurotic Organization* (San Francisco: Jossey-Bass, 1985), *passim*.
16. The model of culture change used here is adapted from A. F. C. Wallace, 'Revitalization Movements', *American Anthropologist*, vol. 58 (1956), pp. 264–81.
17. For an analysis of the symptoms of grieving, see G. A. Arbuckle, *Grieving for Change: A Spirituality for Refounding Gospel Communities* (London: Geoffrey Chapman, 1991), pp. 1–58.
18. Cited by I. Menzies Lyth, *The Dynamics of the Social: Selected Essays* (London: Free Association, 1989), p. 3.
19. See Arbuckle, *Earthing the Gospel*, op. cit., pp. 113–29.
20. Ibid., pp. 116–18; see also N. Cohn, *The Pursuit of the Millennium: Revolutionary Millenarians and Mystical Anarchists of the Middle Ages* (New York: Oxford University Press, 1974), *passim*, and K. Burridge, *New Heaven, New Earth: A Study of Millenarian Activities* (Oxford: Basil Blackwell, 1969), *passim*.

21. P. Arnold, 'The Reemergence of Fundamentalism in the Catholic Church' in N. J. Cohen (ed.), *The Fundamentalist Phenomenon* (Grand Rapids, MI: W. B. Eerdmans, 1990), p. 174.

22. J. Hunter, 'Fundamentalism in its Global Contours', ibid., p. 59.

23. Ibid., p. 63; T. F. O'Meara helpfully defines Christian fundamentalism as 'an interpretation of Christianity in which a charismatic leader locates with easy certitude in chosen words, doctrines and practices the miraculous actions of a strict God saving an elite from an evil world': *Fundamentalism: A Catholic Perspective* (New York: Paulist Press, 1990), p. 18.

24. J. Coleman, 'Global Fundamentalism: Sociological Perspectives', *Concilium* (1992/3), p. 39.

25. I gratefully draw on the insights of R. P. McBrien as presented in his keynote address at the 4th Annual Future of the American Church Conference, Washington, DC, 20 September 1991, as printed in *The Furrow*, vol. 42, no. 12 (December 1991), pp. 679–91.

26. A. de Tocqueville, *L'Ancien Régime* (Oxford: Oxford University Press, 1904), p. 182.

27. See Arbuckle, *Earthing the Gospel*, op. cit., pp. 119f.

28. See 'Dogmatic Constitution on the Church' in W. M. Abbott (ed.), *The Documents of Vatican II* (London: Geoffrey Chapman, 1966), pp. 56f.

29. See P. Hebblethwaite, 'Changing Vatican Policies 1965–85: Peter's Primacy and the Reality of Local Churches' in T. M. Gannon (ed.), *World Catholicism in Transition* (New York: Macmillan, 1988), pp. 39–43; also R. P. McBrien, 'The Church (Lumen Gentium)' in A. Hastings (ed.), *Modern Catholicism: Vatican II and After* (London: SPCK, 1991), pp. 84–95.

30. 'The Revision of Canon Law' in Hastings, op. cit., p. 212.

31. Ibid., pp. 211f.

32. For a conservative overview of the chaos and its causes, see G. A. Kelly, *The Battle for the American Church* (Garden City, NY: Image Books, 1981), and A. R. Muggeridge, *The Desolate City: Revolution in the Catholic Church* (San Francisco: Harper & Row, 1986).

33. See Arbuckle, *Earthing the Gospel*, op. cit., pp. 120–7.

34. See C. J. Mauder, 'Marian Apparitions' in Hastings, op. cit., pp. 280–2; M. T. Walsh offers relevant pastoral comments on Marian visionary cults: 'Medjugorje: A Pastoral Response', *America*, vol. 162, no. 15 (21 April 1990), pp. 403–4, 414; S. L. Zimdars-Swartz, *Encountering Mary: From La Salette to Medjugorje* (New York: Princeton University Press, 1991), *passim*.

35. See *The Catholic Pentecostal Movement: Creative or Divisive Enthusiasm* (Brussels: Pro Mundi Vita), bulletin no. 60 (1975), pp. 30–4.

36. Cited by P. Lernoux, *People of God: The Struggle for World Catholicism* (New York: Penguin, 1989), p. 320. For a critical analysis of Opus Dei, see M. J. Walsh, *The Secret World of Opus Dei* (London: Grafton Books, 1989). M. J. West claims to counter the criticism in his book *Opus Dei: Exploding a Myth* (Sydney: Little Hills Press, 1987), but he avoids the real grounds for concern.

37. See Lernoux, pp. 302–46, and M. J. Walsh, 'The Conservative Reaction' in Hastings, op. cit., pp. 283–8.

38. See comments by P. M. Arnold, 'The Rise of Catholic Fundamentalism', *America*, vol. 156, no. 14 (11 April 1987), pp. 298–302.

39. 'The Postmodern Cultural Transition: Its Challenge to the "Vowed Life" ', Draft Background Paper to Conference of Major Superiors of Men, USA, 8 August 1990, p. 21. See also Coleman, op. cit., pp. 38f.

40. For example, Sean McDonagh records the frustration of priests in a diocese of the Philippines in *The Tablet* (London) (25 May 1991), p. 648.

41. T. Merton, 'Cargo Cults in the South Pacific', *America*, vol. 121, no. 5 (1969), p. 96.

42. See Arbuckle, *Earthing the Gospel*, op. cit., pp. 108–11.

43. See ibid., pp. 86–8.
44. See I. Adizes, *Corporate Lifecycles: How and Why Corporations Grow and Die and What to do about Them* (Englewood Cliffs, NJ: Prentice-Hall, 1988).
45. See D. O'Murchu, *Sharing the Vision* (Birmingham: NACCAN, 1987), pp. 11f.
46. See T. Burns and G. Stalker, 'Mechanistic and Organic Systems' in J. N. Shafritz and P. W. Whitbeck (eds), *Classics of Organization Theory* (Oak Park, IL: Moore, 1978), pp. 207–11; J. P. Kotter, *A Force for Change: How Leadership Differs from Management* (New York: Free Press, 1990), p. 36.
47. See relevant comments by M. P. Hornsby-Smith, *Roman Catholic Beliefs in England: Customary Catholicism and Transformations of Religious Authority* (Cambridge: Cambridge University Press, 1991), pp. 192–6.
48. See John XXIII, opening address to the Council: Abbott, op. cit., p. 716.
49. See P. Hebblethwaite, op. cit. (note 29 above), p. 48; for an overview of Paul VI's approach to inculturation, see A. Shorter, *Toward a Theology of Inculturation* (London: Geoffrey Chapman, 1988), pp. 206–21.
50. See H. S. Hughes, *Sophisticated Rebels: The Political Culture of European Dissent – 1968-1987* (Cambridge, MA: Harvard University Press, 1990), pp. 67–79.
51. Cited by P. Hebblethwaite, 'The Pope's Polish Crusade', *The Tablet* (15 June 1991), p. 728 and 'A Fundamentalist Pope?', *Concilium* (1992/3), pp. 91f.; and A. Nowotny, 'Fortress Catholicism: Wojtyła's Polish Roots' in H. Küng and L. Swidler (eds), *The Church in Anguish: Has the Vatican Betrayed Vatican II?* (San Francisco: Harper & Row, 1987), pp. 21–8.
52. See John Paul II, Encyclical Letter *Mission of the Redeemer* (Boston: St Paul Books, 1991), pp. 109f.
53. See ibid., p. 10.
54. *L'Osservatore Romano* (28 June 1982): cited by Shorter, op. cit., p. 231.
55. Shorter, op. cit., p. 231. S. B. Bevans writes incisively on how John Paul II views evangelization and culture: *Models of Contextual Theology* (Maryknoll, NY: Orbis Books, 1992), pp. 42–6.
56. See J. Ratzinger with V. Messori, *The Ratzinger Report: An Exclusive Interview on the State of the Church*, (San Francisco: Ignatius Press, 1985).
57. See ibid., p. 28.
58. See ibid., pp. 48f.
59. See ibid., pp. 24–6.
60. K. Walf, 'The New Canon Law – The Same Old System' in Küng and Swidler, op. cit., p. 99 and *passim*.
61. M. A. Neal, *From Nuns to Sisters: An Expanding Vocation* (Mystic, CT: Twenty-Third Publications, 1990), p. 89.
62. S. Schneiders, 'Religious Life (Perfectae Caritatis)' in Hastings, op. cit., p. 158.
63. See 'Decree on Bishops' Pastoral Office': Abbott, op. cit., pp. 424–6.
64. Cited by P. Hebblethwaite, *The Tablet* (30 April 1983), p. 401.
65. See Walf, op. cit., p. 97. The US Episcopal Conference was told by Rome that it did not have the skills to write a pastoral letter on peace. See P. Hebblethwaite, 'The Pope and the Bishops', *The Tablet* (30 April 1983), pp. 400–1, and J. Kerkhofs, *Vatican II: Twenty Years On – The Extraordinary Synod, 25 November – 8 December 1985* (Brussels: Pro Mundi Vita, 1985), pp. 47–51; for comments by Cardinal Ratzinger, see *The Ratzinger Report*, op. cit., pp. 59–61.
66. J. Hickey, 'The Bishop as Teacher', *Origins*, vol. 12, no. 9 (1982), p. 142; see A. Dulles for a review of the teaching authority of bishops' conferences: *The Reshaping of Catholicism: Current Challenges in the Theology of Church* (New York: Harper & Row, 1988), pp. 207–26.
67. Submission of Bishops' Conference of England and Wales to the 1985 Bishops' Synod, *The Tablet* (3 August 1985), p. 816.

68. Ibid., p. 814.
69. 'Decree on Bishops' Pastoral Office in the Church': Abbott, op. cit., p. 400.
70. Submission of Bishops' Conference of England and Wales, op. cit., p. 814.
71. See M. Leach, 'New Thought Catholicism: An Idea Whose Time has Come Again', *America*, vol. 166, no. 15 (2 May 1992), pp. 385f.
72. See P. Hebblethwaite, 'John Paul II' in Hastings, op. cit., p. 450.
73. B. Häring, *Evangelization Today* (Notre Dame, IN: Fides Press, 1974), p. 2.

3 Secrecy, orthodoxy and 'witch-hunting'

An excessive concern for orthodoxy in defense of an organization is a symptom of disease within this organization. Orthodoxy without ortho-practice is not salvific; it leads to simplification of truth, to repression and death.

(L. L. Wostyn)[1]

Instead of seeking easy answers and scapegoats, it's time . . . to . . . identify the real problem and the true villains. . . . Sooner or later each of us has to accept . . . that complexity is here to stay and that order begins out of chaos.

(W. Bennis)[2]

This chapter explains:

* why, when cultures disintegrate, witch-hunting flourishes, distracting people from looking for the complex causes of cultural breakdown;

* why secrecy is an integral quality in any witch-hunting;

* the ways in which hierarchical officials and others are using witch-hunting within the Church today in an effort to restore pre-Vatican II values and structures;

* four models of culture within the contemporary Church and ways in which some Church cultures are reacting to the restorationism.

Rapid social, political, economic or religious change renders people highly vulnerable to what are variously called 'crazes' or 'mass enthusiasms', 'group panics', 'group or chaos madness', 'fanatical and apocalyptic movements'.[3] And the mindset of evangelical millenarianism is not confined to people calling themselves religious, but is to be found also within scientific, academic and political groups . People claiming to be logical and rational in their daily lives suddenly become thoroughly intolerant of other people's views. Like-minded people gather avidly to search out (termed 'witch-hunting', 'labelling', 'scapegoating') those who disagree with them and denounce them with such emotive titles as 'dissenters', 'deviants', 'public menaces', 'traitors', 'heretics' or 'orthodoxy-breakers'.

The orthodoxy craze was one of the background themes of the previous chapter because it is markedly prevalent within the post-Vatican II Church; it is one significant symptom of the pervading chaos and a wide variety of Catholics are encouraging the mania. It has gone well beyond the legitimate concern for theological orthodoxy within the Church. In this chapter we look more deeply into the reasons for this chaos madness, describe the qualities of the 'orthodoxy witch-hunters' and explain why, if it is unchecked, it will continue to obstruct or even stop the refounding of the Church in parts of the world.

Understanding 'witches' and 'witch-hunting'

Anthropologically, witch-hunting in modern or traditional cultures has several functions: to explain what cannot be understood, to control the uncontrollable, and to account for the problem of evil personally and in society. Witchcraft beliefs in their many forms tell us why particular persons or groups suffer specific misfortunes – for example, disease, economic depression, social or religious chaos; witchcraft as a theory of causation is concerned to pinpoint the reasons ('witches') for affliction. The term 'witches' (and their activity: 'witchcraft') is used here technically to refer to people believed to threaten *subversively* the established order.[4] Witchcraft fears were behind the anti-Communist craze under Senator McCarthy in the 1950s; earlier, the Nazis labelled Jews as witches or subversives holding back the country from greatness, and millions of Germans believed them. It is the reason why this or that person or group is today labelled as the cause of the chaos in the Church. Aided by the research reflections of anthropologists[5] we now see in more depth why orthodoxy witch-hunting is so prevalent within the contemporary Church.

Anthropologist Mary Douglas reminds us that a simple symbol can contain for people the heart of the whole social system. For Marx it was the city that contained the secret of the capitalist method of production; if we grasp, he says, how a commodity is manufactured, exchanged and achieves its value we will be able to enter into the heart of capitalism. For all societies, however, there is a common symbol that identifies one's adherence to this or that group: dirt or filth. We define what does not belong to our group and equivalently call it dirty, that which is 'out of order or not in the right place' as far as our group is concerned. We are 'clean', others are 'dirty'. We classify people and things according to this measurement most often without thinking about what we are doing. Pots and pans belong in the kitchen, not in the bedroom; shoes must be on the floor, not on the table. Just as we can react with feeling to physical dirt, so we can also to people or ideas that dare to invade our carefully structured world of experienced meaning. What is not in its place, within its boundaries set by the group, is dirty and in danger of 'polluting' all that we hold dear.[6]

In the previous chapter the nature of sects was explained. They are craze movements defining their boundaries with intolerant vigour, and whatever threatens them is marked out as a polluting agent dirtying what is orderly and clean in society. Corrupting agents are to be named, ridiculed, gossiped about, persecuted or eliminated. Sect leaders seek the backing of official authorities to carry out their persecution and society at least condones this persecution, providing it with further legitimacy. An atmosphere of fear develops; people continue assenting to the persecution lest they also be named and destroyed. Truth and objectivity lose out. As long as the group is protected from the source of evil, nothing else matters, no matter what moral or physical violence the innocent experience; the preservation or the restoration of the status quo must be achieved at all costs. The hysteria of the crazes produces all kinds of shoddily prepared evidence against the people already judged as heretics or deviants; false confessions, the destruction of people's reputations, even moral or physical torture and death, are encouraged or tolerated for the sake of the 'sacred' cause or the preservation of the group's purity.

Secrecy in these mass crazes is a potent weapon of control *and* escape. For example, since for witch-hunters the cause of social purity or orthodoxy is the all-important factor, the more secret the preparation of evidence against the accused the better, placing the latter's defence at a distinct disadvantage. People are encouraged to 'inform' secretly on others, even at times, if need be, inventing or twisting evidence. Those who fear becoming the target of scapegoating themselves either keep their true beliefs secret while struggling to conform outwardly to the purity norms of the group (even to the extent of appearing more orthodox than anyone else), or else they seek refuge elsewhere.[7] During the McCarthy period in the 1950s, when Communist-baiting politicians were able to force out of the US State Department Foreign Service officers who were considered insufficiently passionate in their anti-Communism, the Central Intelligence Agency used its special claim to secrecy to make itself a sanctuary for independently minded specialists. Ernest Becker notes that scapegoating can evoke such fears for self-preservation that even friends are falsely (and often secretly) accused, or their persecution is assented to lest one suffer the same fate. We have but to reflect on secret police (Stasi) activity in the former East Germany to see to what extent fear and secrecy can go against family bonds and friendships; the force was 90,000 in strength with a further 200,000 'unofficial co-workers'.[8] Little wonder that witch-hunting transforms open societies into worlds of jealously guarded and fear-evoking secrets in which truth, trust and friendships are shattered.

The Church's history of support for witch-hunting is a sad one indeed and no amount of apologetic arguments can ultimately remove the stain of guilt. Heretics, Jews, the poor and lepers had for a long time one thing in common, particularly from the eleventh century on: they were felt to threaten the religious/social/political fabric of the times in one way or another, thus they had to be named and marginalized – or even worse. Given the beliefs of those days the supposed deviants had to be the destructive agents of evil spirits or eventually even the devil himself. All these movements of social purity sought (and commonly obtained) for effective campaigning the support of the ecclesiastical and emerging civil authorities. The Inquisition was established in the first half of the thirteenth century, and though it did not often try cases of witchcraft itself, it nonetheless provided the manual needed to define the symptoms of unorthodoxy. In 1484 Pope Innocent VIII issued the famous bull *Summis Desiderantes Affectibus* that authorized two inquisitors to destroy witchcraft in Germany. They published in 1486 the *Malleus Maleficarum* ('Hammer of Witches'), which set out the ways in which the witches or devil-worshippers were considered to act and laid down how they should be prosecuted. Appalling injustices were inflicted on people branded as witches. Open disagreement with this witch-hunting craze or the call for reasonable discussion and reflection on the causes and practice of witchcraft was extremely dangerous. Those who dared to question the abuses were often themselves attacked as agents of the devil, and few could withstand socially or politically such fearsome accusations and their consequences.[9]

To summarize, the following are some significant factors to be found in witch-hunting throughout history.

1. The process of guilt avoidance

Witch-hunting is the process of passionately searching for and eliminating evil agents believed to be causing harm to individuals or groups, and as a craze it rises and fades in reaction to chaos and its eventual control. The greater or more intense the chaos or social upheaval and consequent fears of the unknown, the more frequent and persistent is the witch-hunting.

Historian Robert Moore says that as the use of money became more general in the Middle Ages, so the involuntary poor became starkly socially defined by the lack of it.[10] The presence of the poor caused the rich to fear that they would lose their own wealth through the revengeful machinations of the impoverished, so the poor must be identified and isolated, lest they pollute with their presence the emerging wealthy class. Hence there developed 'massive legislation and considerable antipathy [towards the poor] on the part of the establishments of many countries in the later middle ages'.[11] Likewise, considerable witch-hunting occurred from the sixteenth century through to the early eighteenth when Europe was experiencing rapid socio-economic changes: the Reformation, the founding of modern science, the emergence of the individual over against the group. Social unrest was an inevitable consequence of these radical changes and they threatened the social and religious cohesion of traditional society, thus the causes of these threats had to be discovered and eliminated. More than fifty thousand people were executed as witches in this period and a similar number underwent witchcraft trials, but more were acquitted or died, before sentence.[12]

The McCarthy anti-Communist movement had much of the emotion, fear, prejudice and injustices of witch-hunts of previous centuries. The cultural and political climate within the United States provided the right precondition for the McCarthy sect to emerge, because following the Second World War, as Eastern Europe succumbed to oppressive Communist dictatorships, many Americans wondered about their own future as a free nation. Senator Joseph McCarthy publicly stated that there were 205 Communists working to undermine the American way of life and he branded the Democratic leaders and intelligentsia as accomplices. Thus began a fierce witch-hunting craze that caused suffering to thousands of innocent people with the unquestioning co-operation of many politicians, the mass media and millions of American citizens.[13]

When people witch-hunt for the causes of the anxiety and misfortunes of their chaos they are able to relieve themselves of any guilt for what is happening; they lay the blame *simplistically* on others, believing that if only such deviants can be found and punished their tribulations will disappear. For example, today the American car industry is in major crisis and anti-American witches are assumed to be the cause. Consequently, Japanese industrial giants are singled out for the blame and the United States government is called upon to do something about it. Very simple! But American car manufacturers are not looking at the *real* causes of the downturn in their industry – for example, lack of creativity, arrogant self-satisfaction coming from past successes, shoddy workmanship, unsuitable designs and inflated salaries for top executives. The true witches or villains are within, but few want to look in that direction because it would demand painful internal conversion and restructuring of their operations. Warren Bennis describes it like this: in the past 'The auto industry said that government fiats were murdering it. Today, it begs the government to kill the foreign competition.' And he adds another example of scapegoating: 'When the White House goofs, it blames the media'.[14]

No human group is exempt from this guilt transference. I find it alive and well in religious congregations refusing to ask the right questions about the cause of their chaos, preferring to blame this or that member of their communities simply because they are prepared to be pastorally creative and therefore different! How often do I hear comments like: 'If only Father X would stop doing this pastorally new thing and be closer to us in this community. Then we could move together as a community and be true religious!' So often the real problems are complex, and if honest questions were asked by religious it would mean a lot of hard work, radical Gospel conversion, living in ambiguity, and lifestyle changes. And few of us are prepared to take such leaps in faith.

In witch-hunting crazes the leader has tremendous power but he/she will survive only as long as there are enough people, with sufficient fears of the chaos and a desire for simplistic solutions, to sanction them. Hitler could not have persecuted the Jews or McCarthy innocent people, if they had not had a sufficient power base to begin with. The leader's gift is his/her ability to feel the malaise of people and simplistically and convincingly pinpoint its assumed evil cause. When the craze dies down the leader tends to be blamed and people conveniently forget how they co-operated with him/her.

2. The qualities of the 'witch'

The characteristics of the witch, that is the person or group believed to be causing the suffering, are commonly the same throughout history, namely people on the margins of society: known non-conformers to the status quo, creative people who challenge traditional ways of thinking or doing things, those who have little or no access to the power structures (e.g. women, the poor or those who are handicapped). It is interesting to note that in the entire history of witch crazes at least three women were accused for every one man accused. In the patriarchal society of Europe, women had little legal or political power and were thus highly vulnerable to witchcraft accusations; if anything went wrong, women must be at fault since they had no other way of seeking redress.[15] So a witch bewitches others out of revenge, guilt, ill-will, envy, jealousy or the desire for power; the accuser is prejudged to be in the right and the assumed witch to be wrong and the cause of evil.

3. Orthodoxy show trials

The actual search for witches, their identification and the formal laying of charges against them are ritual ways of restating and reaffirming a society's collective values; the 'heretics' or 'deviants' become ritual scapegoats. This explains why there are periodic Marxist show trials (e.g. in the former Soviet Union, in the Cultural Revolution of Maoist China and contemporary China), academic/political/religious purges, and even, at times, American Congressional investigations or Royal Commissions in some British Commonwealth countries. A similar type of ritual process occurs when truly prophetic people threaten, or question, the political/academic/religious attitudinal or structural status quo. The prophets are felt to pollute the accepted system of belief or customs; they are ritually 'dirty', 'dangerous' – for example, Old Testament prophets, Jesus Christ himself (who had to be executed *outside* the city), St Joan of Arc, Gandhi. Their open condemnation and marginalization (e.g. exile, imprisonment, death) ritually reaffirm the fragile solidarity and boundaries of the threatened group.[16]

Application of theory to the post-Vatican II Church

We have seen that the post-Vatican II Church has slipped into the stage of chaos, the period before any radical revitalization can begin. The English and Welsh bishops' preparatory document for the 1985 bishops' synod summarized the tensions, polarizations and teaching challenges resulting from the Council. They said that the tensions arising from efforts to maintain unity in diversity cannot be resolved simplistically and quickly. They admit symptoms of chaos: a 'lack of tolerance and a certain fundamentalism' leading to 'strong expressions of extreme minority views in the Church'; many Catholics are 'rightly disturbed' by such things as the 'lessening in reverence for the Eucharist' and the loss of popular devotions. All this has made the task of bishops and bishops' conferences 'in protecting legitimate diversity' a difficult and delicate one because they 'often face criticism, misunderstanding and misrepresentation'.[17] Behind these words one senses both the pain that the bishops experience as they struggle to foster a legitimate diversity within their local churches and, at the same time, the need to avoid theological and pastoral witch-hunting and instant condemnations in an effort to solve the complex challenges arising from the Council. Vocal extremes within the English and Welsh Church are wanting the bishops to lead a witch-hunting craze and the latter will have none of it.

These bishops assume that every group, including the Church, has the right to define its boundaries, or what is or is not considered to be orthodox. But in boundary setting two principles must be kept always in the forefront: that what is stated to be orthodox is in fact authentically orthodox; that the process of discerning what is or is not orthodox follows the religious and secular norms of truth and objectivity. The examples given above of witch-hunting ignored these principles, and within the Church today the pressure to turn to orthodoxy witch-hunting is very real indeed. The English and Welsh bishops are aware of this and are not prepared to give way, but in various parts of the Church the above two principles are being ignored, causing pain and injustice to many people.

There are two levels at which theological or pastoral scapegoating is especially active within the Church today, namely at the grassroots and the hierarchical levels especially in Rome. Both represent a fearful group in the Church seeking the simplistic and instant order of a bygone Catholic culture. The more that witch-hunters at the grassroots know that Rome favours restorationism, the more avidly they go about their work of scapegoating. Even Cardinal Ratzinger admits that his view of the world comes from alarmist condemnations and reports flowing across his desk. Scapegoaters at the grassroots level go about their task in all kinds of ways – for example, by confidentially reporting 'disobedient' priests to their bishops or, if that does not work, to the local apostolic nuncio (or directly to Rome itself). Diocesan newspapers can be avenues for scapegoating, especially when people complain in letters to the editor on matters like the following: the failure of priests to wear the Roman collar or use the correct vestments; involvement in social justice programmes instead of 'real priestly work'. I was once branded as a Communist in a Catholic weekly because I dared in 1971 to oppose sporting contacts with South Africa. Commonly there are explicit or implicit threats like the following accompanying these letters: 'unless the Roman collar is worn and the sisters return to being proper sisters (i.e. sisters who wear formal habits and who do what the clergy tell them!) God will not give vocations and our young people will continue to leave the Church'.

At the Church's hierarchical level the emphasis on witch-hunting is far more serious because it is deliberately planned and sanctioned from the top. Under Paul VI, theologians like Küng, Schillebeeckx, Gutiérrez and Boff were not condemned or warned, but under John Paul II the insistence on what is considered orthodox theology and the scapegoating of theologians like the above began in earnest.[18] James Provost, Professor of Canon Law at the Catholic University, Washington DC, notes that Roman documents for several years have systematically dealt with issues like christology, liberation theology and biomedical research, but always from a rather narrow theological stance. Any disagreement with Rome's theological stance evokes a witch-hunting craze. Provost comments:

> The rejection of any type of 'dissent' from non-infallible positions has been severe, despite the exception made for many years in the case of Archbishop Lefebvre. There has been an on-going harassment of theologians, without an apparent consistent purpose, which often appears as an attempt to appease influential minorities.

While acknowledging issues of orthodoxy are a legitimate concern of papal authority, Provost comments that the way this authority is being used on occasions 'has the appearance of a defensive effort to exercise centralized control – defensive against the "evil" world in contrast to the Second Vatican Council's views . . . defensive of a very limited school of theology'.[19]

The victims of the theologians' witchcraft are perceived by Rome as the Church itself and the integrity of papal authority. As in all orthodoxy crazes, respect for truth and human rights is apt to suffer, as the following description of the judicial process conducted by the Congregation for the Doctrine of the Faith to assess theological orthodoxy indicates: the Congregation is prosecutor, judge and jury; the person being investigated is not told of the inquiry until stage thirteen (of eighteen stages); the defendant is unable to choose his/her defender or even know his/her identity, nor is there access to material relating to the allegations against the accused; no publicity is permitted concerning the proceedings and there is no right of appeal.[20] And injustices can occur even in the choice of the reasons for condemning theologians. For example, when Leonardo Boff was first silenced in 1985 by Cardinal Ratzinger, as head of the Congregation, he was told that there were no errors or heresies in his writings. Yet in the cardinal's letter it was said that 'The Congregation feels obliged to declare that L. Boff's options, here analysed, are such as to endanger the sound doctrine of the faith, to promote which is the task of the same Congregation'.[21]

Notice the constant recourse to secrecy by the Congregation in the judicial process. Recall that secrecy is a powerful weapon of control in witch-hunting crazes and it is particularly characteristic of cultures that are strongly hierarchical: by elites in order to hold on to their privileged position through possession of special knowledge, and by non-elites in order to defend themselves against the intruding power of the elite. Egalitarian cultures, however, stress values of openness and publicity.[22] Little wonder that the more Rome tries to restore the pre-Vatican II hierarchically vertical structures, the more it opts for greater secrecy.

There are times when secrecy is essential, for example to protect the welfare of a person or group, but it must not be habitually used as a cloak for anything any organization does or wants to keep from public gaze. And the habit of secrecy often leads to a very unpleasant quality – the justification of infringing laws and human rights 'for the sake of the common good'. Oliver North developed that human disease in the Irangate scandal, as did many of the Watergate conspirators, up to and including the President himself. Secrets give power of control over others, even more so when those who cultivate them are accountable to no public group; secrecy was used to intimidate victims in the Inquisition and this is still the case. There is no Gospel reason whatsoever to justify the present form of judicial process for investigating theologians since the Congregation is not publicly accountable to anyone. The Church is not above the Gospel and it is imperative that we respect human rights everywhere, first and foremost within the Church itself, otherwise it contradicts what it is trying to preach.[23] It is time to break away from the ideas and values that found their roots in the burning times of the Inquisition.

The undeniable fact is that Rome is obsessed with using secrecy as a weapon of control. In 1985 the English and Welsh bishops allowed their preparatory submission on the state of their local churches to the forthcoming synod of bishops to be published in full. It was an excellent document – clear, honest, challenging and positively critical of themselves and Rome. The hope was that other episcopal conferences would follow their example of openness. Rome immediately forbade other submissions to be published. Cardinal Ratzinger argues that the hiding of criticism of the Church is to preserve the faith of the faithful 'beginning with the poor and the most vulnerable'.[24] I think this is rather an insult to 'the poor and most vulnerable', as my work in Third World countries has shown me such people are particularly attuned to the weaknesses of their clergy and bishops. So also now in the West the human inadequacies of the clergy, bishops and religious are everywhere to be seen, for example the poverty of our sermons and administrations, the sad sexual and financial scandals. There is little 'the poor and the most vulnerable' do not know, yet their faith remains an inspiration to those of us who claim to be so materially secure and better theologically informed.

It is not the protection of the faithful that Rome is so concerned about, rather it is the fear of being called publicly to be accountable for its actions financially, pastorally and administratively. It is energetically resisting this accountability, despite suspicions (intensified because of secrecy) surrounding such recent scandals as that involving the Vatican Bank under Archbishop Paul Marcinkus. Through invoking the principle of the need to protect the 'simple faithful', Roman administrations are able to do almost anything they wish – appoint bishops according to their criteria alone, investigate and condemn theologians with no resource to appeal, protect fundamentalist movements (e.g. Opus Dei) from the 'interference' of diocesan bishops. It had been hoped that the bishops' synods could call Rome regularly to be accountable, but as these international gatherings have also been domesticated by the curia, that hope has not been realized. There is a chasm separating the curia from the faithful at the grassroots, and as long as it remains secrecy will be maintained as an instrument of on-going control and denial of reality.

Theologians Richard McCormick and Richard McBrien, in their analysis of the 1990 Vatican Instruction on the Ecclesial Vocation of the Theologian, provide a further disturbing insight into how Rome is using secrecy to control and orientate the Church back to its pre-Vatican II structures. Theological reflection according to the Instruction is to be the preserve of a select, safe few. This, McCormick and McBrien argue, is contrary to Vatican II.[25] The Council recognized that all believers can contribute to theological reflection and progress when it expressed the hope that lay people, not just clerics, be well informed in the sacred sciences. It then said: 'In order that such persons may fulfil their proper function, let it be recognized that all the faithful, clerical and lay, possess a lawful freedom of inquiry and of thought, and the freedom to express their minds humbly and courageously about those matters in which they enjoy competence'.[26] This encouragement to all within the Church to ponder theologically is a consequence of the Council's respect for the Church as the people of God; all by baptism journey with Christ, enjoy the presence of the Holy Spirit, and have the right to share that experience for the support and growth of the Church. In the Instruction, however, this model of Church is downplayed and replaced by the hierarchical or pyramidal pre-Vatican II theology.

The consequence of this model reversal in the Instruction is to make theology a 'privatized' discipline, that is, it is reduced to a gnostic-like science or a secret to be shared by the hierarchical magisterium and a docile group of theologians. They must confine their writings to professional journals and avoid speaking with the media. But this is an impossible restriction in an age that specializes in mass-media communication because, as

Ladislas Örsy rightly says, professional theological gatherings are open to journalists, and religious news editors read theological publications. If theologians have any personal difficulties with Church teaching, notes the Instruction, they must not discuss them openly but go instead to magisterial authorities and be counselled by them, but there are simply no structures within the Church to permit this type of informed dialogue to occur.[27]

Sadly, the guidelines of the Instruction are a formula for theological mediocrity, arid pastoral reflection, or the stifling of any realistic effort to dialogue with today's complex world; the process of refounding the Church in this atmosphere is extremely difficult. McCormick and McBrien quote Avery Dulles who says that the effort to crush dissent 'inhibits good theology from performing its critical task, and is detrimental to the atmosphere of freedom in the Church'.[28]

These theologians are correct. Freedom of speech is being more and more controlled and the Instruction's insistence that theology must be kept in the hands of a very select group is only reinforcing this atmosphere of intimidating secrecy within the Church. Even bishops themselves feel coerced by the secrecy imperative, yet they rarely speak out against this trend (with notable exceptions such as Archbishops Rembert Weakland of Milwaukee and Raymond Hunthausen of Seattle), as Bishop Kenneth Untener of Saginaw, Michigan, says:

> But on issues within the church, I am embarrassed. We have seemed fearful to speak on church issues that are right before our eyes, but which are unmentionable. We are like a dysfunctional family, unwilling to talk openly about things that are on everyone's mind even when we are together (at a National Conference of Catholic Bishops meeting).[29]

Cardinal Ratzinger, following the Instruction's publication, expressed the wish that it 'will help create a climate of reduced tension in the Church'.[30] The coercive power of Rome over the Church worked effectively without the faithful questioning its correctness only as long as the latter were aware of only the pre-Vatican II model; with the Council we know there are alternative models of being Church and, since people are now living according to these models, tensions between the people and the centre are bound to increase.

Recall that in earlier centuries witch-hunting was directed especially against the *powerless* within the Church – for example, the poor and women. There are several categories of people today that Rome considers powerless, for example: episcopal conferences, theologians, women and the poor. The first group Rome has apparently subdued with little public reaction from bishops, but the second and third groups are not as powerless as Rome anticipated, because both groups have access to the mass media for their defence. Rome cannot today block the media's support of rights for theologians and women in the Church. Only the poor appear the most defenceless. With Rome's imposition of new bishops to replace a social justice-oriented hierarchy appointed particularly by Paul VI, the lot of the poor is increasingly grim for they have few other leaders to identify with their cause and speak on their behalf to the world. Yet even the poor are reacting – this time with their feet – by joining fundamentalist sects at tremendous speed throughout South America and the Philippines. Fundamentalist missionaries from the United States are attracting more than four hundred converts from Catholicism every hour in Latin America, while Rome remains obsessed with orthodoxy witch-hunting and the appointment of restorationist hierarchies!

Orthodoxy, witch-hunting and models of the Church

Psychologist Eugene Kennedy identifies two cultures of American Catholicism. In Culture One people are more comfortable with the pre-Vatican II model of the Church as a visible institution. However, in Culture Two Catholics see the Church primarily as a mystery of communion in which they feel 'at home in the world instead of embattled with it . . . agents of freedom, rather than only of control, for all that is profoundly human. . . . Faith for them is realized in a social context as much as in church.'[31] This latter culture results from people allowing their faith to interact with the American value system in an evaluative way, which is the process of inculturation. Kennedy's analysis helps to explain why there are tensions within the Church today; the two cultures are just so different that misunderstandings and conflicts between them are inevitable. For example, people belonging to Culture One will see followers of Culture Two as disloyal and theologically unorthodox – an atmosphere ripe for witch-hunting crazes. However, I believe that cultural anthropology also provides additional clarifications about the ways Catholics are living their faith. Before explaining four models of faith-living within the Church today, it is necessary to clarify the notions of 'power' and 'authority' that are applicable to individuals and groups.

Understanding 'authority' and 'power'

Leadership is the process of influencing the action of an individual or a group in an effort to achieve a goal in a given situation. Leadership is an effort to influence, but 'power' is a leader's *potential* to influence; 'authority' is the legitimacy to exercise power. Hence one can have the authority to influence others, but for various reasons have no power to act. On the other hand, one can have the power to affect others' behaviour yet possess no authority for doing so.

Of the many types of authority/power, three major kinds will be helpful in our clarification of four cultures of Catholicism. First, *position* authority is the legitimacy to use power flowing from the status one has within an organization or culture – for example, the United States President has position authority/power derived from his office as legitimized in the Constitution. So position authority means that one has the right to empower a course of action. Of the various kinds of position authority/power, *coercive* permits people to force others to act through fear of punishment, *reward* encourages a response by offering or refusing benefits. The authority to use power in both types can of course be legitimate, but when power is wielded exploitatively or manipulatively it is done so illegitimately – that is, without authority. The second broad category of authority is termed *personal*. This is legitimacy to influence others because of the personal gifts that the leader has – for example, *expert* authority allows one to influence others as a result of one's skills at animation; *information* authority comes from one's knowledge of a subject; *referent* authority is a result of one's attractive personal characteristics that draw people to listen and act. Expert and referent authority/power combined would be equivalent to what we popularly call charismatic authority/power.

Several further clarifications about authority/power are helpful. First, there is the distinction between *unilateral* and *reciprocal* authority/power; with the former, a person or group refuses to receive influence from others, rendering dialogue impossible; with *reciprocal* authority/power, individuals or groups are open not only to giving, but to receiving influence from others, for example ideas, experiences and compassion. Rollo May distinguishes between *nutritive* and *integrative* authority/power (both can be part of position or personal authority/power categories); the former is used *for* or on behalf of another and the latter *with* another. For example, one who fosters a collaborative form of government is exercising an integrative gift; one who acts for the welfare of another person but without his/her involvement is using nutritive authority/power.[32] Rome, when it appoints bishops without due consultation, is using its nutritive authority/power.

Finally, authority/power resides not just in individuals but also in institutions and groups. By institutions we mean 'the established forms or conditions of procedure characteristic of group activity'.[33] As we saw in the previous chapter, institutions and groups or cultures develop lives of their own and they assume or are given the above types of authority and power. For example, groups develop sanctions; that is, reward and punishment systems intended to keep the member's behaviour in line with what groups prefer. And these sanctions can escalate if people do not conform quickly enough. John Paul II when speaking on social justice issues sometimes refers to 'structures of sin'; by this expression he means that institutions or groups have developed, through the concrete acts or omissions of individuals over time, power to influence harmfully those people within their reach.

Cultural models of Church

Mary Douglas has produced a stimulating reflection on the inter-connections between social structure, authority/power, ritualism and cosmology[34] that can aid our understanding of the tensions within the Church today. For example, Catholicism after Vatican II represents from a cultural point of view a distinct swing from a highly articulated social system, existing within a powerfully condensed symbolic universe, to a more flexible and splintered social assembly within a far more diffuse symbolic universe. I now briefly explain the typology of Douglas and then apply it to the contemporary Church.

Douglas founds her reflections on two independently varying social criteria which she terms *grid* and *group*. By *grid* she means the set of rules according to which people relate to one another. For example, there is a grid that regulates how crew members of an airplane should interact. In this case we speak of a *strong* grid, because the rules are unambiguous about how individual crew members must relate to the captain. They must obey or lose their jobs. The second variable is the *group*. This is a community's sense of identity in relationship with people beyond its boundaries; for example, the feeling of group identity of *this* particular plane's crew may be weak (though the grid remains strong), because individual members particularly wish to fly with different personnel and may or may not do so on the next flight. Douglas claims that cosmological ideals and the importance of ritual will differ predictably with the extent to which group and grid are stressed. The social body constrains the way the physical body is seen; thus if there are tight controls over how people are to dress and act bodily, then there will be a rigidly controlled social group and vice versa. Obedience is demanded to the social order. If social control is weak, the body will be at ease, informal, untidy and sloppy as with loose-fitting clothes or unkempt hair. The relation of the individual to society differs with the restraints of grid and group; the more rigid the grid and group are, the more developed the idea of formal transgression and its dangerous results and the less preoccupation there is for the right of the inner self to be freely expressed.[35]

Purity and pollution of both the human body and social body are particular worries of people who are restrained by group and grid. The breaking of purity rules produces dangers for the individual and society; the person and society become ritually 'dirty', so that there must be ritual to take away the impurity and the danger. Witch-hunting is particularly noticeable when the group is strong, but the inner structuring or grid is weak; there is fear that the boundaries of the group will be attacked and broken by disparate and dangerous forces from within. When the group and grid are weak, rules of purity rarely exist, and if they do there is little concern about the consequences should they be infringed. There is a greater concern for inner rather than outer purity. If the grid is strong and the group weak, then magic (that is, the alleged manipulation of forces and powers through secret rituals) provides a reservoir of energy to be tapped by individuals to allow them to triumph over rivals in a competitive milieu. Finally, the varying strengths or weaknesses of the group/grid typology will affect the ways people view the role of the spirit world and the nature of sin in their lives. These points will become clearer as the models are explained below and then applied to the Church.[36]

A reminder to readers before proceeding further. A model aims to illuminate social reality by highlighting emphases and downplaying details or nuances that might interfere with the clarifying process. Reality is interpreted with a model as a measure; and a model is modified or put aside in the light of the data that is being reviewed. Also within any particular local church it is possible that all models of Church culture described below are represented at the same time, though one model will tend to be more prominent than the others. Of course, the situation could change.

Model 1: Strong group/strong grid culture – pre-Vatican II Church

Understanding the strong group/strong grid culture
In the strong group/strong grid culture the boundaries of the group and how individuals are to relate to one another within the boundaries are sharply defined. People are expected to fit into a tradition-based, bureaucratic, hierarchical and patriarchal system which is presumed to have by right the monopoly over knowledge; dependency and conformity are the esteemed qualities. To maintain conformity there are detailed and rigid, morally sanctioned rules about how the human body (and thus the social body) is to be controlled. To break these rules is to risk ritual pollution which the ritual guardians of the system alone can remove. As regards authority/power in this culture model, the following types are particularly influential: unilateral, position (coercive, reward) and personal/information. The hierarchical leaders' task is to maintain the status quo, and for that, personal charismatic qualities are not needed – in fact, they may be dangerous in drawing people away from tradition to a cult of the leader and set precedents for undermining the status quo in the group. Tradition, inasmuch as it sets boundaries and the rules of living, can be said to have within itself a strong position authority/power to coerce individuals into conformity. A potential for orthodoxy witch-hunting exists, but it is infrequently used as long as the group/grid remains strong and the culture stable; people fear to break customs lest the group socially punish them, for example by ostracizing or ridiculing them.

In the religious cosmology of the culture there is a hierarchy of transcendent gods/spirits intimately concerned with the well-being of the culture and its stability. There are intermediary and more approachable spirits helping people to relate to the higher and more remote gods/spirits. The world is maintained in harmony by the gods/spirits who keep the evil forces under control, but people can allow these same powers to enter their lives through sin. Sin is the conscious/unconscious breaking of detailed rules established particularly to maintain the clarity of roles and boundaries within the culture; sexual sins are especially evil because if control over the body is broken there is real danger that the social body will be fractured also. As regards the virtue of justice, it is *legal* justice that is emphasized – that is, the rights of the group or tradition over its constituent members must be maintained at all costs otherwise the group will disintegrate. There are rituals under the firm direction of officials to remove the pollution resulting from sin and to ward off evil forces endangering the predictability of daily life. Examples of cultures approximating to this model are the Israelites as described in the book of Leviticus,[37] the Indian caste system, rural Ireland, and possibly the British class structure in the nineteenth century.

Application to Church

The Catholic Church prior to the Council would reflect many of the qualities of this culture model. For example, the Church in the United States was considered before 1965 as 'the best organized and most powerful of the nation's subcultures – a source of both alienation and enrichment for those born within it and an object of bafflement or uneasiness for others'.[38] This statement is equivalent to saying that the group/grid typology within the American Church was highly effective at that time. Membership qualifications were clearly stated; generally one was born into the faith and over time one became enculturated into a very self-contained cultural milieu with its many distinguishing customs and institutions like schools, clubs, hospitals and universities. Certain particular customs, for example the Friday abstinence,[39] marked one off from 'Protestant enemies' across the boundaries.

In the pre-Vatican II times the Church's mission was also sharply focused and frequently articulated in sermons and popular literature: win pagan and Protestant souls for the Lord. Within the Church, membership was hierarchically graded: Pope, bishops, priests, religious and laity. The laity were to be passive receivers of the expert ritual/religious leadership of the clerical categories and to go about saving their souls in the dangerous secular world through faithfulness to the set of intricate rules and customs. Sin was often synonymous with the breaking of these formally stated regulations, some key ones relating to the maintenance of the culture's boundaries. Thus sexual sins and the crossing of the barriers separating Catholics from non-Catholics were particularly heinous, with the 1917 Code of Canon Law having stopped 'Catholics from participating in disputations or discussions with non-Catholics without the permission of the Holy See' (Canon 1325, 3).

There existed also in the pre-Vatican II culture a complex regulative cosmology and a highly condensed and differentiated symbolic system of

God and the saints, their perceived qualities reflecting the culture's grid/group. God was presented as the remote Almighty and Unchanging One, Creator/Regulator; Christ as the King, Saviour and Judge of a people who break 'the rules'. The Mother of God and the saints were depicted as approachable and understanding beings having particular cultic significance in various needs, for example St Anthony of Padua as the saint concerned for lost things, in contrast to the stern and remote God the Father and the sacrificing, judging Jesus Christ.

The hierarchical officials (Pope, bishops, priests) held considerable position authority/power within the Church. As the essential ritual intermediaries between the laity and Christ they could threaten not to provide their services, even to the extent of excommunicating people from the body of the Church (e.g. for not sending one's children to a Catholic school). If the laity dared smudge the boundaries there were powerful symbols to indicate that they had moved to the edge of the group life and were risking their salvation; thus for a Catholic to marry a non-Catholic within the Church the ceremony had to be held in the sacristy, an uncomfortable and impersonal adjunct to the main church building. The group itself had similar coercive authority/power over individuals; the Catholic community was so strongly bonded that one would fear to break the rules lest one become a subject of gossip, ridicule or even ostracism.[40] In such an atmosphere it was but natural for justice to be considered in this group/grid model primarily as legal justice – that is, emphasizing the rights of the group over the individual.

This model of church culture is open to obvious abuses. For example, the compassionate presence of Christ is downplayed and his role as judge is over-stressed; external conformity to rules can become more important than a personal relationship with Christ; morality is more concerned with sexual and private sins than with social issues of justice and human rights. The authority/power of the ritual/administrative leaders is open to considerable exploitation: 'creeping downward infallibility' becomes an approved way for administrative curial officers, bishops and priests to avoid having to be accountable for their actions to laity and the Church as a whole. And if one is the ritual expert in an unchanging Church, then there is little need to cultivate reciprocal authority/power. One has all the answers before questions are even asked, so why listen to others for solutions to problems! Avery Dulles expresses his concern:

> Without minimizing the charismatic gifts of official leaders [in the Church], we may acknowledge that, in a sinful world, those who hold office will commonly be tempted to employ their power in a dominative and manipulative way. They can easily tend to sacrifice other values to the demands of law and order and to misconceive of loyalty as if it meant merely passive conformity.[41]

In this Church culture, in which there are no in-built public accountability systems for hierarchical officials, 'sinful structures', as defined by John Paul

II, can so easily develop; structures cease to be the means and become instead the ends of church life. Thus ecclesiastical officials could live in princely splendour, or construct richly decorated churches, while being surrounded by people in immense poverty, simply to maintain the Church's status and traditions. It is a culture insensitive to the demands of social justice. Inevitably this model of Church with its emphasis on the maintenance of tradition or the status quo has inbuilt sanctions to discourage pastoral innovation and dialogue with the world. A good symbol of this Church culture is the barque of Peter, tossed around by hostile external forces, but safe, internally intact and under the infallible captaining of the Pope, the Vicar of Christ on earth, assisted by the bishops, priests and religious.

Model 2: Strong group/weak grid culture – the restorationist Church

Understanding the strong group/weak grid culture

In this culture people have the sense of belonging to *this* group rather than to another; there is, however, a lack of clarity about *how* individuals are to relate to one another. There is an ideology of egalitarianism, but as the grid is weak there is considerable inner confusion over roles and access to scarce resources within the group. Authoritarian officials, who keep the boundaries of the group strictly guarded, try to impose an internal sense of order, but to no avail. People will form together loose, social, quasi-egalitarian units to compete more effectively for limited resources, but they are forever intensely suspicious of one another, fearing all the time that people will take advantage of them. They blame others for their problems. Some even feel that people competing with them for restricted resources and statuses are using witchcraft against them. Suspicions eventually lead to feuding – that is, relations of mutual animosity among intimate groups in which resort to violence is anticipated on both sides. The violence does not have to be physical; it can be verbal. Past real or imagined injustices or misunderstandings are recalled to remind all concerned that the 'out-group' simply cannot be trusted to work with the 'in-group'.

Cosmologically the world has no harmony; it is subject to all kinds of warring forces like ghosts, evil spirits and witches. Sin is an evil affecting one's inner self, far more than is the case in the previous model which stressed an external state of pollution as a result of sin. Rituals are of two major types. There are rituals directed by patriarchal figures whose task it is to guard the boundaries of the group by keeping outsiders from entering and those within from escaping. Rituals attempt to impose a mythology of order on the group, for example prior to the disintegration of the Soviet Union the rituals of mass parades before the Lenin mausoleum in Red Square, the witch-hunting and political show trials against those branded for endangering group identity. The second category of rituals includes those at the grassroots conducted by sect or cult leaders in response to the need people have to control fickle and evil forces that forever threaten them. It is important that these unofficial ritual leaders find the right formula, otherwise their intercessory prayers will be ineffective and they personally will lose their guru influence.

The task of the group's officials using their position authority/power is to impose order and maintain it against all attacks; coercive authority/ power leads to oppression, the authorities claiming that the common good requires the use of secrecy, informants and witch-hunting to identify social subversives and infiltrators. Through the use of reward authority/power, the government is able to foster a loyal elite by providing them with special privileges not open to the masses. For them legal justice has priority: the rights of group identity/security over the well-being of the individual. Within the group, however, personal authority/power particularly counts; through specialized knowledge and personal gifts certain individuals are able to win a following in sects and cults claiming to have ways to control Fate. For the masses, justice is synonymous with social justice – that is, the fair distribution of goods/services and access to power structures.

In brief, individuals find life difficult; since the group identity is strong, even if imposed from outside, individuals at least know what group they belong to (e.g. Soviet citizens knew they belonged to the Soviet Union and not to the United States), but as the grid is weak they lack that critical day-to-day identity that comes from an interiorized clarity of internal tradition with its established rules and roles facilitating mutual, predictable interaction. It is a volatile world out of control in which evil forces and spirits aim to crush people indiscriminately. The mythology of internal societal identity that is imposed by paternalistic and authoritarian officials from on high is seen as irrelevant to people's needs at the grassroots. Hence, Communism made little sense to millions of ordinary people within the Soviet Union, but they had to conform externally for fear of punishment.

This type of culture is common to many past and present societies. Scripture scholar Leland White argues that the evangelist Matthew's community illustrates some characteristics of this type; the members felt they belonged to a community of the righteous marked off from the unrighteous. The egalitarian low grid qualities can be seen from the dearth of formal power structures and the barring of rank or achievement statuses within the community.[42] Papua New Guinea in the South Pacific is also of this model. Its government is struggling to impose a national identity on 3 million people who have at least five hundred languages. Internally, however, confusion remains. There are thousands of tribes and clans led not by hereditary chiefs, but by individuals with skills to manipulate groups until a significant following is obtained; while this is happening, however, others are at work to 'dethrone' the leader by offering people a better response in return for their loyalty. In this fragmentary and volatile culture, people feel they are subject to the evil forces of witches that must be detected and destroyed.

The example already given above of the United States during the McCarthy period approximates also to this model. Likewise, the sudden collapse of the Soviet Union into small autonomous or semi-independent states rather aptly points to the relevance of the model. To the outsider the Soviet Union looked indestructible, but it was a country with an authoritarian and paternalistic mythology being imposed upon it by a privileged elite backed up by a military force. The elite claimed the right to interpret and to guard the pure dogmas of Marxism and Leninism against all attackers ('enemies of the people'). However, within the state, the seeds of local nationalisms and independence, as well as a degree of popular religiosity, remained alive despite the oppressive system of state rituals, informants, secrecy and social trials.[43]

The model helps to explain traditional church life in the Philippines, Mexico and South America: popular religiosity provides the grid for the millions of poor, with its saints and fiestas being a source of identity/security within a world subject to evil and fickle forces. The Puebla document of the Latin American Episcopal Conference points to the positive aspects of popular religiosity within local churches: 'At its core the religiosity of the people is a storehouse of values that offers the answers of Christian wisdom to the great questions of life. . . . It creatively combines the divine and the human, Christ and Mary, spirit and body, communion and institution . . . intelligence and emotion.'[44] Popular religiosity is the result of people taking the initiative to indigenize the Gospel message, despite the on-going opposition from Rome. For centuries Rome has been trying to impose its own internal and external structures on these local churches, but with minimal success. Clergy are seen as paternalistic figures having little influence except as ritual practitioners, but even then they can be dispensed with.[45]

Application to Church

I believe this model helps to clarify tensions within the contemporary Church. As a result of Vatican II and other forces, as already explained above, Catholics are experiencing the symptoms of chaos; the grid in Catholic culture is weak, for adherents are no longer able to obtain an identity from the disintegrating pre-Vatican II strong group and strong grid culture. They are prey to all kinds of sect and cult movements within and outside the Church – all offering a quick identity to fit their particular need for meaning. For this reason the restorationism of Rome fits the sect aspirations of some Catholics by offering them a return to a nostalgically remembered, idealized rule-oriented past. The right-wing intra-Church sects are locked in on-going feuds with groups seeking a more open Church, the latter being scapegoated as subversive of orthodoxy, 'agents of the devil', disloyal to the Pope. On a more positive side, the chaos is disposing other Catholics to approach God no longer as the God to be feared, the Almighty One, but as the Merciful Creator; and Jesus Christ as the Concerned One with inexhaustible feeling for a confused people. These

Catholics are assuming responsibility for their own lives, breaking away from an undue dependency on paternalistic ministers; renewal means for them a change of heart, not just a change of structures. Social justice issues become important and thus the social teaching of the Church is seen to be relevant to their experiences.

Roman restorationism makes no sense to this latter group of people who have grown wiser regarding the Council's meaning of Church. Andrew Greeley comments on a recent survey of Catholic opinions in the United States:

> The 'conservatives' are not winning. They have been reduced in the Catholic population . . . to a segment that is both ageing and fundamentally at odds with mainstream America and mainstream Catholic America on issues of race and gender. They may be increasingly influential in the ecclesiastical institution, but their 'restoration' has little impact on the life of the typical U.S. Catholic.[46]

Michael Hornsby-Smith, in his admirable review of English Catholics in the post-Council era, quotes from a study of the international delegates to the Third World Congress for the Lay Apostolate in Rome in 1967: 'Many Catholic laymen want more autonomy, freedom and power in all aspects of their lives. They refuse to be passive and obedient members of the clerically dominated Church. . . . It is not authority as such which is rejected, but authority exercised as domination rather than as service and love.'[47] As a result of his research, Hornsby-Smith claims that this statement would be very acceptable to members of the bishops' advisory commissions, and ordinary Catholics in the parishes, and those attending the special events of Pope John Paul II's visit to England in 1982. The threat of religious sanctions, he says, which earlier had intimidated many Catholics into compliance, no longer has the coercive power to convince or persuade. They can dissent from the Pope on such issues as contraception without feelings of guilt, fear or shame.[48] He concludes that this would never have happened a few years back or at least up to the end of the 1950s. He ends his research study with the following: 'our interview data demonstrated clearly that papal authority was minimal'.[49]

The reality is, therefore, that another way of being Church is struggling to emerge at the grassroots based on the Council's mythology, and no amount of Roman curial manipulation of power or witch-hunting will make these people return to the old Catholic patriarchal or clerical-led group/grid culture. For them, Church is primarily a set of charity/justice relationships based on the person of Christ, not a set of impersonal rules or hierarchical structures. Unless Rome allows collegiality to be the normative way of operating and permits inculturation within local churches, its restorationist approach will further alienate thinking and praying people at the grassroots. Sadly, the more Rome advocates restorationism the more the richness of Catholic traditional piety and spirituality will be seen as synonymous with Roman negativity and paternalism; when people condemn restorationism, tragically this magnificent heritage will also be left by the wayside.

This type of culture is far more favourably disposed to innovation from within than the previous model, but the opposition will be considerable since creativity at the grassroots threatens the rigidity of the control from outside. Within the Church today there are growing tensions between innovative pastoral people at the local levels and ecclesiastical officials at the diocesan and Roman levels. Conflicts will continue to grow the more the centre insists on imposing an outdated mythology of Church.

Model 3: Strong grid/weak group culture – the accommodation Church

Understanding the strong grid/weak group culture
In this type of culture people are sturdily egalitarian-oriented (e.g. gender equality), individualistic, utilitarian and competitive, but they have a very weak sense of belonging or of having obligations to the *group*. People obtain their personal identity from submitting to, and interiorizing, the clearly stated norms and goals of their society's *inner* structure. Individuals form alliances with one another to provide better opportunities for competitive successes, but such alliances are very fragile, since they are held together only for the self-interest of the individuals themselves. These alliances break apart once more profitable interrelationships appear.

Sin is just negligence or the making of mistakes through one's own fault in the personal mission to succeed or achieve one's destiny; it is the failure to take advantage of this or that relationship that will guarantee for me an economic, social or political advantage. Morality in this type might be termed 'Watergate', that is, 'do everything to get ahead, without any concern for the common good, provided one is not found out'. It is a culture that so encourages individualism and self-fulfilment, no matter what the costs to the group, that people will turn to any fad/magic (e.g. astrology) that offers them the secret of instant success. When people speak of justice they primarily mean the commutative or contractual type between equals, for example between individual and individual, individual and group; a culture that fosters a 'my rights first' approach provides lawyers with a flourishing income from litigations in which people are constantly suing one another for supposed personal injuries. Authority/power is strongly of the position type within the grid system, that is, whoever has the ability or status to assist me to get ahead is to be cultivated; personal authority/power is also of critical importance because only the personally industrious and creative can make use of society's internal system. By comparison the group, for example the state or Church, has little authority/power; its main task is to help the individual realize his/her goals.

Religion within this culture model reflects the basic stress on the grid over the group. Since cosmic forces in whatever form do not intrude into people's lives, so secularization flourishes; if gods or spirits do exist, they are befriended for the benefit of individuals in pursuit of success. The society has the potential for millenarian movements – that is, for enthusiastic crazes under the direction of charismatic leaders (e.g. tele-evangelist Jim Bakker), offering a quick and 'miraculous' short-cut to the desired goals of the individual. These movements are generally short-term, but when they are at their peak their leaders (e.g. the radio orator and anti-Roosevelt/New Deal Father Charles E. Coughlin of the 1930s) can rival or threaten the authority/power of the officially appointed leaders belonging to the grid/group hierarchy (e.g. political leaders). Traditional rituals are critically assessed according to the utility principle: will they advance my position in society? If they feel right and useful, then let's accept them and see what happens. Gods and spirits are therefore seen as 'enablers in my journey of success'.

Traditional Melanesian culture within Papua New Guinea, referred to in the previous model, *prior* to colonialism, fits this model rather well (including the secularization emphasis) and still does so today wherever the central government's presence is weak.[50] Likewise, the mainstream United States. Robert Bellah and others in their book *Habits of the Heart* seek to analyse the values of middle-class Americans.[51] One key strand emerging in their findings is a widespread acceptance of Lockean-inspired utilitarian individualism and a lack of consensus over values that bind people together for the sake of the group. This consensus deficiency is an extremely weak foundation on which to build a community in which individual rights are balanced by the legitimate demands of the common good. The authors' description of American society fits rather well our model of the strong grid/weak group culture, for example: vigorous individualism; a philosophy of self-fulfilment; a manipulative use of individuals or organizations to achieve fulfilment; secularization.

Application to Church

This model can be applied to the Church wherever Catholics significantly and uncritically adopt cultural values that conflict with Gospel/tradition imperatives. Thus within Melanesian culture in the South Pacific, especially as it is lived at the village level, the Church's sacraments or rituals have been absorbed into the Melanesian value system often without modifying the latter, as the following comment of a villager records: 'Christianity's rituals must help foreigners to be so successful because they have so many boats, houses and cars; therefore we will use these rituals, so much stronger than our traditional rituals, to become more powerful than other villages'.

Within the United States the same utilitarian approach is adopted when Catholics select only those beliefs and practices that do not conflict with the mainstream values of the culture, manipulating the Church to fit their personal aspiration. Thus the Church, with its rituals and institutions, becomes a junior partner 'in my struggles for achievement' in society. The Church is just another organization to be evaluated not in faith, but by the requirements of utilitarian individualism. Thus the clearly stated and frequently repeated Church stand on abortion means little to a significant percentage of American Catholics today, so well have they accommodated to current secularist values; one survey records that 54 per cent of Catholic men and 41 per cent of women believe that one can be a good Catholic without obeying the Church on abortion.[52] Catholic schools are popular provided they exalt the virtues of self-discipline and individual achievement; the moment they insist on issues of social justice or the welfare of the common good they are seen as irrelevant and obstructive of individual success in this world.

The restorationist Church can appeal to Catholics of this model inasmuch as it stands for the tradition of self-discipline, a sense of personal destiny and a forcefulness and sharp clarity of presentation of the Church's mission, provided of course it downplays anything that might encourage a social conscience. Thus the Church is especially loved when it condemns 'social activists', commented one American Catholic devotee of this model of Church. 'These people are dangerous socialists', he said, 'since they keep insisting on the need for a social conscience and justice. After all, the poor, if they want to be good Americans, should solve their own problems with some hard work on their part!' American Catholics of this type abhor any reference to 'sinful structures', the work of liberation theologians, and Basic Christian Communities in South America and the Philippines, for all these run against the values of their accommodated faith.

Model 4: Weak grid/weak group culture – intentional Christian communities

Understanding weak grid/weak group culture

A culture of this type is strongly egalitarian in social relationships and in gender, with minimum pressure from structures within and at the boundaries of the group. Generally, communities of this type emerge only under the inspiration of some charismatic leader, who denounces the oppressive rigidity of the grid/group traditions or structures of a dominant culture from which escape is sought. Dress codes and rigid rules of conduct based on tradition are considered irrelevant; far more important is the interior conversion and effective commitment of members to the group's vision/values resulting in what sociologically are termed *intentional communities*. There is government by direct democracy or consensus; the authority/power types within this model are predominantly personal and reciprocal, the latter being reflected in the openness of the group to new insights, dialogue and outsiders.

Personal identity according to this model comes from an awareness of one's self-worth and potential for change, not from a culture's traditional internal and boundary structures. Religion is highly personalized; a personal relationship to gods/spirits and to other people who have the same values as oneself is what counts and thus rituals are unimportant, unless they reinforce that sense of relationship or emerge out of the events of daily living, in which case they are very simple in structure. The world is inherently good, and if there are problems they are due to traditional grid/group structures that have stifled the good or prevented it from emerging in people's lives. Love, not 'depersonalized justice', motivates people's lives and sin is not based on external measures but rather on what one feels is wrong. If justice is stressed it is the pursuit in common action of social justice so that all may benefit. This type of culture is open to considerable innovation, and dissent is welcomed, because both are seen as essential requirements for growth.

Concrete examples of this model are the early Christian community in Jerusalem (cf. Acts 1:12ff.), religious congregations in the first stage of founding enthusiasm (e.g. St Francis and his early followers), counter-cultural communities or communes throughout history (e.g. the commune movement in the late 1960s in the West), and religious communities at the authentic refounding stage. Scripture scholar Gerd Theissen, in writing on the early Palestinian Christian communities, pinpoints their counter-cultural witness:

> [A] small group of outsiders experimented with a vision of love and reconciliation in a society which had been put out of joint, suffering from an excess of tensions, pressures and forms of aggression, in order to renew this society from within. The men involved were not lacking in aggressiveness themselves, nor were they untouched by the tensions of their time. . . . A good deal of aggression could be transformed into criticism of riches and possessions, Pharisees and priests, temple and tabus, and thus be made to serve the new vision.[53]

If the fervour is to be maintained, members must face the challenge to build suitable structures and group identity that do not crush the original enthusiasm. This is not an easy challenge and it is rarely successful unless commitment to the ideals of the original founding group is vigorously maintained. Mao Tse-tung realized how institutionalization can stifle the initial revolutionary fervour of his followers; thus he ruthlessly instigated the Cultural Revolution several years after his conquest of mainland China in 1949. John XXIII initiated a revolution against ecclesiastical institutionalism to return the Church to the dynamic virtues of Christ-centred love, justice and service in a changing world.

Application to Church

The model is helpful in understanding the contemporary rise and inner dynamics of 'churches from below', such as prayer groups, 'house churches', refounding religious congregational communities, Basic Christian Communities (BCCs).[54] Normally 'churches from below' develop in reaction to the perceived poverty of Gospel values in society and/or the Church. For example, in Figure 3.1, notice how BCCs are counter-cultural to what are seen as the depersonalized or clericalized structures of the restorationist mythology and the injustices within civil society. The initiative to start a BCC

91

	Restoration Church mythology	Basic Christian Communities
1. Structure	Hierarchical	Democratic
2. Doctrine	Very important; tradition-based	Not important; Gospel/experience-based
3. Conducted by	Clerics/ patriarchal	Laity: male and female
4. Social origins	Middle and upper class: supporters of social/ economic/political status quo	The poor becoming aware of rights/obligations
5. Sacraments	Instruments of individual salvation	Signs of Gospel love/social justice
6. Religious values	Stress individual piety	Stress common action
7. World	Evil/withdrawal	Involvement for justice/dialogue
8. Centre of Church	Rome; perfect society	The poor; pilgrim Church
9. Power	Position power: hierarchical/ tradition; unilateral	Position power: baptism; personal; reciprocal
10. Theology	From above	From below
11. Liturgy	Tradition-based/ oriented to transcendence of God	Life-based/ oriented to immanence of God
12. Spirituality	Remote from the world	Integrated with life

Figure 3.1

often comes from bishops, priests or religious. However, once these lay-centred communities become self-moving, they inevitably begin to criticize traditional ecclesiastical structures according to Gospel values – much to the surprise and at times annoyance of those who initiated them.[55] There is a similar pattern within communities of religious congregations of a refounding type; they may begin with the blessing of superiors, but the latter may quickly discover that no one, even themselves, is spared the Gospel critiques of the refounding groups.

For many intentional communities, especially BCCs, God in Christ is an understanding Liberator, the one with whom the oppressed of this world can identify: 'He has sent me to proclaim liberty to captives, sight to the blind, to let the oppressed go free, to proclaim a year of favour from the Lord' (Lk 4:18–19). Theology becomes a 'theology from below' – the result of people reflecting on their experience of life in the light of the Gospel. Liturgies are simple and mirror the living faith experience of the members and the model of the Church as a pilgrim in this world. Pilgrims have little room for the baggage of titles or formal dress. All members recognize that on the basis of baptism they are called to evangelize through diverse ministries. Every member has a particular role within the group; so also do clerics, but they are not singled out for special status or influence beyond what their sacramental duties require of them.[56]

The more the return of the pre-Vatican II model of the Church is stressed, the greater the temptation for intentional communities formally or informally to cut themselves off from the parent organization (e.g. the institutional Church, religious congregation). If this happens it is most unfortunate for all concerned. The communities will lose contact with rich Catholic traditions that they can no longer distinguish from the impersonal and unreformed parent organization; on the other hand, the parent organization will lose the chance to revitalize itself from within because these Christian communities are integral to the vital charismatic structures of the Church. Without these structures in operation, the Church's evangelizing energy withers. One local church in Australia recognizes this danger and asserts that one of its priorities is the promotion of intentional communities 'within which people can find a sense of belonging, develop a spirit of community and offer support to one another in deepening their faith, transforming their world and building up their Church. In order to bring this about the archdiocese [of Adelaide] has given priority to the provision of opportunities for leadership formation.'[57]

Summary

The potential for witch-hunting in the sense described is within every human heart. Down through the centuries people have blamed and punished others for misfortunes that are in fact usually a result of complex causes. By passing the blame for our afflictions on to others, we conveniently distract ourselves from the real causes and the efforts we must make to remove them.

Anthropologists point out that this tendency to blame other people for our hardships is particularly rife in times of cultural disintegration. We are tempted to look for simple and instant reasons for this chaos so we turn to people who are on the margin of society. They are seeking revenge for their powerlessness, we say. This type of reaction to chaos is to be found today within the hierarchical Church bent on restoring the pre-Vatican II model of Church; for example, theologians and the women's rights movement are being particularly marked out as the evil ones who cause the present malaise. It is also happening at the grassroots where individuals or groups actively search out this or that person pre-judged to be a 'traitor to the Church', 'polluting the Church with unorthodox liturgies and ideas', 'disloyal to the Pope'. Secrecy is a deplorable companion of any witch-hunting and it is being actively used by restorationist officials, just as it was in earlier times of orthodoxy witch-hunting within the Church. Energy that should be used to refound the Church within today's world of indifference, secularism and secularization is being directed instead inwards and wasted.

However, various forms of being Church (e.g. Basic Christian Communities, refounding religious life communities) are emerging that are directly opposed to the restorationist mythology. To survive and grow they need to limit their involvement with restorationist-oriented parish or hierarchical structures. Often they are marginalized by these structures because their simple lifestyles and their concern for faith/justice involvement are too threatening to the restorationists. The effect of this isolation or marginalization is that a kind of informal schism is emerging within some particular local churches.

Other Catholics, seeing restorationism and the poverty of preaching and liturgical worship in parishes as contrary to the Council's values, are forming less-structured support and worshipping networks, for example house churches. Others sadly find no meaning or hope in the Church because restorationism is so irrelevant to their lives, thus they move outside the Church to other religions or sects. And there are others who have become so accommodated to the secular values of the societies in which they live that the pursuit of these values has become a religion in itself. Little wonder that Karl Rahner prophetically claims that the 'future of the Church cannot be planned . . . by the application of generally recognized principles: it needs the courage of . . . creative imagination'.[58] In other words, the Church as never before in modern times desperately needs 'authority' and 'pathfinding' dissenters.

Notes

1. L. L. Wostyn, *Doing Ecclesiology: Church and Mission Today* (Quezon City, Philippines: Claretian Publications, 1990), p. 20.
2. W. Bennis, *Why Leaders Can't Lead: The Unconscious Conspiracy Continues* (San Francisco: Jossey-Bass, 1990), p. 113.
3. See R. Knox, *Enthusiasm: A Chapter in the History of Religion* (Oxford: Oxford University Press, 1950), *passim*; A. R. Cardozo, 'A Modern American Witch-Craze' in M. Marwick (ed.), *Witchcraft and Sorcery* (London: Penguin, 1982), pp. 469–76.
4. See A. Akeroyd, 'Witchcraft and Sorcery' in A. and J. Kuper (eds), *The Social Science Encyclopedia* (London: Routledge & Kegan Paul, 1985), pp. 899f.

Anthropologists commonly distinguish between witchcraft and sorcery: the former is assumed to operate through an inherent and generally unconscious power of the witch, the latter through the action of magic which anyone can use who has the 'right' spell. To prevent unnecessary complexity I avoid this distinction in this book.

5. For an overview of witch-hunting, see Marwick, op. cit.; J. B. Russell, *The Encyclopedia of Religion* (New York: Collier Macmillan, 1987), pp. 415–27; R. H. Winthrop, *Dictionary of Concepts in Cultural Anthropology* (New York: Greenwood Press, 1991), pp. 321–4; E. E. Evans-Pritchard, *Witchcraft, Oracles and Magic among the Azande* (Oxford: Clarendon Press, 1937); M. Douglas (ed.), *Witchcraft Confessions and Accusations* (London: Tavistock, 1970); M. Frelich *et al.* (eds), *Deviance: Anthropological Perspectives* (New York: Bergin & Garvey, 1991), pp. 93–8; for an excellent overview of the contrast between the theory/practice of witchcraft and Christian values, see A. Shorter, *Jesus and the Witchdoctor: An Approach to Healing and Wholeness* (London: Geoffrey Chapman, 1985), *passim*.

6. See M. Douglas, *Purity and Danger: An Analysis of the Concepts of Pollution and Taboo* (London: Routledge & Kegan Paul, 1966), *passim*.

7. See Cardozo, op. cit., p. 469.

8. See E. Becker, *Escape from Evil* (New York: Free Press, 1975), p. 109; also S. Talbot, *Time* (14 October 1991), p. 39; and J. O. Jackson, 'State of Treachery', *Time* (3 February 1992), pp. 24–6.

9. See H. R. Trevor-Roper, 'Witches and Witchcraft: An Historical Essay', *Encounter*, vol. 28, no. 6 (May 1967), pp. 13–34.

10. See R. Moore, *The Formation of a Persecuting Society: Power and Deviance in Western Europe, 900–1250* (Oxford: Basil Blackwell, 1987), pp. 98f.

11. J. Boswell, as cited by Moore, op. cit., p. 98.

12. See K. Thomas, *Religion and the Decline of Magic* (New York: Charles Scribner's Sons, 1971), p. 561; also M. H. Wilson, 'Witch-Beliefs and Social Structure', *American Journal of Sociology*, vol. 56 (1951), pp. 307–13.

13. See Cardozo, op. cit., pp. 472–5.

14. Bennis, op. cit., p. 113.

15. See Russell, op. cit., p. 420; Thomas, op. cit., p. 561.

16. See G. A. Arbuckle, *Earthing the Gospel: An Inculturation Handbook for Pastoral Workers* (London: Geoffrey Chapman/Maryknoll, NY: Orbis Books, 1990), p. 103.

17. *The Tablet* (London) (3 August 1985), p. 815.

18. See P. Hebblethwaite, *The Vatican* (Oxford: Oxford University Press, 1986), pp. 82f.

19. J. Provost, 'The Papacy: Power, Authority, Leadership' in B. Cooke (ed.), *The Papacy and the Church in the United States* (New York: Paulist Press, 1989), p. 205.

20. This description comes from B. Quelquejeu and is quoted by R. A. McCormick and R. P. McBrien, 'L'Affaire Curran II', *America*, vol. 163, no. 6 (8 September 1990), p. 128; also C. Boff, 'The Value of Resistance' in H. Küng and L. Swidler (eds), *The Church in Anguish* (San Francisco: Harper & Row, 1986), p. 229.

21. Cited by Scrutator, *The Tablet* (14 September 1985), p. 949.

22. See D. N. Levine, *The Flight from Ambiguity: Essays in Social and Cultural Theory* (Chicago: University of Chicago Press, 1985), p. 33; for some reflections on secrecy within the Church, see M. H. Crosby, *The Dysfunctional Church: Addiction and Codependency in the Family of Catholicism* (Notre Dame, IN: Ave Maria Press, 1991), pp. 100–2.

23. See Paul VI, Apostolic Letter *Evangelii Nuntiandi* (Sydney: St Paul Publications, 1982), p. 42.

24. Cited by Scrutator in *The Tablet* (14 September 1985), p. 949; see comments by A. T. Padovano, *Reform and Renewal* (New York: Sheed & Ward, 1990), pp. 1–23, 129–43.

25. 'Theology as a Public Responsibility', *America*, vol. 165, no. 8 (1991), pp. 184–9, 203–7; for helpful comments on the Instruction, see F. A. Sullivan, 'The Theologian's Ecclesial Vocation in the 1990 CDF Instruction', *Theological Studies*, vol. 52, no. 1 (1991), pp. 51–68.
26. 'Pastoral Constitution on the Church in the Modern World' in W. M. Abbott (ed.), *The Documents of Vatican II* (London: Geoffrey Chapman, 1966), p. 270.
27. See L. Örsy, 'Magisterium and Theologians: A Vatican Document', *America* vol. 163, no. 2 (21 July 1990), pp. 30–2.
28. Cited by McCormick and McBrien, op. cit., pp. 186f.
29. See ibid., p. 184, and *Origins*, vol. 21, no. 2 (1991), p. 38.
30. *Origins*, vol. 20, no. 8 (1990), p. 119.
31. *Tomorrow's Catholics, Yesterday's Church: The Two Cultures of American Catholicism* (New York: Harper & Row, 1988), p. 25.
32. See *Power and Innocence* (New York: Norton, 1972), pp. 105–9.
33. R. M. MacIver and C. H. Page, *Society* (New York: Rinehart, 1947), p. 15.
34. See particularly the following studies by M. Douglas: *Natural Symbols: Explorations in Cosmology* (New York: Pantheon Books, 1970); *Purity and Danger*, op. cit. (note 4 above); *Cultural Bias* (London: RAI, 1978). J. V. Spickard has criticized her typology used here for a lack of sufficient empirical support. However, as models to help frame experience I believe they have considerable relevance to this study (and to others). See J. V. Spickard, 'A Revised Functionalism in the Sociology of Religion: Mary Douglas's Recent Work', *Religion*, vol. 21 (April 1991), pp. 141–64.
35. See Douglas, *Natural Symbols*, op. cit., p. 102. For a helpful overview of the relationship between power, chaos and ritual, see D. Kertzer, *Ritual, Politics and Power* (New Haven: Yale University Press, 1988), *passim*.
36. I am particularly helped in the development of the models by Scripture scholar B. L. Malina, who masterfully applies Douglas to the Scriptures: *Christian Origins and Cultural Anthropology – Practical Models for Biblical Interpretation* (Atlanta: John Knox, 1986). I will also be using summaries of the models of Douglas that I have previously published: G. A. Arbuckle, *Out of Chaos – Refounding Religious Congregations* (New York: Paulist Press/London: Geoffrey Chapman, 1988), pp. 137–50, and *Earthing the Gospel*, op. cit., pp. 55–7; for an incisive analysis of how the models of Douglas can be applied to witchcraft accusations in the letter of St Paul to the Galatians, see J. H. Neyrey, 'Bewitched in Galatia: Paul and Cultural Anthropology', *Catholic Biblical Quarterly*, vol. 50 (1988), pp. 72–100; Neyrey also uses Douglas's models to clarify the interconnection between christology in the Johannine community and the latter's alienation from the synagogue and its revolt against various practices of Christians: *An Ideology of Revolt: John's Christology in Social Science Perspective* (Philadelphia: Fortress Press, 1988).
37. See Douglas, *Purity and Danger*, op. cit., pp. 54–72.
38. J. Cogley, *Catholic America* (New York: Image, 1974), p. 135; for an overview of the pre-Vatican II Church in England, see M. P. Hornsby-Smith, *Roman Catholic Beliefs in England: Customary Catholicism and Transformations of Religious Authority* (Cambridge: Cambridge University Press, 1991), pp. 190–209.
39. See Douglas, *Natural Symbols*, op, cit., pp. 37–53.
40. See H. Brody, *Inishkillane: Change and Decline in the West of Ireland* (London: Faber & Faber, 1986), p. 178 and *passim*.
41. A. Dulles, *A Church to Believe In: Discipleship and the Dynamics of Freedom* (New York: Crossroad, 1982), pp. 36f.
42. See L. White, 'Grid and Group in Matthew's Community: The Righteousness/Honor Code in the Sermon on the Mount' in J. H. Elliott (ed.), *Semeia* 35:

Social-Scientific Criticism of the New Testament and its Social World (Society of Biblical Literature, 1986), pp. 61–89.

43. See the excellent overview by C. Lane, *The Rites of Rulers: Ritual in Industrial Society – The Soviet Case* (Cambridge: Cambridge University Press, 1981).

44. 'Final Document of the Third General Conference of the Latin American Episcopate, Puebla' in J. Eagleston and P. Scharper (eds), *Puebla and Beyond* (Maryknoll, NY: Orbis Books, 1979), pp. 185f.

45. See the overview by F. Houtart and E. Pin, *The Church and the Latin American Revolution* (New York: Sheed & Ward, 1965), pp. 177–244.

46. A. Greeley, 'Who are the Catholic "Conservatives"?', *America*, vol. 165, no. 7 (1991), p. 161; see also W. D'Antonio *et al.*, *American Catholic Laity in a Changing Church* (New York: Sheed & Ward, 1989), *passim*; see the helpful analysis by A. Dulles, 'Catholicism and American Culture: The Uneasy Dialogue', *America*, vol. 162, no. 3 (1990), pp. 54–59.

47. J.-G. Vaillancourt, *Papal Power: A Study of Vatican Control over Lay Catholic Elites* (Berkeley: University of California Press, 1980), p. 294, as cited by Hornsby-Smith, op. cit., p. 207.

48. See Hornsby-Smith, op. cit., pp. 207f., and by same author, *The Changing Parish* (London: Routledge, 1989), pp. 173–86.

49. Ibid., p. 209.

50. See C. D. Rowley, *The New Guinea Villager* (Melbourne: F. W. Cheshire, 1965), *passim*.

51. See R. Bellah *et al.*, *Habits of the Heart: Individualism and Commitment in American Life* (New York: Harper & Row, 1986) and *The Good Society* (New York: Alfred A. Knopf, 1991), pp. 111–24, 163; see also relevant comments by Bellah, 'Leadership viewed from the Vantage Point of American Culture', Address to US Bishops, *Origins*, vol. 20, no. 14 (1990), pp. 218–23.

52. See D'Antonio *et al.*, op. cit., p. 66; for an example of Christianity being accommodated to a traditional culture, see D. Freeman, *Margaret Mead and Samoa* (Cambridge, MA: Harvard University Press, 1983), pp. 174–99.

53. G. Theissen, *Sociology of Early Palestinian Christianity* (Philadelphia: Fortress Press, 1978), p. 110; for an overview of the problems of modern intentional communities see R. M. Kanter, *Commitment and Community: Communes and Utopias in Sociological Perspective* (Cambridge, MA: Harvard University Press, 1972), *passim*.

54. See T. P. Rausch, *Radical Christian Communities* (Collegeville, MN: Liturgical Press, 1990), pp. 170–90. Leonardo Boff sees the emergence of Base Communities as a way of 'starting the church again': 'We are not dealing with the expansion of an existing ecclesiastical system, rotating on a sacramental, clerical axis, but with the emergence of another form of being church, rotating on the axis of the word and the laity' (*Ecclesiogenesis: The Base Communities Reinvent the Church* (Maryknoll, NY: Orbis Books/London and Glasgow: Collins, 1986), p. 2.

55. See Arbuckle, *Earthing the Gospel*, op. cit., pp. 86f. See also M. Azevedo, *Basic Ecclesial Communities in Brazil: The Challenge of a New Way of Being Church* (Washington, DC: Georgetown University Press, 1987), *passim*, and M. Adriance, 'Agents of Change: The Roles of Priests, Sisters, and Lay Workers in the Grassroots Catholic Church in Brazil', *Journal for the Scientific Study of Religion*, vol. 30, no. 3 (1991), pp. 292–305.

56. See G. Gutiérrez, *We Drink from Our Own Wells: The Spiritual Journey of a People* (London: SCM Press, 1984), *passim*.

57. 'Your Kingdom Come', Report of the Working Party for the Future Pastoral Care of the Archdiocese of Adelaide (April 1991), p. 14.

58. K. Rahner, *The Shape of the Church to Come* (New York: Seabury Press, 1974), p. 47.

4 The transforming leadership of 'authority dissenters'

[There] is no Christian principle to the effect that the conservatives must always be in the right when a choice has to be made between [them and future-oriented people].

(Karl Rahner)[1]

Let me say to you what I will say to the bishops of my own church: I hope you have the courage . . . not to be intimidated by the confusions of our culture and do not fall back too readily on our central cultural stereotypes of leadership – the manager or the therapist.

(Robert Bellah)[2]

This chapter explains:

- the main emphases in contemporary writings on the nature/qualities of leadership;

- the problems that can arise in 'leaderless communities';

- the nature and qualities of transforming leadership according to Vatican II;

- a spirituality of transforming leadership.

'We must recognize and understand the world in which we live . . . its often dramatic characteristics. . . . Profound and rapid changes are gradually spreading around the whole world . . .' and we must 'seek continually for more suitable ways of communicating doctrine to people of our times', so declared Vatican II in proclaiming the primary task of the Church.[3] What a challenge! The Church must have the ability to be stable, but dare to risk prophetically. I believe there is an abundance of ideas, especially at the grassroots of the Church, about ways to respond prophetically to this challenge; but there is also a dearth of able leadership able to use these ideas and guide them to fruition, often because there is widespread confusion over the most appropriate leadership style for change. So the questions is: as restorationists are declining to accept the challenge, what kind of leadership must people who hold official positions in the Church adopt if they wish to take the Council's evangelizing values seriously by creatively responding to the most urgent and non-ephemeral needs of today? In other words, how can official leaders become 'authority dissenters' or refounding leaders within the Church? This chapter seeks to answer this question, at least in an introductory way.

Defining leadership

Leadership is hard to define. Its nature varies in any given situation with the qualities of the leader, the group, the goals and tasks that have to be done, and finally the environment itself. Therefore leadership that succeeds depends on the willingness of a group to choose leaders able to take on the style of leading suited to the overall purpose of the group at a particular time. This is generally termed 'situational leadership'; that is, there are particular occasions in which the leader needs to delegate, persuade, provide directives or foster participation/collaboration.[4] Where what has to be done is uncertain or ill-focused, as will be the case in times of change in which considerable innovative skills are required, a *transforming* style of leadership is necessary – one based on trust and mutuality. The task of the transforming leader is primarily to foster a collaborative or participative atmosphere in which this trust and mutuality exist as the prerequisites for creative action or strategies for change.[5] Transforming leadership for participative pastoral government is the preferred style within the Vatican II documents. I now summarize the major insights of the contemporary literature on leadership, raise the sometimes thorny issue of 'leaderless communities', then define more precisely the nature and qualities of transforming leadership. In a later chapter a specific object of this style, namely collaborative government, will be examined from a more practical angle.

Bookshelves are today groaning under the weight of more and more publications on the art of leadership. And with these books there comes an array of new terms and catch phrases leaving the average worker in the Church utterly bewildered, for example: 'hands-on, value-driven',[6] 'heroes of innovation', 'rites and rituals of leaders in corporate cultures',[7] 'servant leadership',[8] 'transactional/transformational leaders', 'intrapreneurs'.[9] Despite the diversity of language, the following threads run through these publications:

- change is a fact of life and leadership for change must be an integral part of all organizations today;

- leaders must be able to shape and share a vision with others;

- leaders must have the ability themselves or through others to strategize their vision into concrete plans for action;

- leaders must realize that people belong to cultures that tend more to obstruct creativity and change;

- leaders must call people to be accountable for their behaviour according to the vision and strategies they have accepted.

It is assumed in this chapter that leaders are necessary, but this is an assumption that at times is seriously questioned. For example, it is increasingly common for members of religious congregations to belong to 'leaderless' communities. It is felt that people are mature enough not to need formally designated leaders and all matters of importance can be dealt with through regular meetings or direct democratic action. The following two case studies illustrate some of the difficulties that can arise in such communities.

Case study: direct democracy has its weaknesses

Nine sisters decided not to have a leader in the community and to work all decisions out through meetings. For the first few months all went well, but later several sisters were unable to attend the meetings regularly because of work commitments. On hearing of decisions made in their absence, they complained that they had not been involved. Others complained that there were too many meetings to decide on matters of little importance. After a year, the group agreed to appoint an official leader and set guidelines for her to follow.

Case study: unofficial leaders manipulate

An apostolic community of religious priests felt that no community leader was necessary; they all had different ministries and agreed that matters relating to the running of the community could be settled at monthly meetings. At first, there was no trouble, but in time tensions emerged; some felt that far too much work was being left to them while the others found all kinds of excuses not to be present at meetings or, if present, to avoid community works. The former felt manipulated, but there was nothing they could do, one summing up what happened: 'We started with enthusiasm but as the strains developed we turned into a simple boarding house – even worse, because the house became dirty and repairs were left unattended. A leader did emerge, but a negative one, because he would rally a group around him and block every effort for the rest of us to get the real issues of community out in the open. As for common prayer – well, that went pretty early.'

Every group needs a leader whose task it is to listen to the group's needs and to ensure that something is done about them. The leader is *usually* an individual formally appointed in some way and readily identifiable to

100

members of the group. Sometimes, however, the leader is able to be the *group* itself and this happens when members of the group forming an intentional community share a common vision and communicate frequently and well with one another. To permit ease of communication the group needs to be relatively small. The unified group assigns tasks, including the duty of representing the group on specific occasions, and calls members to be accountable for them. In the first case study above, the members have not articulated and interiorized a common vision. Hence they do not form an intentional community and are unable therefore to assign tasks to one another. In the second case study, a common vision and commitment by members to the group are also lacking; individuals suffer because the group has no approved way through which members can be effectively called to be accountable for their actions. So 'leaderless' communities are possible, provided the following qualities in a group are operative: the group is small; members commit themselves to a common vision; effective accountability structures are in place.

Normally, therefore, groups need formally appointed leaders. Of course in view of its size and of the structures established by Christ, the Church commonly needs formally chosen leaders. However, in order to avoid the abuses by ecclesiastical leaders in the past, Vatican II has opted for the transforming style of leadership at all levels of the Church.[10] Thus the Council at least expects the following qualities to be present: a strong emphasis on consultation through dialogue and structures of accountability. Restoration theology distrusts these characteristics and prefers its chosen leaders to be without them.

Transforming leadership

A working definition of a transforming leader most suited to the needs of the contemporary world is: one who moulds and communicates a task-oriented vision for community growth, providing transforming focus to the actions of others so that they are able to foster within themselves their own potential for change.[11] The transforming leader understands the following needs:

1. The need for a vision, strategies and accountability

For the transforming leader the only constant in today's economic, political, social and religious world is change and the 'only stability possible is stability in motion'.[12] No business firm, no organization of any kind, including the Church, can ignore the reality of radical uncertainty at the heart of all change. Innovate or die. There are no exceptions, as Vatican II admits particularly in its Document on the Church in the modern world.

Decision-making for the transforming leader is consequently primarily *proactive* – that is, the leader anticipates the challenges of change and is able to influence its direction through visioning, and strategizing rather than being its slave. Thomas Reese, when reflecting on the method of government within the United States Catholic hierarchy, concludes that a 'characteristic of episcopal governance is that it is primarily reactive and not proactive'. It is a style, he says, which is not necessarily negative, but there are serious drawbacks since a bishop is so overwhelmed by day-to-day issues there is no time for updating theologically or long-range planning. If long-range planning is occurring, 'it is usually in response to a perceived crisis such as the decline in the number of priests'.[13] In effect, this means that bishops are primarily managers, not leaders, and this has serious consequences in the long term for the Church in the United States.

In contrast to transforming leadership, Burns speaks of 'transactional leadership'; this is a type of leadership concerned with the smooth day-to-day running of the organization. This is the leadership of the manager whose primary task is to prevent the complexity of a modern organization degenerating into total chaos; they take details like financial planning, quality control, staffing and market research, and then give order and consistency to them. For managers, systems and structures are all, and change is not integral to their role. The transforming leader challenges the status quo to face up to change in the environment, the manager bows to the status quo. Stephen Covey clarifies the difference in the following way: 'Management is doing things right; leadership is doing the right things. Management is efficiency in climbing the ladder of success; leadership determines whether the ladder is leaning against the right wall.'[14]

But a word of warning. It is not leadership *or* management, but *both*. A transforming leader needs systems and structures behind him/her under the direction of some gifted manager, otherwise the leader does not have the necessary space and time to clarify a much-needed vision for the group. This alone is sufficient to warrant a leadership *team* in which there is someone with transforming leadership skills and others with management gifts, as it is extremely rare for the qualities to be found in the same person. The leader's primary task in the team is to lead by keeping his/her eyes on the future and for this to happen he/she needs to have the right type of team manager. If the primary task of a leader is ill-defined or not repeatedly articulated and interiorized, the temptation will be for a would-be leader to slip into a primarily managerial role. If that happens the group disintegrates, as it lacks a direction-inspiring vision: 'Where there is no vision, the people perish' (Prov 29:18, KJV). The inability to accept the need for leaders *and* managers is a sure recipe for catastrophe, since to be overled and undermanaged is just as dangerous as being underled and overmanaged.

For a leadership team to exist, however, both leader and manager must exercise reciprocal authority/power – that is, they must be aware that they need each other and express this openly in dialogue. A significant factor contributing to the collapse of intentional communities in the Church is their failure to establish suitable internal management structures. Consequently, the transforming leader becomes so burdened by management issues that he/she lacks the freedom to go about his/her primary task. A group can live neither on visions nor by managers alone![15]

The University of Notre Dame, Indiana, is synonymous in the public mind with Father Theodore Hesburgh who, as president, turned the institution into a major American university. Explaining how he instilled his vision of a revitalized university in students, alumni, faculty and the general public, he said: 'The very essence of leadership is for you to have a vision. It's got to be a vision you articulate clearly and forcefully on every occasion. You can't blow an uncertain trumpet.'[16] Hesburgh was successful because he was never known to 'blow an uncertain trumpet'. He exercised leadership by direction-setting; that is, by repeating what he wanted the university to become *and* believing it could become that.

By a *vision* I mean: a mental passage from the known to the unknown, creating the future from a mass of existing facts, hopes, dreams, dangers, and opportunities.[17] On the other hand, a *strategy* is a plan for the use of resources in order to implement in concrete terms a group's vision.[18] A strategy for the future that is only a *re*presentation of what already exists is not a vision, because a vision is the reframing of what is already known but with connections with what is previously unknown. Dr Christiane Brusselmans, the designer of the Rite of Christian Initiation of Adults (RCIA) after Vatican II, created a refounding or transforming vision for evangelizers that recognized the need for converts to move slowly through the conversion process with and into the ecclesial community. The old rite did not fit the restored mythology of initiation, but no one knew how to create the appropriate process. Brusselmans developed a vision and strategies for action, and today people in vastly different cultures feel the vision 'makes sense to them', so it is worth trying. A vision to be effective must be understandable – that is, presented in ways that can be followed – but it also needs to be vague enough to allow initiative. And that is just what the RCIA provides for people in different cultures.

The following case study from the Old Testament further illustrates that a vision and strategies must be interconnected, and unless the would-be transforming leader has the space to dream, his/her role will be reduced to that of uncreative management.

Case study: Moses *must choose – manager or leader!*

Moses was appointed by Yahweh to lead his people into the promised land, so Moses needed ample reflection, space and time to listen to and interpret Yahweh lest he stray from his primary task. In fact Moses the leader was becoming so absorbed in routine or maintenance work – the task of a manager – that creative listening to Yahweh was becoming impossible. It was Jethro, the father-in-law of Moses, who noticed that Moses' leadership powers were in serious danger of being suffocated by his excessive involvement in routine or managerial matters. Jethro said: 'You will only tire yourself out, and the people with you too, for the work is too heavy for you' (Ex 18:18).

Jethro then describes the vision-setting and strategy-creating role that Moses should be fulfilling as a leader: 'Your task is to represent the people to God, to lay their cases before God, and to teach them the statutes and laws, and show them the way they ought to follow and how they ought to behave' (v. 19f.). Jethro then advises Moses to allow the people to choose God-fearing men to manage the day-to-day affairs: they will be 'put . . . in charge of them as heads of thousands, hundreds, fifties and ten' (v. 21). Only difficult matters that relate to Yahweh's vision for his people are to be referred to Moses. 'If you do this', advises the perceptive Jethro, 'you will be able to stand the strain, and all these people will go home satisfied' (v. 23).

Notice the warning of Jethro: if Moses strays from his primary task not only will he become tired, but also 'the people with' him. If Moses does not know what he is supposed to be doing this confusion will be mirrored in the people's lives and they will became weary, disillusioned and angry. So Moses took the advice to keep to his primary task of listening to the Lord, because only then would he know Yahweh's plans for his people beyond the chaos.

Hierarchically and pastorally the Church is *over-managed*. A mechanistic culture (as described in Chapter 2) is again being imposed on the Church in which ecclesiastical officials are chosen primarily to be managers. The Council's vision of transforming leadership founded on collegiality and openness to the world is being slowly suffocated, and if perchance transforming leaders are selected they are nonetheless expected to fulfil managerial roles. We need a few modern Jethros to challenge the Church to recognize the need for transforming leaders supported by appropriate managerial structures as envisaged by Vatican II. Without this, the Church's refounding will remain stalled.

Accountability is as essential for change as the idea of leadership. It is not sufficient to enunciate a fine vision and strategies and have people interiorize them. People must be regularly called by leaders to be accountable for what they have accepted. This is a hard task, demanding of the leader an ability to see where and when their followers stray from the vision and/or escape into unreality. The following case study illustrates what can happen when the leader neglects to call people to be accountable to a vision.

Case study: an initial formation programme disintegrates

Several years ago a provincial chapter, under the inspiration of the congrega-tional leader, formulated an inspirational vision for the initial formation programme of the province. Criteria for the assessment of candidates to the congregation were attached to the vision. Over a period of time, however, successive congregational leaders neglected to call the formation staff to be accountable to the vision and the criteria, thus allowing unsuitable or ill-formed religious to be professed. Several of these professed members have left and those that remain are apostolically negative forces within the province.

In this case study not only did congregational leaders neglect to call the formation staff to be accountable for their actions, but the province, for example through provincial chapters and other bodies, also failed to call their official leader to act responsibly in view of the chapter's vision on formation. Accountability is a two-way process. In this case study the pastoral consequences of the disregard for the requirements of account-ability have been disastrous, causing injustices to the particular professed religious and the people they were appointed to serve. The impor-tance of leadership and accountability will be further emphasized in this book.

To summarize our pivotal insight thus far: the primary task of the trans-forming leader is to lead, not to manage.[19] He/she as part of the leader-ship role must call members of the group to be accountable to the vision they have accepted. If that is not done, the group will fragment and become involved in all kinds of activities, but not within the terms of the primary task of the group as set out in the group's vision. Energy that should be directed to refounding projects is then dissipated on projects not directly related to the group's primary task, as the following case study illustrates.

Case study: rhetoric conflicts with reality

In the revised constitutions of an active congregation of women, the primary task of the foundress was re-articulated: to preach the Gospel to the materially poor. The constitutions had been enthusiastically received within the congrega-tion, but several years after their approval the congregation was still adminis-tering schools for the wealthy and in a very professional way. The superior general assented to this and never challenged the congregation to face the contradiction between its constitutions and its involvement in schools for high-income families. Some ideas on ways to live out the constitutions in today's world had been discussed, but no move had been made to implement them. Several religious had transferred to other, more open, congregations, in frustration over the inaction – and even deliberate blocking of any initiative – to be true to the founding vision.

The case study highlights the denial within the group and what can happen to pastoral innovators blocked from creative action. Above all, it points to the failure of the official leader *to lead*. All sisters were doing good things evangelically, but not the *right* things.

2. The need to empower people

Transforming leadership is a response to the need people have for a sense of purpose, meaning or a vision that raises them in their work above the daily grind of routine. Inspired by this leadership, people are empowered to become more active themselves, more creative in the control of their own lives through interacting with others in trust and mutuality, more confident to lead and/or support evangelizing thrusts.

Psychologist Gordon Lawrence distinguishes between leaders acting by the 'politics of salvation' and those by the 'politics of revelation'. Leaders of the first type exercise their leadership in order to 'rescue' or 'save' people from oppressive structures without really consulting or drawing on the experience and expertise of the people themselves. Sometimes leadership of this type is necessary, in which case it is what we referred to in the previous chapter as the exercise of nutritive or position authority/power. But the danger is that this type of leadership can become the *normal* way of acting instead of the exception, and this is precisely what is to be seen within the restorationist Church today. In contrast, the transforming leader prefers to act according to the criteria of the 'politics of revelation'; that is, he/she aims to develop those processes that encourage the responsible exercise of authority, both individually and collectively, so that people become *generative* of ideas and the agents of their own growth and that of the group.[20] This latter style of leadership, so desired in intentional communities, is preferred by Jesus himself. Often Jesus, out of respect for the freedom of the person, goes out of his way to avoid imposing his own healing power on people; for example, he knows the sick man at the Pool of Bethesda has been ill for decades, but still he asks him 'Do you want to be well again?' (Jn 5:6). The sick man begs for healing and is restored to health, his self-worth enhanced. Ponder how Jesus tells us to pray: 'Ask', 'Knock', 'Search' (Lk 11:10) – and *then* he will answer. He also searches for us: 'Look, I am standing at the door, knocking. If one of you hears me calling and opens the door, I will come in to share a meal at that person's side' (Rev 3:20). He knocks, but *we* must open the door, for he will not push against our freedom, and then he will be revealed. The Spirit uses the same transforming leadership at the annunciation when Mary's consent is freely sought; when she gives it, there is revealed to her gifts beyond human imagination, which inspire her to praise and glorify God for the sensitivity shown to her and humankind (Lk 1:26–55).

Case study: leadership for structures of 'revelation'

In the mid-1960s I researched into the reasons for the successful development of credit unions (small-scale people's banks) within the Fiji Islands, South Pacific, under the direction of Jesuit Father Marion Ganey. Their prosperity contrasted with the frequent shortcomings of the co-operative movement initiated and directed by a paternalistic colonial government. There was a twofold reason for Ganey's success: his ability to impart a vision of a people running their own lives; and the establishment of a suitable management infrastructure through which members could regularly call their officials to be accountable for their leadership and vice versa.

One middle-aged informant summarized the effectiveness of Ganey's leadership skills in this way (the other villagers nodding in agreement):

> When Father Ganey comes into the village we all feel ten feet taller and ten years younger! Somehow or other he is able to enter right into our hearts and spark off the conviction that we can control our own destiny and not depend on others for handouts. He taught us how to set up structures of our own, under our own management, to learn how to save, to be in charge of our own lives. If we fail, we know why. We used to blame others for our mistakes, now not so much. This is why we like credit union. It helps us grow up to be real people!

Another informant, with tears in his eyes, told me what membership in the village credit union did for him: 'I got a loan on the basis of my good character. Never before have I ever felt trusted.' Another: 'It is like meeting Jesus Christ. Now I know what Jesus means when he sets captives free. I am no longer dependent on the hand-outs of others because now I am in charge of my growth in co-operation and trust with others.'

The case study speaks for itself. The credit union movement provided these villagers with 'structures of revelation' through which they could experience what it means to be truly human. Through an articulated and communicated vision these people claimed their own authority/power to decide for themselves how they are to live. Up to that point, paternalistic government agencies had consistently sabotaged this authority/power for self-direction.

While the transforming leader is sensitive to the potential for growth, he/she is acutely aware that there are forces of resistance at work within the individual and the culture of the group inhibiting or obstructing people from claiming rightfully their own authority. The above example of paternalistic colonial structures illustrates this point. However, recall a key point from the previous chapter – just belonging to any culture renders us subconsciously wary of the dissenter's vision of change for we fear that we might lose our cherished identity, status and power. Earlier in my applied research I would, after appropriate field work study, somewhat naïvely present lengthy and detailed reports on the changes religious congregations or dioceses must face in order to remain apostolically relevant; I assumed that the resolutions carefully formulated and assented to by the contracting agencies would be quickly implemented. After all, I said to myself, they wrote the resolutions themselves and they are printed for all to see! Unfortunately I did not take sufficiently into account the deep-seated fears of change that would emerge once people returned to their communities/homes following 'successful' workshops on the reports. During the journey home participants had a chance to realize what they would have to give up if they carried out the resolutions they had made so enthusiastically to change their lives and apostolic structures. True leaders expect the in-built resistance to change and seek the necessary skills to use creatively this fear of the new.

3. The need for personal authenticity

Leaders need to testify to their belief in the vision by living it themselves. In the above case study (p. 107), Ganey, as a transforming leader, could energize Fijian villagers to rise above their poor self-image because he believed in his own heart in the creative worth of a human being. And people sensed his authenticity, as only the oppressed can do so well. As one informant said: 'He speaks our language poorly, but we do not have to speak with him to feel his belief in our inner worth as persons'. That is why another could say that he 'felt ten feet taller and ten years younger' when Ganey entered the village. Pope John XXIII exuded this same gift of inner integrity, and also Mother Teresa. In brief, 'a total pragmatist cannot be a transforming leader',[21] no matter how well-trained in debating techniques, public oratory or interpersonal communication skills. Ultimately, personal authenticity for a transforming leader within the Church finds its source in an intimate relationship with the Lord born of contemplative prayer and asceticism. The would-be leader may have the jargon to transform leadership and mastery over the most up-to-date techniques of communication, yet, lacking a burning love of the Lord, may be 'no more than a gong booming or a cymbal clashing' (1 Cor 13:1).

4. The need for community-oriented innovators

The transforming leader, to fulfil his/her primary task of confronting a group with the need for innovation, recognizes the urgency of engaging creative and refounding persons, not just managers, in this process. The leader can encourage, nurture, nudge and inspire a group to move, but unless he/she has these creative persons at all levels in the organization to break through the rigidities of custom and denial, nothing will take place.

Frequently, 'creativity is seen as the generation of unique solutions to problems through the discovery of previously unobserved relationships between known factors or the insightful revelation of solutions to previously unsolvable problems'.[22] This definition is unsatisfactory as it is too limited in scope. Creative, even revolutionary, ideas can exist at least vaguely in organizations for years, but because no one assumes responsibility for them nothing happens. Often what is lacking is not creative ideas, but their *application* through innovative people.[23] Readers must have had the experience of seeing mission statements of dioceses or religious communities on walls of rectories, churches or convents – ornately printed and elegantly framed, but few are doing anything about implementing them. Fine dreams, but no action! Thus when I speak of creativity I am referring to 'dreamers who do' – that is, those rather rare people who are gifted at both dreaming up the new *and* doing. This obvious conclusion is little appreciated, otherwise I think people would have put a stop long ago to more and more meetings until the resolutions of the previous ones had been implemented.

A second clarification is important – namely, the distinction between *innovative* persons and *adaptors*. Both are creative persons and needed, especially the innovative or refounding type; both threaten the group because they dissent from the acceptable ways of doing things, but it is the innovator that particularly endangers the group's security and is thus the least liked. The adaptor takes a disciplined and methodical approach to the solution of problems according to traditionally accepted practices, but with more zest and initiative than usual. Every manager needs adaptors, but they are maintenance or renewal people; their aim is to keep the organization running, but a little better than before.

Some problems – especially the challenge to relate to a rapidly changing environment – demand people with totally new pastoral approaches to give the group a dramatically new direction. These are innovative or refounding persons as described earlier in this book. For example, the priest who seeks to improve his methods of preaching the Gospel in the pulpit, according to the best contemporary public speaking methods, could be called an adaptor. However, the priest who, recognizing that pulpit preaching only reaches the already converted, invents a method of evangelizing on the streets of cities is an innovator whose style or methods will be considered unorthodox by the adaptor. To be effective, the innovator is a community-oriented person, not an *individualist*; that is, he/she, though personally creative, knows that refounding cannot be done alone. With their various gifts a team is able to work out the details, experiment and evaluate the progress of the innovative insight in reality. St Paul is very much aware of this need for a community approach within the Church: 'Now Christ's body is yourselves, each of you with a part to play in the whole. And those whom God has appointed in the Church are, first apostles, secondly prophets, thirdly teachers . . . after them, miraculous powers, then gifts of healing, helpful acts, guidance, various kinds of tongues' (1 Cor 12:27–28). Prophets need teachers to help communicate the message, and teachers need prophets to articulate for them what needs to be taught.

A word of warning. Old Testament prophets were covenant-refounding persons, loving Yahweh dearly, praying and yearning above everything else to build a community of believers committed to worship, mutual love and justice. Yet in their lifetime there were others who claimed to be prophetic but were in fact dangerous agitators; in their hearts they were enemies of the people and their welfare.[24] Likewise, within the Church today there are agitators; these people are not refounding persons because they lack the virtues indicative of authenticity: 'joy, peace, patience, kindness, goodness, trustfulness, gentleness and self-control' (Gal 5:22). They may use the language of refounding, but because they lack authenticity they are dangerous to themselves and to others. The blunt and worldly-wise advice of a leadership adviser is relevant to us:

> Guard against the crazies. Innovation is seductive. It attracts interesting people. It also attracts people who will distort your ideas into something monstrous. . . . A change-oriented administrator should be damned sure that the people he or she recruits are change agents but not agitators. . . . Eccentricities and idiosyncrasies in change agents are often useful and valuable. Neurosis isn't.[25]

As we look back on the recent history of the Church we see examples of truly creative people who have struggled to live out the virtues listed by St Paul, resisting the temptation to become agitators as a consequence of being marginalized for their writings or actions. Thus we have Henri de Lubac, John Courtney Murray, Yves Congar, Dorothy Day, Pierre Teilhard de Chardin. Eventually they were listened to, but there are others who, once marginalized, have little or no influence. The discernment of the authentic refounding person as opposed to the agitator is difficult, and ultimately it can only be done in faith and prayer, as I explain elsewhere.[26]

5. The need to foster responsible dissent

Innovators are *dissenters*; that is, they offer alternative ways of acting to a group. However, a fundamental cultural anthropological insight often repeated in this book is: culture has an anxiety-reducing purpose and it will naturally resist change simply because any change is anxiety-evoking, even if the refusal to allow change may lead to the destruction of the culture itself. The predictability of culture is the swamp that can mire even the most creative of leaders. Hence, the dilemma: all cultures need dissenters who offer alternative ways of doing things if they are to continue to live, yet cultures have an inbuilt resistance to change and will normally do everything possible to obstruct the fear-creating alternatives of dissenters. The Church, like any organization or culture, cannot escape this dilemma: it is a 'treasure in pots of earthenware' (2 Cor 4:7). The restorationist Church is opting not for the future, but rather for what it considers to be the fear-lessening cultural status quo, in which the proposing of alternative ways of evangelizing and administration are strictly limited. Thus the restorationist Church shows the signs of an ageing culture (see Chapter 2).

In order to understand dissent's role in change we need to appreciate better the ways in which *open* cultures cultivate it for their survival. As a small boy in New Zealand I lived close to a Maori village and I would at times sit and watch in amazement how Maori people came to decisions. They deliberately fostered discussion and dissent before important decisions were made that would affect the whole group. Speakers presented their points of view or alternative proposals, often with considerable vehemence; this was encouraged provided it was done with the aim of achieving resolution through *dialogue* and *amity*. Meetings would go on for hours, even days, until finally a consensus emerged. As Maori people view it, to argue with or over a person is a compliment of the highest order, since it shows that he/she matters. For them, truthfulness and accountability are far more important than banal politeness. How different, I thought, to the ways of the dominant white New Zealander's culture. We want rapid decisions according to the majority vote or sometimes imposed from the top, so we find the Maori way of deliberation and cultivation of dissent too long and conflictual. However, the efforts to prevent dissent emerging in the long term leaves people angry, distrustful and prey to bickering and feuding. The Maori way is also the Japanese method of decision-making; they deliberately create discussion and dissent as an avenue to consensus, though the style is far less confrontational. Japanese business groups are very conscious that most organizations will risk death rather than encourage nonconformists who question the relevance of the status quo. Hence in order to survive they deliberately foster an ethos of dissent. Thus the principle is the same across cultures: there can be no worthwhile decisions unless there is first disagreement.[27]

Consensus, as expressed in Maori and Japanese societies, is not synonymous with unanimous aggreement; rather, it is a decision that appears most acceptable to the group as a whole. Consensus results from authentic dialogue, which is 'that address and response between persons in which there is a flow of meaning between them in spite of all the obstacles that normally would block the relationship'.[28] It is that interaction between people in which each one aims to give himself/herself as they are and seeks also to know the other as the other is. Dialogue is authentic, therefore, if three conditions are met: people feel they understand the position of others; they also feel that others understand their points of view; and thirdly, there is a readiness on the part of all to accept what is decided because it was reached openly and fairly. To assume that consensus is always synonymous with unanimity can be a dangerous mistake, because the latter may or may not be attained through dialogue.

If there are no dissenters in the process of decision-making, then *group-think* can rarely be avoided. Groupthink is a deliberately pejorative expression which is defined as a decline in mental efficiency, reality testing, and moral judgements as the result of group pressures.[29] During groupthink, people attempt so hard to agree with one another that they avoid looking at alternatives lest there be division in the gathering. Groupthink can evoke a sense of righteous well-being in the group's culture that is quite ill-founded. Would-be dissenters are silenced as a result of fear of punishment by the group; often, potential dissenters are so flattered by the attentions of others that they feel too embarrassed to express disagreement in the group. The more amiability and *esprit de corps* there is among the members of a decision-making or advising ingroup, the greater the risk that groupthink will be substituted for independent critical thinking; consequently, decisions are made not on facts but on fantasy. Irving Janis argues that groupthink caused the Bay of Pigs disaster in Cuba: President Kennedy's advisers assumed a unanimous position when it did not exist; conformity took place out of a sense of mutual loyalties to the group.[30] John Gardner, after years of research into leadership, comments on the need to foster dissenters from outside the group to avoid the seductive power of groupthink: 'Only from outside can one be sure of disinterested criticism, astringent appraisal, the rude question. Only from outside can one expect judgments untainted by the loyalty and camaraderie of insiders, undistorted by the comfortable assumptions held within the walls.'[31]

Case study: a diocesan senate trapped in groupthink

A bishop called a meeting of his senate to seek its advice about the building of a new cathedral. After some preliminary superficial discussion, he said: 'My sense is that there is general agreement about going ahead. I presume no one really objects to this work in honour of the Lord.' In fact, two did have reservations but felt that in the light of the overall agreement in the group it would cause less trouble not to speak. And, they said to themselves, 'we depend on the bishop for promotion'. When the news of the building was published there was a bitter public outcry from other priests, religious and laity. Questions like the following emerged: 'What about catechetical programs that are already poorly funded?' 'Do we really need a cathedral when there is a large parish church already in the city centre?' 'What is the morality of constructing an expensive building when this country is so poor and underdeveloped?' All very valid questions.

The bishop's mistake was to take a group of priests that by background and status was too like-minded, and the resulting groupthink was so strong that the two possible dissenters lost the courage to speak up. The bishop did not want to 'reality test' his insight for fear of it being rejected. This reinforced the senate's desire to conform to his wishes. Fortunately, alarmed by the stormy reactions from outside the senate, he finally listened to the dissenting voices; the cathedral was never built, but instead a multi-purpose pastoral centre was constructed in the poorest section of the city. The bishop was overheard to remark: 'What a pity this idea did not come up earlier in the senate! I wonder if the senate is made up of too many people who think the same.' Having taken professional advice, he changed his method of decision-making by deliberately cultivating dissent as the way to make wise judgements. He also found that when conflicts are brought out into the open, a good many just disappear; petty matters that had loomed large are exposed for what they are and the real issues take priority.

The critical role of dissent in pastoral discernment is far from being a new insight in the Church. Think of what would have happened if St Peter had forbidden St Paul and others to raise at the Council of Jerusalem the critical issue of the evangelization of non-Jews. If that had occurred, the Church would have remained a little sect confined to Jewish people. Through St Ignatius Loyola particularly, we have come to see that the way of dissent should be a normal method of decision-making for the Christian. For Ignatius, as for all Christians, the overriding need is: what is God asking of me or this group? In order to be able to hear the Lord speaking we must spend time in prayerful reflection during which we deliberately propose all kinds of alternatives without pre-judging any of them. Yet all this is impossible if we are not willing to enter into ourselves to discover the obstacles to true listening to the Spirit: the interior chaos of prejudice, fear and sinfulness. The Christian, as he/she gradually begins to be freed of these interior barriers, is able to evaluate the alternatives and slowly feels comfortable with the one that he/she senses is what God wants. A modified discernment process, deliberately aiming to evoke dissenting views for evaluation, is precisely the method adopted by the US bishops for the writing of their key pastorals, for example on peace. It does not lessen their authority. On the contrary, it enhances it because the method, based on the people of God model of Church, recognizes that the Holy Spirit speaks through the legitimate gifts and concerns of everyone within the body of Christ; and people come to own the document that they feel able to comment on.[32]

In brief, dissenters reframe things we take for granted by offering new ways of viewing issues or by putting them into contexts that we did not previously think possible. Dissenters expand our imaginations. They are upside-down thinkers, terribly annoying to us when we are too attached to the security of our ideas or habits, but very necessary if we want to know what God wills of us. The leader who does not cultivate an atmosphere in which dissent is valued risks the judgement that he/she wants to be God, and no right-minded person, versed in the lessons of Genesis, wants to have that said of him/her!

6. The need to claim one's authority/power

In Chapter 3 I clarified the meaning of authority and power. These two words within the contemporary Church have so many negative connotations that to speak of 'claiming one's authority/power' means that a cool discussion on authority and power is even more difficult to achieve.

However, we cannot avoid these words or the phrase because I firmly believe that the failure of leaders and followers to own their respective authority/power is further exacerbating the chaos in the Church today. Readers will recall that authority, from whatever source it comes, gives legitimacy to the use of power. A clearly indicated authority (or authorities) in a group is essential for the stability and progress of that group; authority sets the limits, draws appropriate boundaries, provides structures to allow the group to fulfil its primary task. People (e.g. bishops, senates, episcopal conferences, parish councils, individuals on the basis of baptism) who have legitimately been given the power to act and direct the group administratively and/or prophetically must recognize or claim this authority. So often in times of change and chaos people in authority fear to own and exercise their authority out of fear that the group will punish them in some way or other. Unfortunately, because of people who have abused their authority, the word 'authority' has become incorrectly synonymous with 'authoritarian'. The latter word simply means a way of improperly using authority.

There are several biblical examples of leaders who for a time refused out of fear to claim and use the authority/power given them. Moses, having tried every trick he could to refuse Yahweh's command to lead the Israelites out of Egypt, finally said in desperation: 'Please, my Lord . . . send anyone you decide to send!' (Ex 4:13). At this, Yahweh became angry at Moses' reluctance. Jonah has the same hesitancy, so he 'set about running away from Yahweh' (Jon 1:3). Gideon is so fearful of owning the authority given him by Yahweh that at one point he hides in the wine-press. There is a similar dithering or unwillingness on the part of many leaders in today's Church to accept their position and personal authority/power to lead. The consequence is disorganized and dispirited dioceses, parishes and religious communities. There are times (generally rare) when one's position authority/power must be formally used – that is, with an implicit or explicit threat attached to the directive given – but the pastoral effectiveness of its use will depend on how one's personal authority/power is employed (e.g. by way of love, understanding, empathy, compassion).

Case study: a diocese with low morale

Five years ago a diocese held a synod after two years of detailed planning and widespread consultation of priests, religious and laity. After a vision statement and strategies for action had been produced, people left the synod enthusiastic and willing to participate in the renewal of the diocese. Within eighteen months, though, the high morale and hopes of action had evaporated; people had become angry, frustrated, feeling betrayed that after all their efforts nothing substantial had resulted from the synod. The bishop had vigorously supported the synod, but kept putting off the recommendations he had assented to. He did not, he said, 'want to hurt anyone'. He would agree to all kinds of plans proposed to him by priests and religious which either had nothing to do with the synod's strategies or directly went contrary to them. 'If only he would do what he alone can do – make decisions for structural changes – to allow us to get on with the job!' said one informant.

Note the basic cause of the frustration: the inability of the bishop to be a bishop! People say he 'is a good man, kind to all', but unless he acts as only a diocesan leader can, his 'goodness and kindness' are misplaced. No substantial renewal can occur in his diocese until he makes the decisions that he alone can make after appropriate dialogue/consultation. Now he feels frustrated himself because his kind qualities no longer contribute to good morale in the diocese. The more he uncritically gives way to requests and refuses to make necessary, though unpopular, decisions based on the synod's pastoral vision, the more angry and cynical people become. He himself now feels isolated and bitter. Yet he has only himself to blame.

We need to examine further this critical and delicate issue of the need to claim one's authority/power. Robert Bellah, in the quotation at the beginning of this chapter, warns the United States Catholic bishops to avoid falling into the cultural trap of becoming just managers or therapists. His warning applies not only to bishops, but to all who are called to lead in today's Church (e.g. religious congregational leaders). They must be ever aware that their primary task as transforming leaders is to lead the people of God; it is not to be bursars, managers, therapists, real estate developers. They will seek to lead, even when making difficult decisions, through winning the consent of people rather than through the use of fear or the creation of dependent relationships so common in the pre-Vatican II Church. This is what the 'politics of revelation' is all about – namely, engaging with others to raise one another to higher levels of motivation and morality. It is a *moral* issue in that it elevates both the leader and the led to new levels of human interaction through a process that is challenging and uplifting. Transforming leadership demands an on-going honesty with oneself: What is my motivation? Do I fear making difficult decisions in view of the primary task of my leadership, because I fear offending people and then they will not like me?

Case study: parishioners claim their authority

A mission church in one section of a large geographically spread parish was suddenly closed by the decision of the pastor after no consultation with the local parishioners. The church was to be sold. The pastor told them they must travel 30 miles each Sunday to mass at the central church. The parishioners were angry not only regarding the way the decision was made, but also because many of them had limited transport facilities available to them. Many refused to accept the decision and travelled long distances to petition the bishop's intervention. Permission for the church to remain open was granted, but no mass would be available; on their own initiative, though, the people arranged – with the bishop's blessing – Sunday prayer services.

Despite their limited knowledge of theology, the parishioners claimed the authority to act based on their common baptism; they refused to submit to the authoritarianism of the pastor.

Case study: a cardinal accepts his authority

After finishing a major study of cultural prejudice among white Catholics in New Zealand at the request of the episcopal conference, I was asked by reporters of two television stations to answer questions for prime-time national news. I hesitated, fearing, that on such a delicate topic I would unwittingly do harm to the Church by the information I would give. I expressed my fears to Cardinal Reginald Delargey, the head of the bishops' conference, but he replied: 'Gerald, this is not your report, it is ours. We commissioned it and we accept the responsibility for its findings. Go out and share what you think should be said. We support you!'

I found the cardinal's action a refreshing experience, because after conducting surveys for other agencies in the past, I frequently found myself standing alone with reports because no one would assume responsibility for their challenging conclusions. People wanted to blame me for their own problems rather than confront the awkward reality themselves; their leaders assented to and intensified this scapegoating, fearing to own their own authority/power to challenge the group's denial. In the next case study a bishop accepts his primary pastoral responsibility to his priests. He could call them to holiness simply because he himself placed prayer in his own life as *the* priority; his authenticity showed through to his men.

Case study: calling to integral salvation

A bishop, on taking over a small diocese, found low morale among his priests. They had not been visited personally for years, except by the diocesan business manager to check on properties and books and a brief visit by the previous bishop for confirmations. The priests felt neglected, tired and uncertain about how to serve the Church in difficult times. The bishop cancelled all major appointments for three months, delegated routine work to others, and then visited his men to listen to their concerns; he also arranged retreats for the following year that he himself led. Many priests began to feel appreciated and understood by their bishop, who helped during the retreat and afterwards to call them to a deeper union with the person of Christ. One informent remarked: 'Before the bishop talked *at* us, if we ever saw him. This one speaks of his own personal love of Christ, *his* struggles to come closer to him. This is good and touches us where we most need help.'

The emphasis on persuasion in transforming leadership does not mean that the leader's task is merely confined to directing discussion groups or making inspiring speeches; it means the hard task of goal-setting and calling people to be responsible for what they have committed themselves to. Recall the times in which Moses was tempted to turn aside from the primary task of leading the Israelites into the promised land. The people made Moses the scapegoat for the chaos they were experiencing: 'Was it for lack of graves in Egypt, that you had to lead us out to die in the desert? What was the point of bringing us out of Egypt. . . . We prefer to work for the Egyptians than to die in the desert . . .' (Ex 14:11–12). He did not panic or flee, but kept to the primary task of calling the people clearly – with no ambiguity – to follow Yahweh's vision for them.[33] In later times we see the Israelites trying to trick the prophets into doublespeak – that is, language that pretends to tell people the truth but does not do so. 'It is language', writes William Lutz, the inventor of the term, 'that makes the bad seem good, the negative appear positive, the unpleasant appear attractive or at least tolerable.'[34] So they tempt the prophets: 'Do not prophesy the truth to us; tell us flattering things; have illusory visions; turn aside from the way, leave the path, rid us of the Holy One of Israel' (Isa 30:10–11). The prophets will not be seduced by the people's flattery or fantasies: 'This is a rebellious people, they are lying children' (Isa 30:9). Nor would the apostles tolerate doublespeak. Listen to James: 'If you mean "yes", you must say "yes"; if you mean "no", say "no"' (Jas 5:12).

In modern times Douglas McGregor, an industrial psychologist, had long believed that the primary task of the leader was to give people the greatest possible scope to exercise their freedom and to flatter them with fine words; but after a spell as a college president he changed his mind. His comments are apposite:

I believed . . . that a leader could operate successfully as a kind of adviser to his organization . . . duck the unpleasant necessity of making difficult decisions . . . that 'good human relations' would eliminate all discord and disagreement. I couldn't have been more wrong. . . . [A] leader cannot avoid the exercise of authority any more than he can avoid responsibility for what happens to his organization.[35]

The message is clear: you cannot be an authority dissenter if you varnish the truth to please people. Ownership of your authority/power means naming denial and other aberrations for what they are – untruths.

7. The need for appropriate knowledge/skills

The transforming leader needs competence (knowledge and skills) and commitment (attitudes and beliefs) and it is the first that is commonly overlooked in the Church. The type of knowledge and skills will depend on the particular leadership role one is expected to fill.

Case study: poor theology frustrates pastoral planning

A reactive-management bishop was concerned to formulate a vision for the diocese and wanted to found it on Vatican II orientations. With the aid of his senate he formed a vision statement; but, as he studied little, he did not realize it was based on pre-Vatican II values. Dissidents favouring the Council had been marginalized on the senate. Two years previously, the bishop had ordained three new priests – though he had been a little uneasy about them because they seemed generally out of touch with the people pastorally. However, he thought God would do something about it and 'make them come right'. Within a year, complaints came in about the authoritarian attitudes of the new priests, but the senate reassured him 'because the people will learn the right things from these men'.

This case study, from a diocese in an affluent Western country, sadly illustrates the danger of good will without sound theological knowledge. Here, an entire diocese is put at risk because the bishop is theologically ill-equipped. If the bishop really owned his authority/power he would himself seek, before formulating a vision statement and ordaining ministers, skilled theological advice about the nature of the Church according to the Council and the qualities needed in contemporary candidates for the priesthood. The following case study exemplifies how easy it is for a leader to be entrapped in the fantasies of a group.

Case study: colluding with a group's fantasies

A bishop with moderate restorationist qualities was loudly praised on his
transfer to a new diocese by a vocally abrasive group of restorationists. Over
time, this group kept reminding the bishop that his strong leadership was
providing a much-needed direction to the diocese. The more they applauded
him the more he colluded with them in their fantasies of what the Church
should be today. At present, he is as strident as the group is over the necessity
of restorationism in the diocese. Since he will hear no contrary views, the diocese
is becoming increasingly and openly polarized. Non-restorationists consider the
situation hopeless.

Once we admit the necessity for diversities flowing from inculturation and
for principled dissent, any attempt to foster a thoroughly homogeneous,
unargumentative, non-disputatious Church is out of the question.
Morever, it is evident from the previous chapter that there are at least four
ways of being Church today. Leaders, therefore, require skills to develop
within a pluralist Church a workable degree of unity. From experience I
find that groupthink and other forms of denial are so devious and subtle
that a future-oriented leader will need skilled outsiders or consultants to
help himself/herself be open to positive dissent. In this last case study, the
bishop had lost all objectivity and non-restorationists knew this, but no one
would confront him with the fact of his polarizing leadership. Not only the
bishop, but also his non-restorationist advisers, required the advice of consultants on how best to approach the problem. The conflictual situation
could not be resolved by amateurs alone. In Chapter 8 I explain the role
of these consultants in more detail.

8. The need to apply the axiom 'the new belongs elsewhere'

Having found the creative pastoral agents, the task of the official transforming leader is to position them where their talents can be most produc-
tive for the Church. The official leader becomes the 'political' sponsor and
protector of these agents by changing or forming new structures to allow
the latter to work. In the next chapter I argue that since the obstacles within
existing structures to the refounding process are often so considerable, this
'protection' and the encouragement to establish new structures are
necessary if the refounding projects are to have the space in which to succeed. Instead of having to lose apostolic energy battling to explain their
insights to colleagues frightened of the new ideas, the creative pastoral
agents protected by their authority dissenter(s) (e.g. bishop(s) or congregational leader(s)) can be left in peace to get on with the task of apostolic

innovation. This is an application of the axiom 'the new belongs elsewhere' (to be further explained in Chapter 5).[36]

9. The need for reflection and 'not-knowing'

True Gospel leadership occurs only when one has learnt the art of follower-ship; that is, the journeying inwards with the Lord to acknowledge one's own chaos of sinfulness, prejudices and fear. In this world it is a journey that can never end. Followership is primarily a way of being face-to-face with the Lord in faith, admitting our powerlessness and our desperate need for the Lord's grace, sensitive to his on-going forgiveness and compassion. If deep in my heart I become aware of manipulative tendencies in my leadership, despite the rhetoric I give to others, I have self-knowledge of immense worth. Mary is a model of transforming leadership because she would enter deep within herself and there acknowledge her own need of the Lord; in opening herself to the Lord in this way she discovered that nothing is impossible to those who love him: 'she treasured all these things and *pondered* them in her heart' (Lk 2:19). Ultimately the quality of a person's integrity is what determines authentic leadership, not whether or not he/she holds a position of authority.[37] Mary is the Mother of God, but that is not the primary cause of her greatness, as her Son tells us: 'a woman in the crowd raised her voice and said, "Blessed the womb that bore you and the breasts that fed you!" But he replied, "More blessed still are those who hear the word of God and keep it!"' (Lk 11:27–28).

Psychoanalyst Wilfred Bion strongly advises his colleagues to admit at times in their clinical work that they do not know the answers to the problems confronting them. He tells them to sit in the darkness of *not-knowing*:

> Discard your memory; discard the future tense of your desire . . . to leave a space for a new idea. . . . Instead of trying to bring a brilliant, intelligent, knowledgeable light to bear on obscure problems, I suggest we bring to bear a diminution of the light – a penetrating beam of darkness. . . . Thus, a very faint light would become visible in maximum conditions of darkness.[38]

To sit in the liminality or the darkness/chaos of 'not-knowing', without distractions or the escapism of busyness, is the way to new insights.

If this process is necessary for the pursuit of ordinary human knowledge or the answers to problems, much more so is it valid for those who seek to discover God's will for them as leaders within the Church. In fact, in the mystery of God's plan the way to true wisdom is also through admitting 'not-knowing'. Reflect on the story of Job. His secure world suddenly disintegrates when he loses everything: wealth, health and family. He admits his chaos and inability to understand the reasons for his afflictions: 'I have months of futility assigned to me, nights of suffering to be my lot' (Job 7:3). While sitting in the darkness of the not-knowing, Job discovers an energizing hope beyond human imagination: 'I know that I have a living Defender. . . . He whom I shall see will take my part' (Job 19:25, 27). Jesus in his agony in Gethsemane acknowledges his own not-knowing in the midst of incredible darkness of soul. What is the Father asking of him? Why do his chosen disciples not understand his agony of darkness and offer him consolation? Jesus rests in the chaos of desolation and discovers a newness and confidence in response to his prayer: 'The hour has come. . . . Get up! Let us go! My betrayer is not far away' (Mk 14:41–42). Not surprisingly, therefore, the advice of the fourteenth-century author of *The Cloud of Unknowing* remains just as relevant for today's Christian leader: 'So set yourself to rest in this darkness as long as you can, always crying out after him whom you love. For if you are to experience him or to see him at all, insofar as it is possible here, it must always be in this cloud.'[39]

10. The need for rituals of mourning

One of the most important, and most neglected, tasks of a leader is to offer space to people to grieve over that which has died or is no longer apostolically relevant. When one accepts the reality of loss, with all its pain and anger, and allows it to go, then the new has room to enter. If losses are not owned up to they remain to haunt the living, trapping people unwittingly in the past.

Case study: an archbishop surprised by the pain of loss

Rome decided to divide a long-established archdiocese into three dioceses. The archbishop announced the decision by letter at Sunday Masses, mentioning in passing that Rome's unexpected decision would be seen 'by all as a blessing on the local church'. To his surprise, the decision evoked a spate of angry phone calls and letters to the local newspapers; the degree of anger of these spontaneous responses puzzled him. So he published another letter to the faithful, pointing out that Rome's decision was to be expected because he could not care for such a large area any longer. The reactions this time were even more fierce.

What had the archbishop done wrong? He had failed to communicate with the people for two reasons: first, Rome had made a decision that affected people's lives and they had not been consulted, so the anger they expressed reflected their grief at the loss of an opportunity to become part of an important pastoral decision. Second, the decision having been made without their involvement was communicated rationally and bluntly to them with no reference to the losses the division would cause them. For generations, families had been associated or identified with the name of the archdiocese and suddenly one day they find this link broken. The archbishop eventually recognized the pain and its causes and wrote a third letter to the people, apologizing for his insensitivity; in effect, this letter became a quasi-public ritual of mourning. People now felt a little more at peace with the decision. In Chapter 7 I will consider more fully the need for rituals of grieving.

A spirituality for leadership in refounding

Within the Gospel, Jesus Christ is at pains to stress the principle that authority/power presupposes service and sacrifice. When the sons of Zebedee seek the first places in the Kingdom, Jesus responds by asking them a very awkward question: 'Can you drink the cup that I shall drink, or be baptised with the baptism with which I shall be baptised?' (Mk 10:38). They did not grasp his radically new insight into the role of leadership – namely, transforming leadership by way of integrative and reciprocal authority/power through which people reveal to themselves the richness of growing through service to others. Thus in contrast to the position authority/power of coercion commonly practised in Palestine and much desired by the sons of Zebedee, Jesus proposes this axiom: 'anyone who wants to become great among you must be your servant, and anyone who wants to be first among you must be slave to all' (Mk 10:43–44). During the last supper he reiterates that authority/power among his followers must be one of service for the building up of community: 'For who is the greater: the one at table or the one who serves? The one at table, surely? Yet here am I among you as one who serves!' (Lk 22:27).

So accustomed are the apostles to authority being synonymous with dominative or coercive power over others, together with the status privileges attached, that they cannot grasp the meaning of Jesus' instructions. Thus he does what he preaches, hoping that they will understand his message; he personally exemplifies kindness, service, humility and love for others to a degree beyond imagination: 'I have come so that they may have life and have it to the full. I am the good shepherd: the good shepherd lays down his life for his sheep' (Jn 10:10–11). The apostles finally understood, and in their own teaching they repeated the theme, that authority/power is synonymous with service – the service of listening and persuasion, not exploitation on account of one's position: 'Do not lord it over the group which is in your charge, but be an example for the flock' (1 Pet 5:3). It is St Paul who spells out that only through love can we begin to depth the incredible demands that Christian dialogue commits us to: 'Love is always patient and kind; love is never jealous; love is not boastful or conceited, it is never rude and never seeks its own advantage, it does not take offence or store up grievances. . . . It is always ready to make allowances, to trust, to hope and to endure whatever comes' (1 Cor 13:4–7).

History shows, however, that the Church throughout the centuries has at times lost sight of this inspiring servant/dialogue vision of authority/power by embracing the oppressive values and practices of feudalism, absolute monarchies and imperialism. Vatican II, in calling itself a pastoral gathering, opted to return the Church to the servant model of leadership. Because the Church is the people of God all share in the priestly, prophetic, and royal authority/power of Christ and hence have their own particular roles within the mission of the Church. Bishops and priests have a responsibility to represent this authority/power, but its exercise must always be modelled on that of Christ the Servant. As in all transforming leadership, it is the *purpose* that is crucial: the building up of the Christian community, the primary means being listening, example and persuasion. Speaking of the role of bishops, the Council stresses their listening or servant quality, saying that they 'govern the particular churches . . . by their counsel, exhortations and example, as well, indeed, as by their authority and sacred power. This power they use only for the edification of their flock in truth and holiness.'[40] Paul VI takes up the Council's repeated emphasis on dialogue – the medium of transforming leadership – within the Church and further clarifies it in his first encyclical, *Ecclesiam Suam*: 'Before speaking we must take great care to listen not only to what people say but more especially to what they have in their hearts to say. Only then will we understand them and respect them, and even, as far as possible, agree with them . . .'[41]

The grace of leading according to the servanthood model must characterize both the authority and pathfinding dissenters within the Church. However, there are other qualities, for example the admission of one's absolute dependence on the Lord, that form together a distinctive spirituality in those people committed to the refounding process.[42] It is not a spirituality of escape from the world of uncertainty characteristic of restorationists. Rather, it is a way of sustaining dissenters in their uncharted faith journey into a world of cultures that are increasingly unreceptive to the faith/justice message of Jesus Christ (see Figure 4.1). It is a world of extremes of wealth and poverty and of oppression in many forms. While many people believe that technology can solve all problems, countless others have lost all hope in human ability to provide meaning in their lives. Religious sects and fundamentalists withdraw into the securities of the past and private piety.

Responsible dissenters, however, foster communities marked by such qualities as: the prophetic involvement in the faith/justice issues; prayer that acknowledges their human powerlessness before God; a commitment to work with people of different denominations and religion. Yet these communities cannot develop, unless the dissenters themselves are imbued with a deep interior and ascetical life that allows them to be open to God and to the ever-changing pastoral needs of their neighbours. It is a spirituality that breeds a Paul-like apostolic hope and toughness: 'We are subjected to every kind of hardship, but never distressed; we see no way

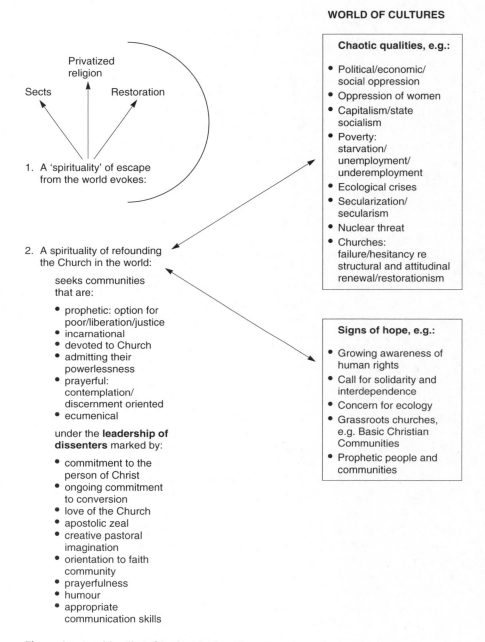

Figure 4.1 A spirituality of leadership for refounding

out but we never despair; we are pursued but never cut off; knocked down, but still have some life in us; always we carry with us in our body the death of Jesus so that the life of Jesus, too, may be visible in our body' (2 Cor 4:8–10).

Summary

Today the emphasis in leadership has moved from management in order to control groups to a transforming style that aims to bring the best out of people and to respond quickly to change. A leader moulds and communicates a task-oriented vision which gives direction to the work of others. If the leader fails to provide this vision, the strategies to realize it and appropriate accountability structures, the group becomes confused and de-energized.[43] The primary task of the Church's leaders is to articulate according to the transforming model of leadership the vision of a believing, worshipping and serving community, bringing the Gospel into interaction with the ever-changing world of today. Appropriate apostolic strategies cannot develop if officially appointed leaders are not prepared to foster responsible dissent within believing communities.

However, the cultural forces inhibiting this creative dissent cannot be over-stressed. For example, if we take creativity as the variable and examine the world of ecclesial and secular cultures in any age, only one out of four types has an unquestioning concern for it. The four models of culture are: power, role, person and mission.[44] In power cultures, for example the Church and religious congregations in pre-Vatican II times, pastoral creativity is allowed only at the top – and even that is limited by the rigorous constraints of tradition; the role culture, the preferred culture of restorationism, is a bureaucracy that by definition aims to maintain the status quo and discourage all dissent. In the person culture the individual is the central figure and all is directed to his/her welfare no matter at what cost to the common good. This type of culture, in which creativity exists primarily for the individual, is fundamentally alien to the Church's community-oriented nature. Only where mission cultures exist is there an atmosphere conducive to the emergence of creativity through dissent. In this culture the primary aim is to respond to needs 'out there' through flexible and innovative ways by people working together for that purpose, sharing talents, fostering creative dissent, encouraging one another; leadership in this culture is transforming.

The majority of cultures, including the culture of the restorationist Church, belong to the first three types and are based on mythologies of control that obstruct or restrict creativity, especially of the quantum leap kind needed for refounding. People in the Church with a special obligation to be transforming leaders (e.g. bishops, congregational leaders), therefore, are called to foster radical culture changes and, as anthropological studies show, this is an onerous task requiring competency, commitment and courage. Jesus chose a transforming form of leadership for mission and refused to adopt the coercive styles of the leaders around him. We can do no better for 'A servant is not greater than his master' (Jn 15:20).

Notes

1. K. Rahner, *The Shape of the Church to Come* (New York: Seabury Press, 1974), p. 49.
2. R. Bellah, 'Leadership Viewed from the Vantage Point of American Culture', Address to the US Catholic Bishops' Conference, *Origins*, vol. 20, no. 14 (1990), p. 220.
3. 'Pastoral Constitution on the Church in the Modern World' in W. M. Abbott, *The Documents of Vatican II* (London: Geoffrey Chapman, 1966), pp. 202, 269.
4. See P. Hersey and K. Blanchard, *Management of Organizational Behavior: Utilizing Human Resources* (Englewood Cliffs, NJ: Prentice-Hall, 1982), pp. 149–92.
5. See J. Heap, *The Management of Innovation and Design* (London: Cassell, 1989), pp. 69ff.
6. See T. J. Peters and R. H. Waterman, *In Search of Excellence: Lessons from America's Best-Run Companies* (New York: Harper & Row, 1982).
7. T. E. Deal and A. A. Kennedy, *Corporate Cultures: The Rites and Rituals of Corporate Life* (Reading, MA: Addison-Wesley, 1982).
8. R. K. Greenleaf, *Servant Leadership: A Journey into the Nature of Legitimate Power and Greatness* (New York: Paulist Press, 1977).
9. G. Pinchot, *Intrapreneuring* (New York: Harper & Row, 1985); for a detailed review of leadership issues, see B. M. Bass, *Handbook of Leadership: Theory, Research, and Managerial Applications* (3rd edn; New York: Free Press, 1990).
10. See relevant comments by J. W. Gardner, *On Leadership* (New York: Free Press, 1990), pp. 141ff.; L. P. Carroll, *To Love To Share To Serve: Challenge to a Religious* (Collegeville, MN: Liturgical Press, 1979), pp. 36–40; M. Wolff-Salin, *The Shadow Side of Community and the Growth of the Self* (New York: Crossroad, 1988), pp. 61–8.
11. This definition is based on J. M. Burns's insights into transforming leadership: *Leadership* (New York: Harper Torch, 1978), *passim*.
12. J. W. Gardner, cited by R. H. Waterman, *The Renewal Factor* (New York: Bantam Books, 1987), p. 213.
13. T. Reese, *Archbishop: Inside the Power Structure of the American Catholic Church* (San Francisco: Harper & Row, 1989), pp. 349f.
14. S. Corey, *The Seven Habits of Highly Effective People: Powerful Lessons in Personal Change: Restoring the Character Ethic* (New York: Simon & Schuster, 1990), p. 101.
15. See J. P. Kotter, *A Force for Change: How Leadership Differs from Management* (New York: Free Press, 1990), pp. 3–18; W. Bennis, *On Becoming a Leader* (Reading, MA: Addison-Wesley, 1989), pp. 44–9; S. P. Robbins, *Organizational Behavior: Concepts, Controversies, and Applications* (Englewood Cliffs, NJ: Prentice-Hall, 1989), pp. 302–35.
16. Quoted in *Time* (18 May 1987), p. 68.
17. See C. R. Hickman and M. A. Silva, *Creating Excellence* (New York: NAL, 1984), p. 151, and R. Beckhard and R. T. Harris, *Organizational Transitions: Managing Complex Change* (Reading, MA: Addison-Wesley, 1987), pp. 45–56.
18. See clarifications by P. Avis, *Authority, Leadership and Conflict in the Church* (London: Mowbray, 1992), pp. 113f.
19. For an understanding of 'primary task', see E. J. Miller and A. K. Rice, *Systems of Organization: The Control of Task and Sentient Boundaries* (London: Tavistock, 1970), pp. 25–8.
20. Quoted by brochure: *Social Dreaming for the Management of Change: A Programme of Dialogues*, Grubb Institute, London, July 1989.
21. C. Handy, *An Age of Unreason* (London: Random Century, 1989), p. 107.

22. T. A. Luckenbach, 'Encouraging "Little C" and "Big C" Creativity' in A. D. Timpe (ed.), *Creativity* (New York: Facts on File Publications, 1987), p. 84.
23. See T. Leavitt, 'Creativity is Not Enough', *Harvard Business Review* (May/June 1963), pp. 72–83.
24. See G. A. Arbuckle, *Out of Chaos: Refounding Religious Congregations* (New York: Paulist Press/London: Geoffrey Chapman, 1988), pp. 46–62.
25. W. Bennis, *Why Leaders Can't Lead: The Unconscious Conspiracy Continues* (San Francisco: Jossey-Bass, 1990), p. 148.
26. See Arbuckle, op. cit., pp. 118–24.
27. See J. Medge, *The Maoris of New Zealand* (London: Routledge & Kegan Paul, 1976), pp. 257–9, and R. T. Pascale and A. G. Athos, *The Art of Japanese Management* (London: Allen Lane, 1982), pp. 116–76; also Bennis, op. cit., pp. 121–36.
28. R. L. Howe, *The Miracle of Dialogue* (New York: Seabury Press, 1963), p. 37; also see R. Wynn and C. W. Guditus, *Team Management: Leadership by Consensus* (Columbus, OH: Charles E. Merrill, n.d.), pp. 40–7.
29. See D. R. Forsyth, *Group Dynamics* (Pacific Grove, CA: Brooks/Cole, 1990), pp. 294–315; and C. Handy, *Understanding Voluntary Organizations* (London: Penguin, 1990), pp. 62–4.
30. See I. L. Janis, *Victims of Groupthink* (2nd edn; Boston: Houghton Mifflin, 1982).
31. Gardner, op. cit., p. 130.
32. See R. Weakland, 'Where Does the Economics Pastoral Stand?', *Origins*, vol. 13, no. 46 (1984), p. 758.
33. See G. A. Arbuckle, *Grieving for Change: A Spirituality for Refounding Gospel Communities* (London: Geoffrey Chapman/Maryknoll, NY: Orbis Books, 1991), pp. 151–6.
34. W. Lutz, *Doublespeak* (New York: HarperPerennial, 1990), p. 1.
35. D. McGregor, 'On Leadership', *Antioch Notes* (May 1954), pp. 2f., as cited by W. Bennis, *Beyond Bureaucracy: Essays on the Development and Evolution of Human Organization* (New York: McGraw-Hill, 1966), p. 70. I am grateful to A. Bain *et al.* for clarifying the words 'authority' and 'authoritarianism' as used in this section. See their book *Paper Houses: The Authority Vacuum in a Government School* (Melbourne: CollinsDove, 1992), pp. 23–5. See also W. R. Bion, *Attention and Interpretation* (London: Tavistock, 1970), *passim*.
36. See Arbuckle, *Out of Chaos*, op. cit., pp. 40, 125.
37. See relevant comments by J. Hagberg, *Real Power: The Stages of Personal Power in Organizations* (Minneapolis: Winston Press, 1984), pp. 149–74, and R. Kelley, *The Power of Followership* (New York: Doubleday, 1991), *passim*.
38. W. R. Bion, as cited by P. J. Casement, *Learning from the Patient* (New York: Guilford Press, 1991), p. 358.
39. J. Walsh (ed.), *The Cloud of Unknowing* (New York: Paulist Press, 1981), p. 121.
40. 'Dogmatic Constitution on the Church' in W. M. Abbott (ed.), *The Documents of Vatican II* (London: Geoffrey Chapman, 1966), p. 51.
41. *The Papal Encyclicals: 1958–1981* (Raleigh, NC: Pierian Press, 1981), p. 153.
42. See G. A. Arbuckle, *Earthing the Gospel: An Inculturation Handbook for Pastoral Workers* (London: Geoffrey Chapman/Maryknoll, NY: Orbis Books, 1990), pp. 208–20.
43. See Miller and Rice, op. cit., p. 28.
44. See C. Hardy, *Understanding Organizations* (Harmondsworth: Penguin, 1985), pp. 186–96.

PART TWO
The Church in Miniature: The Refounding of Religious Congregations

[Religious] embody the Church in her desire to give herself completely
to the radical demands of the beatitudes. . . . [They are] a challenge
to the world and to the Church . . .

(Paul VI)

5 Challenging restorationism: refounding religious congregations

It is from chaos that God created and recreates. So our situation does not call for a restoration. . . . The solution [to the chaos in religious life] cannot be found in going back, but in refounding.

(John M. Lozano)[1]

There is a chaos in many religious congregations but it is a calcified chaos.

(Mary Jo Leddy)[2]

This chapter explains:

- in-depth some of the key tensions and barriers to pastoral creativity common to the wider Church;

- why religious life must challenge contemporary restorationism;

- why historically religious congregations are founded and refounded at times of chaos in the Church and society;

- the qualities of leadership needed for the refounding of religious congregations;

- the various ways in which religious are reacting to the chaos in religious life, including the possibility of congregational schism;

- the meaning of the operational axiom 'the new belongs elsewhere'.

Religious congregations are the Church, as the people of God, in miniature. People come together to live the radical values of the Gospel, to be devoted totally to the person of Christ and his Kingdom values, and to share that experience with others even if it costs them their lives in imitation of their Master. They are dissenters because, in contrast to worldly values and customs, they offer alternative Gospel-based examples.

No one is to be spared the dissenting critique of their lives and message – not even the Church itself. 'Religious orders', writes Johannes

Metz, 'are a kind of shock therapy introduced by the Holy Spirit for the Church as a whole. Against the dangerous accommodations and questionable compromises that the Church . . . can always incline to, they press for the uncompromising nature of the Gospel and of the imitation of Christ.'[3] This is the enthralling theory of religious life. If religious life is strong, then so is the Church. If it is weak or accommodating to worldly values and lacking apostolic dissent or imagination, then so is the Church itself.

Religious life: mirrors the chaos in the Church

Part Two of this book looks at religious congregations within the Church today. As explained in the introduction, by analysing the present state of religious life at some depth, we are able to see in sharper focus some of the issues and barriers to refounding the Church at all levels (e.g. within parishes, dioceses, episcopal conferences), as considered in Part One. And by further refining the insight into the process of refounding religious communities through the leadership of authority and pathfinding dissenters, it is possible to grasp a little more clearly the ways in which leaders and evangelizers throughout the Church should be reacting to the chaos within itself and the world. In brief, this part of the book takes religious life as a case study to uncover lessons helpful for the refounding of the Church at large.

The major types of religious congregations (monastic, mendicant and apostolic) have emerged historically in response to periods of significant chaos/corruption within and outside the Church.[4] (See Figure 6.1 on p. 160.) People like Benedict, Dominic, Francis of Assisi, Teresa of Avila, John of the Cross, Ignatius Loyola and Mary Ward, burning with love of the Lord, zeal for his Church and immense creative imagination, made quantum leaps in the theory and practice of religious life. They consciously set out to remind the Church of its primary task to preach and live the message of Christ within the world. Theirs was a martyrdom of prophecy because the Lord tested them, most often through the marginalizations and condemnations of the very people who should have been their most radical supporters – fellow members of their congregations and/or the Church's hierarchy itself. Their visions were so profound and expansive that people took fright at the challenge of the risks demanded for their implementation. Hence the opposition aroused by people like Francis of Assisi, John Baptist de la Salle, Madeleine Sophie Barat, Cornelia Connelly, Guillaume Chaminade, Jean-Claude Colin, Edmund Rice, Anne Marie Javouhey, Teresa Maxis Duchemin, Mary McKillop, Pierre Teilhard de Chardin.

Religious women as foundresses have suffered by the very fact of being women in thoroughly patriarchal cultures and Church. Thus Mary McKillop, the saintly foundress of the Josephite order in Australia, was excommunicated for a period of time in the 1870s by a local bishop. Much earlier, in the seventeenth century, Mary Ward planned a congregation in which women could be active and apostolic with no cloister, something unheard of for women until very recent times, but she was incarcerated by ecclesiastics for a period of time for daring to think so creatively. Mary Ward's insight was based on her unshaken faith in the ability of women to do great things in and for the Church. She wrote: 'I would to God that all men understand this verity, that women, if they will, may be perfect and if they would not make us believe we can do nothing and that we are but women, we might do great matters'.[5]

Since, as described in previous chapters, the Church and the world are experiencing symptoms of chaos – for example, the disintegration of meaning systems, violence, malaise, a sense of drifting without goals, fundamentalism, secularism – the conditions are right for dramatically new types of religious life to emerge and for old authentic forms to be revitalized. One could reasonably expect that religious congregations are prophetically leading by word and example in constructive criticism of the present restorationism within the Church, because restorationism is itself a corruption of power – well-intentioned, but corruption nonetheless. The authority/power of church leadership that should be calling for an all-out, effective missionary thrust into the world is instead directing its energies inwards in an effort to restore a Counter-Reformation façade.

On the part of religious congregations, however, there is no lack of rhetoric, for example at provincial and general chapters, about the need to respond to the contemporary apostolic challenges. Certainly at the level of theory or rhetoric, as concretized in new constitutions, religious generally accept the values of Vatican II. But I believe that, with some exceptions, religious communities are simply not owning in practice the radicality of the Gospel message as set out so extensively in their constitutions and vision/mission statements. The Executive Summary of the Study on the Future of Religious Orders in the United States comments:

> Perhaps the most striking discrepancy in the portrait of the future of the social institution of religious life that emerges from [the study] . . . relates to commitment to the poor. The random sample of members reveals at most a moderate commitment to participate in an activity which has become increasingly an espoused mission for many religious orders and quite explicitly by the church.[6]

The chaos in religious life mirrors the malaise in the wider Church; just as there is denial and escape-from-the-world theology or restorationism within the Church, so also in religious congregations. Meanwhile, congregational membership continues to decline dramatically, especially in the Western world; for example, in the United States membership in religious orders has dropped 40 per cent since 1962. This brief review of religious life needs further explanation.

Refounding in religious congregations: overview of model

Refounding, readers will recall, is a process – whether in the Church or in religious life – whereby Gospel values are applied to the most urgent, non-ephemeral needs of today, under the inspiration of persons who see what has to be done and can make it happen. By 'non-ephemeral' we mean that the movements go to the very heart of the problems – for example, personal or structural greed; refounding people seek to live Gospel virtues and to inspire others by their radical example that Christ is the ultimate source of all meaning and the end of all life itself. A refounding movement within religious life occurs under three main conditions: first, members are experiencing the confusion and malaise of chaos. Second, they actually acknowledge the chaos and admit in the very *depths* of their hearts their own inner powerlessness to act without the Lord. Within their converting hearts they identify with the psalmist: 'From the very depths [i.e. of my chaos] I call to you, Yahweh: Lord, hear my cry' (Ps 130:1–2). Third, there is a leader (or leaders) who is able to articulate and implement a radical way of Christian living and people are prepared to follow him/her.

Are such movements alive within the Church today? Are existing religious congregations refounding? Since Vatican II, I do not see any radically *new* form of religious life emerging overall that is *outward-looking* and confronting constructively the challenges of the contemporary secularizing world. Perhaps it is too early for any large-scale movement of this kind. As explained earlier, there are sects such as Opus Dei and the Neo-Catechumenate, but they do not fit the requirements for refounding movements and they do not see themselves as religious congregations (see Chapters 2 and 3). What of the refounding of *existing* congregations? Though I find some examples of refounding persons, such as the late Pedro Arrupe, Jesuit superior general,[7] and some examples of profound refounding within some congregations, I generally feel that most religious communities have yet to begin the process of refounding. Many may never begin because they lack the passion and refounding fire to do so.

I have elsewhere explained at length a five-stage model showing the history of religious life since Vatican II,[8] but it can be summarized briefly in the following way (see Figures 2.1 and 2.2 on pp. 44 and 49 for background and accompanying explanations):

- Stage 1: initial unease following Vatican II about the future of religious life (1965–7 +).

- Stage 2: attempts to counter the growing anxiety resulting from change through legislative/political action (e.g. experimental constitutions) or structures imposed by Rome (1967–1970 +).

- Stage 3: symptoms of chaos (e.g. paralysis, confusion of goals, despair, denial) (1970–?).

- Stage 4: various self-help movements in reaction to the chaos under the inspiration of differing forms of leaders (1972–?).

- Stage 5: a revitalized religious life emerges clearly and confidently based on the values of Vatican II. I believe this stage has yet to be reached and may still be a long way off; it may even be unrealizable by most religious commmunities.

To appreciate the enormity of the chaos in religious life we need to be aware of what Vatican II did to the then existing creation mythology of religious life. Prior to Vatican II, for several centuries religious were portrayed mythologically as the spiritual elite in the Church who had separated themselves from an evil world. As Pope Urban II stated in 1092, religious are the 'strong' ones: 'from the beginning the Church has always offered two types of life to her children: one to aid the insufficiency of the weak, the other to bring to perfection the goodness of the strong'.[9] With Vatican II, religious are no longer to be seen as the spiritual elite because all the baptized are called to holiness; secondly, the world is to be seen not as something wholly evil, but as the arena in which religious must be in the forefront of inculturating the Gospel. The Council, having rightly undermined a distorted mythology of religious life, could provide no immediate substitute; all it did was to challenge religious to go back to the person of Christ, the founding vision and the needs of the world and begin the painful process of creating a mythology based on the values of the Council. Inevitably the radical destruction of the prevailing mythology of religious life produced initial unease and anxiety as the implications of the change had their impact. Then the chaos hit as the first attempts to contain the anxiety through legislative chapters and decrees failed. An inevitable identity crisis of catastrophic proportions resulted and thousands started to leave. Why be a religious if one can be holy – even apostolically *more* effective – in the world?

As explained in Chapter 2, a model highlights emphases that are detectable at particular times rather than at others. As regards the model of religious life since Vatican II, I believe that stages 3 (chaos) and 4 (self-help) are particularly evident today, with both existing at the same time in religious communities. I will now concentrate on these two stages.

1. Understanding congregational chaos

The following are some of the significant, unedited symptoms of chaos that religious have shared with me in numerous workshops on religious life in the First and Third Worlds since 1986:

'We have a vision, I think, but few are committed to it.'

'We are all doing "our own thing", no vision, no commitment to the group; feeling of fatalism – nothing will work.'

'Bewildered at the loss of friends/houses/apostolates.'

'Numbness/paralysis/weariness: feeling of lostness/helplessness.'

'Personal and group grief unresolved.'

'We cannot let go in our hearts the glories and securities of the past. They haunt us.'

'My congregation places far more stress on visibly being linked to our communities than to the demands of mission.'

'On-going anger without knowing the precise cause.'

'Let's pray more and all will be well.'

'Sense of drifting without goals and objectives as religious and congregationally.'

'Group and individual depression; feeling of just clinging to life.'

'Blaming/scapegoating administrations and others.'

'Denial, the inability to admit there is any real chaos.'

'Feeling envy at the success of fellow creative religious.'

'Excessive individualism; my rights at all costs.'

'Joking relationships in community; real issues unaddressed.'

'Busyness – to hide pain or to avoid facing the chaos.'

'We choose leaders who we know will do nothing, but just try to keep the peace.'

'Polarizations due to unresolved ecclesiological differences.'

'Feuding/manipulation of power blocks to hold on to symbols of the past.'

'Weariness with more meetings to "discuss the future" or the "charism".'

'Over-dependence on pseudo-psychological techniques.'

'An unreal optimism about the future: "God will provide".'

'Inability of leadership teams to lead.'

'Dreams of a messiah to get us out of the mess; he/she will tell us what to do.'

'Addictive behaviour, e.g. overeating and drinking.'

'Identity through being miserable: "Don't want anyone to do anything because they will take us into the unknown. Better the misery we know."'

'Superficial or joking relationships in community.'

'Emphasis on structural changes; conversion is unimportant.'

'Nostalgia for the secure structures and symbols of the past.'

'Burn-out felt to be synonymous with the virtue of religious life martyrdom.'

'Never-ending discussion over the nature of community and how to live it.'

'Marginalization of innovators.'

'Feeling of being subjected to overwhelming violence as women religious within a patriarchal Church.'

'Pain because communities de-energize creative pastoral people.'

'Pain over lost opportunities for evangelization.'

'Neurotic communities: inward-looking, de-energizing, joyless.'

'Seeking gimmicks to get us out of the mess.'

'We have fine chapter documents and mission statements, but nothing happens.'

'We need better chapter documents and vision statements.'

'Trivialization of serious issues; serious discussion is impossible.'

'Escape into sects/cults, e.g. the latest "Marian visions".'

136

I ask participants of workshops on religious life to check the list and indicate what symptoms, if any, apply to their experience. Invariably, religious acknowledge that the vast majority of these indications of chaos fit their own congregational experience. The above symptoms of chaos can be summarized as follows:

- a lack of clarity about the nature and role of contemporary religious life; fear of the new;

- a vigorous individualism;

- lack of commitment to a shared vision;

- poverty of leadership;

- personal/group dysfunctional behaviour, e.g. envy, denial;

- real difficulties in achieving a reasonable personal self-image because the loss of identity is so great;

- just surviving as a person is hard – concern for religious life values is a luxury;

- a concern for congregational identity/belonging takes precedence over mission;

- the failure to grieve over losses in religious life;

- pastoral paralysis;

- the marginalization and de-energizing of pastoral innovators.

I will now move on to explain some of these symptoms of chaos.

Repeatedly, religious admit to being confused about the nature and role of religious life within the contemporary Church. At times they feel over-whelmed by phrases like 'we must be prophetic in today's world' because they do not know how and where to begin such a challenge. 'How does the call to be prophetic differ from what every Christian is called to do?' said one religious. They feel numbed, paralysed, even depressed. One religious summarized this: 'We are without fire or passion, for how can we be dynamic when we don't know who we are or where we should be going as religious!' If people are confused about the nature of religious life, then they will naturally be uncertain over the role of their respective congregations. In their study of religious life in the United States, David Nygren and Miriam Ukeritis confirm this symptom of the chaos: 'It is fair to say that members of religious orders do not experience an overwhelming sense of clarity concerning their congregation's policies and procedures'. These authors also found in their study that members of 'religious orders find a high degree of satisfaction from membership in their congregation'. At first sight this appears to be a very positive conclusion, but there is a particularly negative aspect to it: 'In many instances what holds them to their commitment to religious life is a sense of affiliation that is stronger than their sense of purpose or mission. . . . The high need for affiliation . . . may, in fact, stifle the creativity necessary to move groups into the future.'[10] This confirms my own experience. The following case study illustrates the problem.

Case study: belonging is more powerful than mission

Over a period of a year members of a clerical religious congregation were invited to attend weekend workshops on their founding vision and 85 per cent enthusiastically did so. Early the next year the local episcopal conference exhorted priests, religious and laity to attend one of two five-day workshops on what they considered to be 'the most urgent pastoral need in the nation: racism, multiculturalism and inculturation'. In view of such enthusiasm for their charism, it was expected that a high percentage of the clerical congregation would attend; the founder in fact had asked that his congregation be especially dedicated supporters of the local churches. Only 3 per cent of the province accepted the bishops' invitation despite the convenient timing and siting of the workshops.

The reason for such a low percentage response is contained in the answers that members of the province gave to the question: 'why did you enjoy the workshops on the founding vision?' The responses could be summarized in this comment: 'The founder's vision gives us a feeling of belonging to an esteemed group'. The congregational workshops had helped to revitalize the members' sense of belonging or affiliation, but had done nothing significant to convert them to the mission of the founder.

The faith development theory of James Fowler can throw some light on this case study.[11] The third level of faith is what he calls the Synthetic–Conventional stage; this is a faith that comes from a sense of belonging to a particular cultural group. We believe because the group believes; affiliation to the group and its culture is particularly important in times of chaos when people's identity is seriously endangered. When chaos threatens, people will ritualize their oneness and the traditions that support it with renewed energy. Creative members who dare to challenge the group to adapt their vision and lives to a changing world are marginalized because they intensify the feeling of anxiety within the group that is fleeing the implications of the chaos. The group's reactions in the case study fit the description of Fowler's third level of faith; the bishops' call to evangelization reflects a higher and more detached level of faith, the sixth stage: the Universalizing Faith stage. The bishops were asking people to move out from their secure cultural sense of belonging in order to struggle with new anxiety-creating programmes of evangelization. Despite the verbal assent to the founding vision of evangelization, however, the majority of the province simply lacked the inner conversion to the radical demands of the faith/justice apostolate.

I believe that personal and group envy is an especially significant obstacle to the process of refounding. Envy is not a feeling we readily admit to; in fact, we can be envious without being aware we have this cancerous affliction. Envy is a feeling of sadness/resentment aroused by the desire to have what another possesses and, like witch-hunting, it is especially prevalent in times of chaos; jealousy, on the other hand, is the fear of losing what one already possesses. The envious person experiences an emptiness and a consciousness of inferiority to the person or group envied; envy lessens the ability of people to hope and be hopeful. Because envy is an emotion that is essentially both selfish and *malevolent*, it has destructive results when uncontrolled. This is so dramatically illustrated biblically with incidents such as the killing of Abel by Cain, the abandonment of Joseph by his brothers, and it was 'out of envy that the chief priests handed Jesus' (Mk 15:10) over to Pilate to be crucified. The brother of the prodigal son is consumed with envy for two reasons: to celebrate the return of his brother a calf is being killed which he feels should be his, but more especially he is consumed with sadness because his brother now has a maturity and an adult relationship with his father that he himself does not possess. He wants his brother to be punished for his earlier adolescent selfishness and he even seeks to belittle the joy of his father that he himself yearns to possess (Lk 15:25–30). Paul and Barnabas experienced the sting of the envy of supposedly holy women who colluded with the Jewish authorities to have them removed from a particular town; these women became envious of the apostles' successful preaching and this they could not tolerate (Acts 13:44–51).

Envy is a disease not only of individuals but also of entire groups or cultures. Particularly in group-oriented cultures, the success of individuals (or sub-groups) is seen as a threat to the status quo. Once group envy is aroused, people can blindly and ruthlessly attack the innovators verbally and physically (or through recourse to magical forces in many traditional cultures). Not uncommonly, innovators are ostracized or marginalized from the group; this is an especially potent form of punishment in group-oriented cultures and few innovators can tolerate such victimization for very long. Not surprisingly, therefore, group envy is often the most effective barrier to change within contemporary cultures that are less economically developed.[12] Those who lead the attack on the cultural dissidents will rationalize their viciousness by claiming that they alone are being loyal to the traditions of the group's culture. In fact, often they will see the success of innovators as a symbol of their own poverty of initiative and courage.

As an anthropologist, then, I am not at all amazed when religious say that as innovators they become the painful objects of the envy of others and of communities. There is envy of fellow religious who are able to use the experience of chaos positively (like the prodigal son), by becoming pastorally creative and achieving a deep peace in their lives with the Lord. The envious ones see in this peace and creativity what they should be but are not, and they do all they can to crush the Gospel innovators. My view is that the envy, with its crippling malevolent consequences, is so deeply rooted in the individual and religious group unconscious that sufferers are blind to it. This of course makes it very difficult for envy to be acknowledged and eradicated. Envy is a response to an inner hollowness that can only be filled with the presence of the Lord. St Paul mentions several times how envy is destructive of community and exhorts his listeners to search deep within themselves for its presence: 'All who belong to Christ Jesus have crucified self with all its passions and its desires. Since we are living by the Spirit, let our behaviour be guided by the spirit and let us not be conceited or provocative and envious of one another' (Gal 5:24–26).

One of the dangers that an anthropologist must avoid in fieldwork is too readily assuming that what people say about the life of the group is actually the truth. Without being conscious of what they are doing, the tendency is for people to describe the ideal – assuming it is the same as the reality. They are caught in a group fantasy; that is, a shared image of reality that may or may not be true. This is very much a problem in religious congregations entrapped in chaos. Notice in the above symptoms of chaos the reference to an inability to implement chapter documents and mission statements. Frequently, I find religious in chaos can as groups share fantasies that assume that documents and finely crafted mission statements are being implemented when the opposite is true. Phrases like 'collaborative ministry', 'participative government' and 'refounding our community' are frequently used in documents and discussions and the more often they are repeated the more people believe they are actually being collaborative or participative, when in fact that is not so! In these group fantasies the written word and the reality are the same. No one wants to test the truth of the group fantasy since it would be too anxiety-evoking. This neatly avoids the hard and uncertain task of conversion.

Sometimes I feel that visionary documents of religious congregations are nothing less than attempts to defend the group culture against the anxiety and uncertainty coming from the chaos in which the group finds itself. The fact that nothing radical is done to implement these documents does not seem to worry people; often these statements or documents are updated at successive chapters with great satisfaction by participants who marginalize anyone venturing to question their unreality. Commonly these documents speak of the option for the poor and the need to adjust lifestyles accordingly, but their exuberant writers are blind to how they themselves have become assimilated to the middle-class values of the culture in which they live. A further indication of the chaos is the different ways that the founding vision is used by opposing factions – for example by nativists or millenarianists (as explained below) – to support their particular interests. Statements of the founding person are taken out of context of their original intention and historical circumstances.

Many symptoms of the chaos listed above by religious are typical of neurotic organizations or cultures. A neurotic culture is one that overall is out of touch with reality, having high levels of avoidance and anxiety as the result of traumatic change. And the tendency is for the culture to maintain consistently its complex system of beliefs and actions despite its pathological self-defeating nature. A neurotic culture fosters within its institutions social norms and standards that are not rooted in reality, the breaking of which by individual members results in the application of painful and insidious social pressures to conform. Members implicitly or explicitly work together to maintain the status quo – even if this means 'enjoying' identity-giving organizational neurosis – and push to the sideline those who dare to question inconsistencies in the group's life.[13] My experience is that people in neurotic religious congregational cultures generally choose leaders who will reinforce their unreality. Little wonder that personally integrated and pastorally creative religious in neurotic communities feel themselves marginalized! And their pain is intense. Then there are younger religious who have few or no recruits coming after them; they look ahead and wonder if the future has anything to offer them within neurotic, de-energized communities. Is it really possible, they plead, for these communities ever to change? A loneliness and a fear enters their hearts that few of the older religious are able to grasp or have empathy with.

I find the above symptoms of chaos belong both to men's and women's congregations, but there are some significant additional differences.[14] Especially in the United States, religious women initiated for themselves a process of on-going formation in the 1950s, before the Council opened, with little encouragement from their male counterparts. And this formation has continued, so much so that sisters are now generally far more theologically and pastorally updated than their male counterparts. Also, widespread participation over twenty years in all kinds of spiritual renewal programmes has produced in many religious women a prayerful, yet restless, creative apostolic zeal for the Lord's work and a justifiable anger at being powerless within a patriarchal Church. Pastoral action, despite often high qualifications, is not infrequently blocked to them through clerical intolerance and prejudice. With the decline in the number of priests, however, sisters are increasingly being 'allowed' to be involved in pastoral work and here tensions emerge. If the pastor clings to a pre-Vatican II patriarchal and authority/power model, he feels threatened by sisters who may be far more informed and skilled in collaborative pastoral ministry than himself. Yet sisters generally remain at their posts, sometimes poorly paid (if at all), and in sadness as they see parishioners denied what is their pastoral due.

Clericalism is a significant reason why the role of religious brothers in the Church has been so little appreciated. The belief over the centuries that only the clergy should be involved in proclaiming the word of God and in ecclesiastical administration has inhibited the development of a truly collaborative ministry of brothers and priests. One way for brothers to survive is to 'go it alone', by ignoring the clergy, even developing an antagonism towards clergy as a form of identity; so many fine academic and medical institutions over the centuries testify to their apostolic zeal and creativity. But teaching brothers can become so identified with their institutions that they cannot see more urgent pastoral needs. Often their congregations were founded to serve the educational needs of the poor and in the past a school system was the means. Today it can happen that the only way to reach the poor is through alternative educational institutions. But those who leave the school freely and with the encouragement of congregational leaders can be branded as 'betraying the founding spirit'. Hence a particular challenge for brothers is to separate the original vision of education for the poor from the school as an historical instrument for education. If the vision and the school are seen (wrongly) as inseparable, brothers experience a loss of identity both as individuals in religious life and as members of their congregations should circumstances force them out of the schools.

Clerical religious, in addition to the symptoms of chaos listed above, are apt to experience a malaise unique to them – namely, unresolved tensions between their priesthood and religious life. As John O'Malley incisively points out, [15] the great number of religious orders and congregations since the thirteenth century centre their reason for existence on *ministry* in response to an apostolic need – for example, the catechetical, educational or material poverty of people. This is in contrast to the other form of ministry built on the office/authority of priest or bishop; ministry here is parish- or diocese-centred. As the latter ministry became increasingly powerful after the Council of Trent, it became popular for the clergy to seek to domesticate to their authority or de-emphasize the various ministries of religious. If religious base their identity primarily on the priesthood, the critical prophetic dimension of religious life is diminished – namely, that they be apostolically creative in view of needs transcending the boundaries of an orderly, sacrament-oriented parish.

I believe that many religious clerics following Vatican II chose as the easier option the priesthood, not religious life, as their source of identity. For a few years after the Council the priesthood maintained its traditional status within the Catholic community and often society at large, but that is no longer so and religious clerics find that even the priesthood is under relentless attack. Laity are now eating into the traditional roles of the priest as the source of authority/power and it is no longer so easy to quieten the voices of those calling for an open dialogue on the issue of women priests. With their self-confidence under attack, clerical religious commonly avoid renewal programmes in which well-informed women religious are present. For it is there that their poverty of updated theology and the crisis of their identity as males, religious and priests are poignantly evident. So from two sides religious clerics have an identity problem – the source of deepening pain for them.

Most congregations within the Church today were founded over the last hundred years or so. Unlike the older institutes, for example Dominicans or Benedictines, they have never experienced anything like the present chaos, with the real possibility of extinction in the foreseeable future; from their founding they had known nothing but numerical and geographical growth. Thus they have no tradition to guide them in coping with the present malaise. Moreover, most apostolic congregations of this period paradoxically were never founded. That is, the dynamic founding experience was quickly stifled by an overlay of monastic or conventual traditions that were assumed by Rome to be integral to religious life. Religious communities founded to be actively apostolic were rapidly turned into semi-cloistered institutes. Now that these congregations are discovering the truth about their apostolic founding vision, it is a question not so much of *refounding* as *founding* for the first time.

As explained earlier, an experience of chaos, that is the dramatic loss of identity through the disintegration of predictable symbols, myths and rituals, can be the preface for creative action previously unimagined. But for that to occur people must acknowledge or own up to the chaos; they must admit to their powerlessness, otherwise nothing happens except on-going denial and other forms of dysfunctional behaviour. In biblical language, chaos has immense positive significance, provided people admit its presence and their unending need for the grace of God. Consider, for example, the archetype of all chaos for the early Israelites – the experience of the wilderness, that 'vast and dreadful desert, a land of fiery snakes, scorpions, thirst' (Dt 8:15). When confronted with the chaos of the desert, after bitter suffering the Israelites find out and *admit* the shallowness of their faith on the one hand and the creative, compassionate power of Yahweh on the other. But for the chaos to be a positive encounter the Israelites had to acknowledge its existence and their complete dependence on God. Once they did that, the impossible became possible and new horizons opened up through the mercy of Yahweh.[16]

For the refounding process to begin and be sustained in religious congregations, individual and group acceptance of our outer and inner chaos is required. It demands, as Metz says, an admission of our own infinite poverty which is 'the shadow-image of God's inner infinity' and goodness. In accepting that we are poor, we begin to grasp that whatever power and strength we have are derived from the 'wellsprings of invisible mystery'.[17] In speaking about the radicality of conversion required in accepting the chaos, I like to use the analogy of the alcoholic. Unless he/she admits finally to a sickness and that nothing can be done without the power of God, denial continues to blind the person to the reality of the chaos of his/her disease. What, then, of religious communities – are they admitting to their poverty, their inner and outer chaos? With very few exceptions (to be found particularly in women's congregations) I find considerable unacknowledged denial of the chaos. I readily agree with Mary Jo Leddy that there 'is chaos in many religious congregations but it is a calcified chaos'. Chaos is calcified because few will use it as the Lord would wish – as the springboard to inner and outer personal/congregational conversion. They do anything to avoid the struggle to get out of the malaise; they fear that the risks inherent in change are more anxiety-evoking than the distress inherent in the chaos. Some even enjoy being miserable because at least it gives them some sense of identity! As long as this refusal by religious to own the chaos prevails, restorationism will have nothing to fear from the vast majority of religious.

It is a privilege to meet refounding religious communities who walk 'by faith and not yet by sight' (2 Cor 5:7) because in them I sense an apostolic zeal gripping even the eldest religious, an inner peace, a love of the Lord born of honesty, a lot of hard discernment. For them leadership means the transformational drawing of people out of their superficial tranquillity into the anxiety of the chaos, an awareness of the need for courage and then along the courage-shaped road of refounding itself. They recognize that refounding is a risk-filled process of entering into the heart of the paschal mystery itself for the Lord's mission. It is the re-living of the abandonment of Christ – 'Father, into your hands I commit my spirit' (Lk 23:46) – to discover the freedom and creativity of the risen Lord. This means death to self and to all that is humanly comforting and secure. Refounding is seen as a corporate effort involving transforming leaders (authority dissenters), refounding persons (pathfinding dissenters) and creative individuals in a journey of faith through darkness into light. For communities sincerely committed to refounding, vocation recruitment and the ageing of religious are not *the* issues. The issue above everything else is to know and do what God wants for them. Refounding may in fact end in the death of the community, but it is a death accepted salvifically because in discernment these communities grasp that this is what the Lord desires of them. Consequently, a deep inner peace and freedom for pastoral creativity emerge.

2. Reacting to the chaos: leadership in confusion

In the self-help period (the fourth stage) religious attempt to gain control of the chaos in various ways:

Through nativistic *reactions*
Leaders emerge, claiming that the unquestioning return to the symbols (e.g. habits), myths and rituals of religious life before Vatican II will in some magical way resolve the loss of meaning. Fundamentalist and sect-like, they fanatically assume 'we have the truth and the Pope is on our side'; these communities withdraw from the 'contaminating world', refuse all dialogue with their opponents, and avoid any critique of restorationism in the Church. Prayer is emphasized, but only the pre-Vatican II forms that stress personal/privatized holiness remote from the world's concerns.

Through conservative *reactions*
Moved by the numerical success of the sect-like lay movements, e.g. Opus Dei, leaders encourage the return to pre-Vatican II traditions,

e.g. quasi-monastic structures for apostolic communities, traditional religious habits, though with far less fanaticism than nativistic leaders. Souls are to be converted to the Lord, compassion shown to the poor, but the faith/justice apostolates are to be avoided as irrelevant and dangerous to one's consecrated vocation. Conformist-oriented candidates are attracted to these religious communities because of their above-average needs for security/identity. New forms of prayer are allowed (e.g. as in the charismatic movement), provided they do not lead to involvement in the social apostolate. Liberation theology and inculturation are considered dangerous, 'leftist' ideologies. Criticism of ecclesiastical restorationism is not considered necessary.

Through millenarian *reactions*

All forms of instant-success programmes are offered by leaders (e.g. encounter-group sessions, techniques for bodily relaxation, immediate-union-with-God prayer sessions). Often, in true millenarian style, religious indiscriminately discard as 'old-fashioned' any reference to the past, thus, for example, the great spiritual traditions of St Teresa and St John of the Cross are seen as of no value. Religious, unwilling to face the necessary faith/justice inner conversion, keep feverishly searching from one workshop to another for the 'right leader, or spiritual/professional guru, to describe the latest way to inner peace and a firm sense of direction' for themselves personally and for their congregations. They may even turn to commendable methods of professionally conducting chapters, meetings or establishing goals and objectives, but if unaccompanied by radical conversion these instruments do nothing by themselves to aid religious out of the chaos. Try harder, they feel, and the right miraculous technique will turn up sometime. . . Leaders and followers are so concerned about their own identity issues that ecclesiastical restorationism is of little concern to them.

Through cultural assimilationist *reactions*

Leaders themselves are seduced by the individualism and materialism of the cultures in which they live and encourage fellow religious to do the same; they see their task as therapeutic (i.e. as responding to the individualistic and excessive self-fulfilment needs of religious) (see Chapter 6 for further explanation). If restorationism is criticized, it is only because it is thought to be an obstacle to the pursuit of individualism and personal self-fulfilment.

Through neo-conservative *reactions*

Leaders, once avid supporters of change, but now frightened of the chaos and the extremes of attempted adaptation programmes, believe that only slow, measured, apostolic adaptation to the world will achieve new expressions of religious life. It is assumed that revitalization will be realized by the *whole* community or congregation moving in response to agreed-to mission statements and strategic pastoral planning. Intra-group tensions and conflict are to be avoided at all costs: 'Let the province move when all are ready and willing to do so'. The sense of belonging to the congregation is viewed as more important than the struggle for the religious community to realize its primary task of prophetically 'quantum-leap jumping' into the world. Creative religious, believing that the chaos requires a more radical linking between the Gospel and cultures, are marginalized, since they threaten the group's desire for an orderly approach to refounding. Any critique of restorationism is couched in unchallenging tones.

Through radical *non-conversion-oriented reactions*
Leaders attract others with a vision of a radical, social-justice programme; however, because the values of religious life do not impinge on their consciousness, they see themselves only as social workers/activists or enablers of others. Either they withdraw from religious life or they remain living highly individualistic lives, refusing all efforts to work towards a religious life vision and/or a commitment to one. There is an un-Gospel-like harshness to criticism of restorationism within the Church.

Through prophetic/refounding *reactions*
Others, truly prophets to their congregations, recognize that the only way out of the chaos is through radically new faith/justice, hope-inspired communities and programmes linking the Gospel message with the needs of the world today. Hence, for example, they struggle to be living witnesses to the radical demands of asceticism in opposition to the symbols of consumerism and 'instant spirituality'; living witnesses to the virtue of hope, to counter symbols that seek to negate any redemptive and eschatological power of suffering; living witnesses to the need to dialogue with the world, to counter the elitism/sectarianism of restorationist Catholicism; living witnesses through their lifestyle and attitudes to God's mercy, Jesus Christ, in concern for the alienated, the oppressed; living witnesses to vibrant community life relationships, to counter the symbols of excessive individualism, abuse of authority/power in society and the Church.[18] These prophetic religious see that this demands from them an on-going admission of their powerlessness without the grace of God; they act accordingly and draw others with them. These religious we call refounding persons – authority or pathfinding dissenters within religious communities. Restorationism is critiqued with a boldness of apostolic faith, love and compassion.

Refounding persons as dissenters: clarifications

The nature and role of refounding persons are sometimes not understood. For example, it has been said that 'self-appointed prophets' in the past have abused authority and religious have suffered under their authoritarianism: 'We don't want a return to the past'. Others say that refounding persons are not necessary because the group itself can refound without specially gifted individuals; others comment that refounding persons are dangerous to the group because they are 'strong individualists and want "to do their own thing"'. Some have said that the definition is merely an application of business management techniques to religious life and 'this is dangerous to one's faith', because it means that 'secularism will take over religious life'; some claim that the refounding person is really a restorationist at heart, 'a real conservative', and therefore to be rejected. A close reading of the definition, however, will show that these reservations are groundless. If individuals are 'individualistic', 'millenarian', 'authoritarian', 'restorationist' or 'conservative' as defined here, they are definitely *not* refounding persons! A refounding person is one who:

> in response to the inspiration of the Holy Spirit, in imitation of the 'faith shock' and reaction of the founding person (who originally perceived the gap between the Gospel and the world), *acutely* sees the contemporary chasm between the Gospel and the secularizing cultures; he/she moves, by transforming leadership and creative pastoral strategies, to bridge that chasm, and at the same time *restlessly* summons others to faith/justice conversion – especially members of his/her own congregation – and to share in the vision to go out into the unknown in order to implement the Gospel strategies.[19]

The grace of refounding is an extraordinary gift of the Holy Spirit, to be accepted or rejected by the individual and/or the group itself. The refounding person is solidly rooted in reality – that is, he/she experiences a real pastoral need where the Gospel is not touching the lives of people. And that person undergoes what I call a 'faith shock'; that is, as the original founder grieved over the chasm separating a pastoral need from the Gospel and was determined to do something about it, so also the refounding person relives that experience but in contemporary times. A fellow Marist explained to me his own faith shock:

> One day as I walked through the slums of the city I suddenly felt as though I was back in the rural parts of France last century walking with the founder. I sensed his shock as he looked at the educational and spiritual poverty of the people after the French Revolution. As he acted in faith so I now try to do also in relating to the poor in this slum. I feel the founder walking with me in my work.

Some would call this the reliving of the original charism, but I feel charism as a word has lost its experiential bite through overuse. It has tended to come across as 'a thing' to be studied rather than as 'a dynamic force' to be identified with an re-lived over and over again. We need new words to express the richness of the grace of refounding. Hence I prefer to use the expression 'faith shock' rather than charism.

Refounding persons are not 'revolutionaries', 'restorationists' or 'conservatives' as these words have been defined in this book. Rather, they are dynamic reformers or rediscoverers; there is a movement back to the past, not to stay there, but to derive the faith energy to move forward with pastoral strategies of the quantum-leap kind. Revolutionaries break completely with the past; reformers see the experience of the past as critical for the future. The refounding person's journey of rediscovery is twofold:

- the rediscovery of the power of Christ within himself/herself coming from conversion; that is, the rediscoverer identifies again with the power of the founding myth of *religious life* itself and so with its stress in active congregations on apostolic mobility, flexibility, creativity in response to needs 'out there'; religious are to be at the cutting edge of the Good News and cultures;

- the reformer rediscovers with renewed vitality, and identifies with, the power of the founding myth of the *congregation* itself, and sees, as did the founder, that it is to be applied to pastoral needs here and now. Historian John Padberg writes: 'A refounder will have to insert the fundamental myths of the congregation into the culture of his or her own time, both to make those myths intelligible and, perhaps more importantly, to use those myths as a critique of that very culture and of the refounding itself'. [20]

The refounding person calls others to share his/her conversion and vision, so he/she is not a loner – though the community, refusing to own its inner and outer chaos, may well marginalize him/her so that he/she *appears* to be a loner. The fault rests with the group, not the refounding person. Such a person yearns to build with others a community of fellow believers in the service of the Lord, as would have been the case with the original founding group. As is the situation with refounders of the Church, congregational refounding dissenters aim at pastoral quantum leaps, not merely renewal; with feet firmly within the faith shock of the founder and in contemporary reality, they seek to bridge the gap between the Good News and the world of today.

As for the charge that refounding is merely the application of managerial techniques, little needs to be said. 'Refounders' and 'refounding' are as old as religious life itself, so they are not the constructs of any managerial discipline. Refounding is a faith journey into the paschal mystery for mission today according to the spirit of the original founder. As founders used the technical know-how of their day (e.g. horses and coaches, printing presses), so also do contemporary refounders turn to anything that will help the communication of their message. If faxes help, they use faxes! If training in managerial leadership techniques assists the understanding and communication of the message, then these techniques are enthusiastically used!

Founders and refounders are incarnational people because, as St Thomas

Aquinas says, whatever is true no matter from where it comes is derived from the Holy Spirit. The social sciences may be tainted by the market place, but they also contain truths born out of the experience of sincere people; and strange as it may seem to some critics of these contemporary studies, these truths ultimately have their source in the Holy Spirit. As to the claim that refounding persons will reintroduce the authoritarian style of leadership common to religious communities prior to Vatican II, the answer is simply that such a person does not fit in any way the description given here of an authentic refounding person. The assumption that a group refounds itself and does not need refounding persons is correct in a limited sense; in refounding communities it is sometimes not easy to pinpoint the person with refounding qualities, so united is the group. However, anthropologically there will always be someone articulating the vision of the group and he/she is the one who actively leads, but with a particularly quiet transforming leadership style.

Pastoral planning and its implementation are essential for religious communities in order that resources may be best used apostolically. Planning should foster an atmosphere in a group that allows refounding people to emerge and act. However, if pastoral planning is not seen as the servant of apostolic creativity it becomes an end in itself, an assumed magical way out of the chaos; there is a preoccupation with order, stability and consistency. Plans then become so attractive that we hold to them tenaciously in order to avoid unpleasant, unprogrammed creative surprises. Then creative and refounding persons are marginalized because they are risk-takers given over by definition to producing order-breaking apostolic surprises.[21]

Applying the axiom 'the new belongs elsewhere'

Refounding religious congregations is a co-operative process involving congregational authority dissenters, pathfinding dissenters and renewal people. By 'renewal people' I mean religious who, on entering into their own inner darkness to encounter the saving power of the Risen Lord, become open to creative pastoral action. They do not have the gifts of quantum leap pastoral strategists, but they contribute by their various talents placed at the service of the refounding process and by fostering an atmosphere of openness in the community without which refounding cannot function. Congregational authority dissenters hold a crucial role in the process, as we saw in the previous chapter on transforming leadership, because without them refounding and renewal persons cannot function. As they are concerned for the future of the community, their key task is to find refounding and renewal persons and place them in positions where they can use their gifts. This demands of them an on-going gift of discernment for they cannot lightly name people as prophetically creative; much harm could be done to many people unless authentic discernment is undertaken. It may take a long time, but it needs to be done using, as a measure, the qualities one should expect in prophetic people throughout history.[22]

One major obstacle, and sometimes *the* barrier, to refounding is the inability of the congregational leader to claim his/her authority to lead, as explained in Chapter 4. Admittedly when religious communities are neurotic cultures, the obstacles to the exercise of leadership are immense and often insuperable if the level of group neurosis or dysfunction is extremely high. But I firmly believe that normally something can be done if the leader has the qualities of critical judgement, self-knowledge and maturity to be found in a transforming leader. With skilled assistance and long-term planning, the leader may succeed in facilitating the breaking of the calcified chaos a fraction or more, a revolution in view of the rigidity of the group denial. It can be done, as I have seen it happen several times, despite the fact that these communities were especially dysfunctional. The key to this is: prayer, competency and commitment. If a community's quality of life improves even minimally, then there will be a little less resistance to creative religious in their midst. And that is a blessing!

Congregational leaders need to be sensitive to four potential traps when they decide to confront religious communities with their chaos:

- being insufficiently aware of how difficult it is for a congregational culture to change, even if in the state of chaos. Applied anthropologists would fully endorse the realism of organizational consultant Isobel Menzies Lyth: 'Institutions, once established, may be extremely difficult to change in their essentials and they do actually modify the personality structure of their members, temporarily or permanently. Indeed, to change the members one may first need to change the institution.'[23]

- being seduced into the emotional or fantasy life of the group culture;

- attempting to energize the group when in fact at the *present* time it is unable to be energized; like the alcoholic, the group may need to be left alone to allow the chaos to reach a point when it is to be hoped that some people can no longer deny it and express a need for conversion;

- developing a 'saviour complex', acting as an amateur therapist to the entire group, seeing failure as an insult to one's ability.

Aware that the process of breaking calcified congregational chaos is a slow and problematic one, the leader will need to act courageously as the sponsor or 'political friend' of renewal and refounding persons by using his/her position authority/power to loosen up some structures or form new ones to permit creative people to act. A common temptation is to place creative religious within denying or neurotic communities and expect them to work miracles of revitalization; the miracles will not occur, and the creative people will be de-energized with their apostolic work negated. For this reason I speak of the axiom 'the new belongs elsewhere', a practical guideline with anthropological and scriptural foundations that I first developed in 1988. In brief, the axiom means that a refounding project should not normally be placed in the midst of existing works/structures, where prophetic people would be under constant critical assessment by members of the community and required to waste invaluable energy 'apologizing' for what they are doing.[24] Nygren and Ukeritis express a similar insight when they use the expression 'structural demonstrations';[25] likewise, Donna Markham speaks of 'communities of hope', and Joe Holland writes of 'islands of creativity'.[26] Some case studies will help to illustrate the relevance of the axiom.

Case study: the market place provides an insight

With few exceptions, Japanese firms venturing abroad now prefer to build their own factories, for fear that a takeover would involve a de-energizing culture clash. In buying an existing firm the Japanese found they were taking over an existing negative culture – for example, a history of labour disputes, outdated working practices, and adversarial management. They find it is far safer to build a new firm from scratch, thus developing a culture open to change.[27]

Case study: a wise congregational leader

A congregational leader of a clerical religious congregation decided, with the co-operation of the local bishop, to establish a new form of pastoral care for a minority group that had long suffered cultural/economic oppression. He appointed two of his most experienced priests to plan the project over a period of a year. After listening to the people, the two evangelizers recognized that the members of the minority group had stopped going to the local parish church as the negative influence of the dominant white culture was too strong; the minority group felt unwanted, second-class parishioners, pressured to worship in ways alien to their culture. The two evangelizers, with the bishop's permission, set up a pastoral care structure; this differed from the traditional parish system in that it was formed to fit the needs of the minority group. The bishop and congregational leader agreed to explain and defend the project to the diocese and religious province respectively.

Over the years, successive reports on the pastoral care of the minority group in this case study had highlighted the impossibility (and injustice) of forcing people into what are for them oppressive parish structures. But up to this point no one had been able to devise an appropriate method of evangelizing. The project is slowly developing, but integral to the success of the project is the establishment of bishop-approved, pastorally adapted structures of independence from surrounding traditional parish administrations; secondly, the publicity about the project is the responsibility of the official leadership, namely the bishop and congregational leader, thus freeing the evangelizers to concentrate their energies on the project. This last point is also well illustrated by the following case study.

Case study: avoiding too many cups of coffee

A religious sister had developed over many years a unique form of adult education for a minority culture as part of a diocesan programme. However, the sister hoped to involve her congregation more directly in the project as she felt it fitted the faith shock experience of the foundress. The congregational leadership team thought for some time and replied as follows: 'We think the idea is excellent but we advise you to establish it with two like-minded people of the province a thousand miles away from this city. You know in this city there are 81 members of our congregation; if you establish it here you will be plagued with visits for coffee and telephone calls that will go like this: "Are you sure this is what the foundress would have wanted? Explain it to me." "I am coming around for a cup of coffee, Clare, because I am really worried about the investment made in your project by the province. You tell me why this is being done!"

'After dozens of telephone calls and visits by sisters for coffee you will be exhausted. Our plan then as a team is to give you space to get on with the job. During the early stages of the project we ask you to keep Mary on the team here up-to-date with what is happening. We will keep the province informed. Until you are well under way you are responsible to no other province structure.'

Notice in this case study how the leader sets up an accountability system that is simple and direct. In ageing or chaotic cultures one sure method to control creativity is to insist on the frequent presentation of detailed planning reports: 'Tell us exactly what you plan to do over the next five years! We would appreciate clarification of footnote 3 on page 4' is the type of request pastorally innovative people are likely to get from leaders in mechanistic cultures (as explained in Chapter 2). But a creative person cannot give all the details of a vision; it takes time, interaction within the team, experimentation and evaluation. Hence the wisdom of the above congregational leadership team.

Jesus himself was quite literally commenting on the seductive and crushing power of groups caught up in chaos when he said: 'No one puts a piece of unshrunken cloth onto an old cloak, because the patch pulls away from the cloak and the tear gets worse. Nor do people put new wine into old wineskins; otherwise, the skins burst, the wine runs out, and the skins are lost. No; they put new wine in fresh skins and both are preserved' (Mt 9:16–17). Each successive apostolic community in the refounding process is the new wine, requiring some degree of protection lest it be smothered by existing structures and attitudes of the surrounding ageing organization or culture in chaos. The word of wisdom is: build new structures and foster simple, clear lines of accountability for on-going evaluation to allow space for renewal and refounding people to function. Do not ask them or yourself to do the impossible – namely, to convert that which is presently not open to conversion. Recall the instruction of Jesus to the apostles: 'And if anyone does not welcome you or listen to what you have to say, as you walk out of the house or town shake the dust from your feet' (Mt 10:14). That is, if people are not interested in refounding, even more so if they seek to subvert it deliberately or otherwise, then following Jesus' advice our energies must be unequivocally directed elsewhere. Go wherever there is life, not death: 'Leave the dead to bury their dead; your duty is to go and spread the news of the kingdom of God' (Lk 9:60).

Finally, an analogy with the human body may help to explain the relevance of the axiom. In coronary artery disease progressive obstruction in arteries restricts the blood flow to the heart; if the problem is left unchecked, death is inevitable. Because the welfare of the *total* body has priority, surgeons take healthy veins from other parts of the body, and turn them upside down to make them into arteries that bypass the diseased arteries. The bypass operation, through the use of 'new structures' – that is, the grafted healthy veins – allows the patient to be, as it were, 'refounded'. Having been through this operation I know what this refounding means. Before it, I had little energy and death was a real possibility, but now I even jog! A culture of denial in a religious community is like a diseased artery – the apostolic dynamism of refounding people cannot break through it. If the latter's life-giving actions are to be at the service of the Church and the congregation, then new structures must be established that bypass obstructing individuals and institutions.

Patricia Wittberg notes that '*all* major refoundings are fraught with schism and controversy'.[28] And she quotes Raymond Hostie: 'Everywhere the reform [of the Franciscans] unleashed violent internal opposition. The movement . . . split the entire group in two.'[29] It is true that the application of the axiom 'the new belongs elsewhere' has led at times historically to schism and bitterness. I noted in 1988, by way of example, that reformers may eventually find within their own communities that the obstacles to revitalization are insurmountable, and that they have no option but to break away and establish a separate institute. St Teresa of Avila tried hard to avoid this taking place within the Carmelite congregation, but she finally recognized that 'unless the Discalced are made into a separate province, and that without delay, serious harm will be done: in fact, I believe it will be impossible for them to go on'.[30] The fear of opposition or even schism must not hold back the process of refounding, but it intensifies the need for all involved to be thoroughly honest in their own faith discernment in the Lord. Ultimately a congregation exists to serve the Church, not its own preservation. In the case of Teresa it was refounding not within the congregation but *within* a particular existing tradition, so also the Capuchin reform of the Franciscans in 1529, and later the Recollect reform of the Augustinians.

Because this axiom is so important in refounding, I invite readers to ponder the following propositions:

- If religious communities and their leaders are so calcified in their thinking that they are not open to the frequent application of the axiom, then frustrations on the part of renewal and refounding persons will be so intense that schism becomes a real possibility.

A schism can be *formal*, as happened within the Carmelite order under Teresa, or *informal*, when authentic renewal and refounding people, while remaining in the congregation, nonetheless legitimately withdraw from actively being involved in the hopelessly de-energizing political life of a province's neurotic culture, and instead direct their energy as far as possible to their particular apostolates. Informal schism can also be synonymous with the withdrawal of people of renewal or refounding potential from their own religious communities; the neurotic pressure or the collective madness of the group becomes so personally and apostolically depowering and intolerable that they consider the pastoral needs of the wider ecclesial community have priority. Contemporary restorationism within the Church and religious life may also result in formal schisms within religious congregations; refounding persons may find themselves with no alternative in their discernment but to withdraw from their congregations and build new communities of hope based on Vatican II values.

- I believe that the axiom is being too infrequently applied, especially in men's congregations; the assumption of conservatives is quite widely accepted, namely, that no refounding can take place until the entire religious community is able and willing to move – a hope that can never be realized. This assumption is an aberration of the theology of active religious congregations whose primary task is ministry to the world and not the preservation of congregational unity at all costs.

At the heart of religious life is the commitment to offer oneself in total surrender to God our Creator; involvement in refounding is a rededication of oneself with others to God. No one, however, who is sincere about such an offering will be spared the chance to share in the sufferings of the Lord. And invariably one major source of the pain is one's own congregation – the opposition, the misunderstandings of those people that the refounding person or community yearns to convert.

A refounding person once tried to describe to me the twofold pain he experiences within his congregation. There is the pain that comes from being marginalized within a congregation that preaches charity, but will not give it to him. Describing the negative comments made of him by his confrères and his own reactions to them, he quoted from Jeremiah: 'I heard so many disparaging me. . . . All those who were on good terms with me watched for my downfall . . . but then there seemed to be a fire burning in my heart. . . . But Yahweh is at my side like a mighty hero' (Jer 20:10, 9, 11). The greater pain, however, comes from having to watch his religious community refusing to read the signs of the times, denying the chaos and holding back from conversion. As he contemplates this denial he increasingly feels one with Christ's intense sadness as he looks over the city that will not recognize the seeds of death within its walls: 'As he drew near and came in sight of the city he shed tears over it and said, "If you too had only recognized on this day the way to peace! But in fact it is hidden from your eyes!" ' (Lk 19:41–42).

Summary

Religious life historically flourishes at times of corruption within the Church and society. Today there is a form of authority/power corruption encouraged by restorationists within the Church; for example, the unwillingness of the hierarchical Church to balance its exercise of authority/power with the demands of collegiality. Logically, one could expect to find individual religious and communities challenging this abuse.

Are religious responding to this challenge? Johannes Metz does not think so. He writes with sadness:

> Where today do the religious orders exert a shock-effect within the Church? Where are they passionately concerned to make prophetic criticism within the Church something that counts . . .? Is the crisis in the Church to develop without any prophetic exaggeration, without any religious radicalism?[31]

I agree with Metz. I believe that religious communities overall are not exerting the shock-effects within the Church that their vocation demands. There is little widespread passionate concern to critique the Church according to Gospel values. Prophetic rhetoric – yes, in plenty of vision statements, but little action. Some are trapped in escapist restorationism, others are benumbed by the chaos. And too often leaders – as in other areas of church life – simply do not know how to lead and challenge their communities to become islands of apostolic creativity and prophetic witness.

However, despite the obstacles there are some religious who daily enter into their own inner powerlessness before the Lord and are alive with Gospel vision and creative action that prophetically shocks the Church. They do not shun the pains of misunderstandings and marginalization coming from their own communities and the Church itself. They are not downcast by the chaos around and within themselves, because they dream that the humanly impossible vision of refounding religious life is possible, if they but walk more intimately, powerlessly, yet courageously and prophetically with the Lord. They are prophets who hold God and humankind, as Abraham Heschel writes, 'in one thought at one time, at all times'. They do not accept 'the segregation of God, with the bifurcation of the secular and sacred' nor do they 'worry more about the purity of dogma than about the integrity of love'. They believe that 'God may be more intimately present in slums than in mansions, with those who are smarting under the abuse of the callous'.[32] They also believe that the future of the Church ultimately rests in the building of more and more communities of faith, worship and action. These are not inward communities concerned primarily for their own preservation; rather, they are communities of mission, outward-looking and committed to dialogue with all peoples of good will. In the chapter that follows I explain why so many religious communities are unable prophetically to model to the Church this form of faith-oriented community.

Notes

1. Review by John M. Lozano of my book *Out of Chaos: Refounding Religious Congregations* (New York: Paulist Press/London: Geoffrey Chapman, 1988) in *New Theology Review*, vol. 3, no. 2 (1990), p. 81.
2. M. J. Leddy, 'Beyond the Liberal Model', *The Way Supplement*, no. 65 (1989), p. 50.
3. J. Metz, *Followers of Christ: The Religious Life and the Church* (London: Burns & Oates/New York: Paulist Press, 1978), p. 12; see also an excellent statement on the prophetic nature of religious life by D. O'Murchu, *Religious Life: A Prophetic Vision* (Notre Dame, IN: Ave Maria, 1991).
4. See L. Cada *et al.*, *Shaping the Coming Age of Religious Life* (New York: Seabury Press, 1979), pp. 20–50.
5. Cited by J. Chittister, *The Way Supplement*, no. 53 (1985), p. 66; see J. M. Lozano for a description of the sufferings of founding persons: *Foundresses, Founders, and their Religious Families* (Chicago: Claret Center, 1983), pp. 65–70.
6. D. Nygren and M. Ukeritis, *Origins*, vol. 22, no. 15 (1992), p. 270.
7. See Arbuckle, *Out of Chaos*, op. cit., pp. 163f.
8. Ibid., pp. 65–87, and G. A. Arbuckle, *Earthing the Gospel: An Inculturation Handbook for Pastoral Workers* (London: Geoffrey Chapman/Maryknoll, NY: Orbis Books, 1990), pp. 70–2.
9. Cited by J. M. Lozano, *Discipleship: Towards an Understanding of Religious Life* (Chicago: Claret Center, 1980), p. 53.
10. Nygren and Ukeritis, op. cit., pp. 265, 272.
11. See J. Fowler, *Stages of Faith: The Psychology of Human Development and the Quest for Meaning* (San Francisco: Harper & Row, 1981), pp. 292–303. The relevance of Fowler's analysis to refounding is further developed in my *Out of Chaos*, op. cit., pp. 98–101.
12. See N. Cannon, 'Envy: A Longing for Wholeness', *Human Development*, vol. 12, no. 3 (1991), pp. 5–11; E. Hopper in M. Pines (ed.), *Bion and Group Psychotherapy* (London: Routledge & Kegan Paul, 1985), pp. 341–3; H. Schoeck, *Envy: A Theory of Social Behavior* (Indianapolis: Liberty Press, 1987), pp. 20–3, 40–76; M. Klein, *Envy and Gratitude: A Study of Unconscious Sources* (New York: Basic Books, 1957), *passim*.

13. See M. F. Kets de Vries and D. Miller, *The Neurotic Organization* (San Francisco: Jossey-Bass, 1985), pp. 47–71; U. Merry and G. I. Brown, *The Neurotic Behavior of Organizations* (New York: Gardner Press, 1987). p. 33; also W. R. Bion, *Experiences in Groups* (London: Routledge, 1989), *passim*.

14. See G. A. Arbuckle, 'Through Chaos to Prophecy', *The Tablet* (London) (12 January 1991), pp. 42f. For an overview of the changing roles of women in religious life in the United States, see M. A. Neal, *Catholic Sisters in Transition: From the 1960s to the 1980s* (Wilmington, DE: Michael Glazier, 1984) and *From Nuns to Sisters: An Expanding Vocation* (Mystic, CT: Twenty-Third Publications, 1990); J. P. Dolan *et al.*, *Transforming Parish Ministry: The Changing Roles of Catholic Clergy, Laity, and Women Religious* (New York: Crossroad, 1990), pp. 154–200; L. A. Quinonez and M. D. Turner, *The Transforming of American Catholic Sisters* (Philadelphia: Temple University Press, 1992).

15. J. O'Malley, 'Priesthood, Ministry, and Religious Life: Some Historical and Historiographical Considerations', *Theological Studies*, vol. 49, no. 1 (1988), pp. 223–57.

16. See Arbuckle, *Out of Chaos*, op. cit., pp. 46–62.

17. J. Metz, *Poverty of Spirit* (New York: Paulist Press, 1968), p. 47.

18. See G. A. Arbuckle, *Strategies for Growth in Religious Life* (New York: Alba House, 1986), p. 41.

19. Arbuckle, *Out of Chaos*, op. cit., p. 89.

20. J. Padberg, 'Understanding a Tradition of Religious Life' in G. A. Arbuckle and D. L. Fleming (eds), *Religious Life: Rebirth Through Conversion* (New York: Alba House, 1990), p. 18; for qualities of refounding persons, see Arbuckle, *Out of Chaos*, op. cit., pp. 57–62, 95–111; and O'Murchu, op. cit., pp. 51–8.

21. See R. Stacey, *Managing Chaos* (London: Kogan Page, 1992), pp. 43f.

22. See Arbuckle, *Out of Chaos*, op. cit., pp. 118–24.

23. I. Menzies Lyth, *The Dynamic of the Social* (London: Free Association, 1989), p. 26.

24. See Arbuckle, *Out of Chaos*, op. cit., pp. 40–125.

25. Nygren and Ukeritis, op. cit., p. 269.

26. See D. Markham, 'Communities of Hope', *Origins*, vol. 22, no. 14 (1992), pp. 247–9, and J. Holland, 'The Postmodern Cultural Transition: Its Challenge to the "Vowed Life" ', Draft Background Paper to Conference of Major Superiors of Men, USA, 8 August 1990, pp. 26f.

27. See *The Economist* (UK) (7 September 1991), p. 83.

28. P. Wittberg, *Creating a Future for Religious Life: A Sociological Perspective* (New York: Paulist Press, 1991), p. 31.

29. Translation by Wittberg from *La Vie et Mort des Ordres Religieux* (Paris: Desclée de Brouwer, 1972), p. 151.

30. Letter of St Teresa to King Philip II of Spain, 19 July 1575, in E. Allison Peers (ed.), *The Letters of Saint Teresa of Jesus* (Westminster, MD: Newman, 1950), p. 188.

31. Metz, op. cit., p. 16.

32. A. Heschel, *The Insecurity of Freedom* (New York: Alfred A. Knopf, 1972), p. 92.

6 Living community: essential for refounding

Experts in communion, religious are, therefore, called to be an ecclesial community in the Church and in the world, witnesses and architects of the plan for unity.

(*Congregation for Religious, 1978*)[1]

Community is the process of becoming united through the common experience of a core vision . . .

(*Evelyn Woodward*)[2]

This chapter explains:

- the three major models of religious community that have evolved over the centuries;

- through the use of case studies the importance for refounding that each congregation clarify the model emphasized in the founding mythology;

- why it is impossible prophetically to challenge the Church and society through the 'therapeutic' or 'me-istic' model of religious community.

Religious life communities must demonstrate to Church and society how the demands of authority and collaboration are able to be positively balanced for the common good. But there is considerable confusion among religious today as to the meaning of community. As long as this malaise continues, the process of congregational refounding and of prophetically challenging restorationism in the Church will be frustrated.

Understanding community in religious life

Within social sciences there is a bewildering range of definitions of community, but it is possible to detect four broad categories of definitions. Some make community synonymous with *place*, some with a *set of relationships*; some identify community with the *quality of relationships*. Others like to unite in their definitions *place* and the *quality of relationships*. These four categories of definitions of community are particularly helpful for clarifying the three dominant models of community that have emerged over the centuries in religious life: the monastic or ascetical, the conventual or relational, and the mission models (see Figure 6.1).

Model 1: The 'ascetical' community

Religious in this model are not to be involved in apostolic work with people *outside* the physical boundaries of the local community. The structures and roles of the community – for example the rule, the hierarchical role and authority of the superior, the cultivation of humility, obedience and mutual love, periods of community and private prayer – aim to facilitate the individual's contemplative and ascetical search for God. The fundamental purpose of this type of community is not the work that it does nor a comforting sense of togetherness, but the discovery of the ways of God.

The element of *locality* is integral, however, to the definition of community life according to this model. Monasticism, especially under the inspiration of the Irish Columba and of Benedict (Monte Cassino) in the sixth century, developed according to this model. Benedict recognized the abuses that had befallen the religious life of the desert tradition. Up to this point the eremitical life, living totally alone, had been considered essential for authentic religious life. Benedict and Basil in the West and East respectively now made living in community an essential aspect of religious life and this was, says John Padberg, 'a fundamental refounding'.[3] Religious henceforth would not be permitted to roam freely around the countryside, but they would live their entire lives in designated places, challenged and supported by one another and under the fatherly or motherly authority of superiors. And through the Gospel-based system of authority within monasteries it was hoped that the Church and society would be prophetically called back to Christ, the model for just rulers. This form of religious life fitted in well with the settled nature of the feudal society of the time. Reform movements for men's and women's congregations reinforced the emphasis on ascetical practices and withdrawal from the world. Thus the Cistercians, beginning in the Middle Ages with their Benedictine reform, fled society in order to establish monasteries on the frontiers of its settlements.[4]

Model 2: The 'relational'/'mobile' community

In this model the primary emphasis is on witnessing to the quality of relationships that should characterize a group of Christians living together

Type	Emerged in reaction to:	Community type: qualities
Monastic	1. Abuses of desert religious life	'Ascetical': 'locality' in definition
	2. Development of feudal life	
Mendicants	1. Abuses of monastic life	'Relational'/ 'mobile'
	2. Development of urban life	'Locality' not in definition
Apostolic	1. Abuses of mendicant life	'Mission' or 'relational': 'locality' not in definition
	2. Reformation/new areas of evangelization	
Therapeutic/ me-istic	1. Abuses of above models: depersonalization	Self-fulfilment
	2. Authoritarianism	Independence
	3. Primacy of community over individual needs	Individualism/ inward-looking/ fragmented
Refounding/ transforming	1. Abuses of therapeutic model, e.g.	Mutuality
	– individualism	Interdependence
	– 'me-ism'/ self-fulfilment	Primacy of apostolic needs
	– consumerism	Poverty/preferential option for poor
	2. Restorationism/ fundamentalism in institutional Church	

Figure 6.1 Types of religious life: contemporary examples.

according to the values of the Gospel. Locality is not, according to this notion of religious community, an integral part of the definition of community. The primary stress on *communio*, not on the attachment to a monastic locality, makes it easier for communities to move to points of particular pastoral need.

Historically, the mendicant orders helped to create this model of religious life in prophetic reaction to the chaotic conditions both inside and outside the Church. Within the Church many monastic communities had become, by the twelfth and thirteenth centuries, giant feudal estates, wealthy and powerful, lacking zeal for the Lord and for the ascetical ideals they had vowed to express in their lives. At the same time, in the secular world, the feudal system was beginning to crumble as urban life began to emerge. In reaction to the monastic abuses of poverty, the wealth and corruption of power in the Church, the new mendicant orders consequently renounced communal wealth. This gave them the ability to move when necessary to new areas of pastoral need. The radical poverty of St Francis was not primarily ascetical; rather, it was evangelical and christological. Christ had freely chosen poverty, thus revealing the humility of God himself. Above all, Francis loved Jesus in the crib, on the cross and in the Eucharist because in these realities God's powerlessness, his vulnerability and his littleness were so dramatically revealed. St Dominic, sensing the changing social milieu, attempted a new synthesis of the contemplative life and the apostolic life. In order to permit mobility for ministry in the developing urban society, he widened the scope of dispensations from monastic observances.[5] The female religious orders, however, were to remain cloistered with detailed rules based on the ascetical model.

The relational community aims to provide an ambience in which individuals are able to develop their talents through the encouragement of other members of the community. Hence dialogue, sharing of faith experiences and supportive interaction are especially important for religious under this model. The congregational or community leader's role is to co-ordinate or facilitate the interaction or dialogue between members. In order to provide the space and time necessary for frequent, sustained, in-depth interaction between members, communities need to be relatively small in size. Unlike the first community model (the ascetical type), relational communities are concerned with the world *immediately* around them. They hope that the 'one heart and one mind' Gospel quality of their community life will positively influence outsiders close by. However, concern for the world outside is still somewhat indirect. Community members must primarily concentrate on Gospel relations first among themselves; they are to evangelize in and through the community. The community needs its own locale or physical structure with sections reserved only to itself (though this is not as important as for model 1 above); otherwise, efforts at deep interpersonal interaction would be unnecessarily interrupted.

Model 3: The 'mission' community

The *primary* concern in this model is with the pastoral needs of the world beyond the community. The shape and structure of the community is determined by these needs; therefore the structures (e.g. timetables for community meals and prayers) are highly flexible and adaptable. Whatever is helpful in assisting members to react to changing and pressing pastoral needs is to be encouraged. A physical place or territory is of little or no importance in defining this type of community. What is important is the feeling that members belong to a group of evangelizers prepared to share talents in an atmosphere of faith and to enter into collaborative relationships for ministry to people directly 'out there'.

Historically, Ignatius Loyola in establishing the Jesuits contributed immensely to the formation of this model and it developed for two main reasons. First, there were abuses in existing congregations because religious desperately needed revitalization. Secondly, the models of organization of these same congregations (using the ascetical or relational models) made it difficult for religious to adapt easily to the new apostolic demands of the post-Reformation Church and the evangelization of peoples in far distant places. The primary thrust is no longer a common search for God as articulated in obligatory liturgies, office in choir or the community as such, but instead the emphasis moves directly to the needs of people in the world. Apostolic activity was to be seen 'as a prayer because personal holiness and apostolic activity were not to be separate items in a member's life, but necessarily flowing out of and into each other'.[6]

Women's communities in the sixteenth and seventeenth centuries attempted to develop along these same lines under imaginative women and men: Angela Merici with the first Ursulines; Jeanne de Chantal and François de Sales with the Visitation nuns; Mary Ward with the Institute of the Blessed Virgin Mary; Vincent de Paul and Louise de Marillac with the Daughters of Charity. Sadly, most of these communities were eventually pressurized by ecclesiastics to go back to the cloister in which the call to consecration and prayer in choir predominated over apostolic needs. Only the Daughters of Charity and the Sisters of St Joseph were able to sustain pressure to conform, but only because they opted not to be formally religious.[7]

Most active congregations that have been established since the sixteenth century have designed their constitutions according to this mission model. However, as Rome remained uncomfortable with the model, the founding visions of these congregations, especially but not exclusively of women's institutes, rapidly became submerged under an imposed overlay of monastic or conventual customs. For example, the Society of Mary (Marists), established in France in 1836, had as integral to their creation myth the mystery of Pentecost; Marists were to be apostolically creative and mobile, but very rapidly through the process of myth drift – encouraged by the canonical requirements as set by Rome – this vision was lost and the Nazareth myth of contemplation and hiddenness became the dominant emphasis, a royal road to apostolic calcification for Marists.[8]

To repeat, a physical place is in no way integral to the understanding of community in this model. John Lozano wisely distinguishes 'belonging' to a community and the 'actual living' in a community: 'while . . .

belonging to a local community is a distinctive element [of religious life], actual living in the community is only the normal thing and not essential in the sense that the lack of it would destroy the religious life'.[9] It is helpful to record how Ignatius Loyola saw community according to his apostolic model; his vicar general, Jerome Nadal, wishing to highlight the key value of apostolic mobility, wrote that Jesuits have four kinds of houses: novitiates, mobility, pastoral centres and 'journeys'. Nadal asserted that journeys (apostolic missions, the freedom to go where sent for spiritual/ apostolic purposes and the will to go) are to be *the* example of the most perfect house for Jesuits. Jesuits must be prepared to move immediately from this or that place or apostolate and go to where there are more urgent pastoral needs.[10] At times, according to this model, the pastoral needs may require that individual religious live alone or distant from their community. If religious are to survive in these circumstances they must have a vigorous interior life, a deep commitment to the congregation's vision, a yearning to do everything possible to maintain community links, and a sense of being accountable for their work to their fellow members of the congregation.

Each model described above emphasizes a particular quality that is of lasting importance within the life of the Church: ascetical detachment from this world which is the quality in model 1; the love of God as shown through reverence for one's immediate neighbour, as in model 2; and the accent on the 'outward' (i.e. concern for people who do not know Christ or who need to know him more deeply) distinguishes model 3. In reality, every religious congregation in its constitutions will approximate to one of these three models. However, elements of the other two models will be present in varying degrees. For example, Cistercians were not founded for direct involvement in the pastoral needs of people outside their monasteries, but they must show concern by praying for the world. Also, every religious must embrace ascetical practices if they are to develop union with Christ. If communities concentrate *exclusively* on one model, abuses inevitably follow. For example, a group of religious who belong to a mission-model congregation can become so absorbed with their work of evangelization that they neglect to support one another. On the other hand, another group of religious, whose congregation belongs to the relational/mobile model, may be so committed to their own community/ individual welfare that the world at large is neglected.

Case studies: importance of discernment

The following case studies illustrate why it is important for congregations to discover the particular model of community that is at the heart of their founding experience. Failure to do so leads to unnecessary confusion, needless suffering for individuals and communities, and a weakening of congregational prophetic potential.

Case study: the congregational primary task is confused

> The creation myth of the Society of Mary (Marist Fathers) emphasizes primarily the mission model of community; that is, the model that orientates a particular congregation to respond with speed and creativity to the most urgent apostolic needs of the age, as their constitutions indicate: 'Their call is to be truly missionary: they are to go from place to place, announcing the word of God . . .'[11] The ascetical or monastic model is certainly not for Marists: 'They are ready to carry out these [apostolic] tasks anywhere and at any time . . .'[12] However, Marists must be supportive of one another in ways that 'provide a sign of what the Church is called to be in the world'; in fact, 'The ministry of loving service to each other in community is a primary apostolate'.[13] This stresses aspects of the relational model. Community is not to be *merely* an instrument to support Marists in mission, but it should be also a sign to outsiders of the perfection of the Kingdom to come. This latter quality, however, is secondary to their response to the urgent apostolic needs around them.

The brief extracts from this congregation's constitutions are sufficient to show the importance of two things. First, the need to understand the full mythology of a congregation. The unwary Marist who reads only the last of the above constitutional extracts could well argue that the dominant model of community (and thus the creation/identity myth) for the congregation and for himself must be the relational; the primary apostolate would be 'this group of people living in this house', and the needs of the mission beyond its boundaries are of secondary importance. He would of course be incorrect, as other constitutional texts show. Because in fact the mission model is at the heart of the Marist mythology, community exists *primarily* as a service for individuals in mission; it must be flexible, adaptable to the needs of mission. When Marists cannot live together for reasons of mission, their first community will be their province and they must creatively do what they can to help it become a sign of what the Church is called to be in the world. Secondly, the case study highlights why the framers of new constitutions need to be cautious about the use of words, if needless bewilderment is to be avoided. For example, it would have been preferable not to have used the words 'a primary apostolate' to describe how Marists must relate to one another in community. The word 'primary' can wrongly convey to the unsuspecting the view that the dominant model of Marist community is relational not mission. Consistency in language is necessary if muddled thinking is to be prevented.

The following case studies exemplify what happens in practice when community models become confused:

Case study: the power of non-verbal disapproval

Three sisters are involved in developing new catechetical programmes within their local church. Their work demands that they meet frequently with parents who, because of their working hours, can only be contacted between 8 p.m. and midnight daily. The sisters return to their community about 1 a.m. and are far too tired to be up for morning prayers at 6 a.m. with the other nine sisters. These other sisters are involved together in the apostolate in running a school from 8.30 a.m. to 4 p.m. These school teachers are 'deeply concerned about the religious life' of the catechetical sisters and frequently tell them verbally, but especially through looks, that 'if they cannot regularly be up for morning prayers and Mass, and be present and on time at meals, then they are not living truly religious lives according to the requirements of Mother Foundress'.

However, a review of the constitutions of this congregation shows that the mission model is at the heart of its creation mythology. The school teachers in the community had adopted without question as *the* norm for their religious life aspects of the ascetical or monastic model; anyone not living according to the demands of this model, they believed, could not be an authentic religious! They had searched their constitutions and could readily quote (out of context of course) phrases or sections to 'prove their point'. In fact, only the three catechetical sisters had adopted the authentic mythology of the congregation.

Case study: defining the 'monk'

Father X, a member of a monastic community, believes that his institute is not responding to the signs of the times. In the local church where the monastery is situated there is an increasing lack of clergy, so he feels that the founder of his congregation would certainly have allowed monks to adapt their rule to permit *regular* pastoral work outside the monastery, given the new needs of the times. If permission is granted him, then his presence at community exercises would be at best 'from time to time'.

An inspection of the creation mythology of his institute, however, showed that its founding story is based on the ascetical model. In the mind of the founder, service to the local church – no matter how urgent its pastoral needs – could essentially be realized only through adherence to this model; this required permanent residence in a definite locality, that is, in a particular monastery. Father X had not understood the different types of community – and that he could not move from the monastic model to the mission type and remain a monk.

Community, congregational refounding and Roman restorationism

As explained, refounding is the process whereby a religious community (congregational leaders, refounding and renewal people) struggles to relate the Gospel message to the most persistent and urgent needs of the times. This process assumes that a congregation has a clear and accurate vision of itself, its mission and the community model desired by the founding person. And there must be creative individuals who are willing and able to draw others to live the vision in concrete and relevant ways. Before proceeding further, let me explain some of the implications of these conditions for refounding:

1. In the writing of new constitutions, it is important for general chapters to state with sharp clarity what the dominant model of community is to be for the institute. In their enthusiasm to please all sections of the congregation, general chapter delegates can end up unwittingly causing unnecessary tensions and conflicts for future generations by attempting the impossible: trying to give at the same time primary emphasis to two or three models of community instead of to one model. There is no substitute for thorough historical analysis of the origin and nature of the congregational mythology and for courageous honesty in its presentation.

2. Those who recruit for religious congregations must be objective in the presentation of their respective charisms. For example, if a charism or congregational mythology rests primarily on the mission model, then it should be presented as such, even though with some audiences it might be more attractive to overstress the relational qualities of the charism.

3. Initial formation programmes must be designed according to the requirements of the dominant community model of each congregation. For example, a congregation emphasizing the mission model does not design an initial formation programme that would be suitable for either the ascetical or relational model.

4. Sociologically, locality is not normally an essential quality for defining community. This is also the case in religious congregations, except in those institutes that approximate to the ascetical model. However, there is still a tendency within congregations of the mission emphasis to consider those religious who, for legitimate reasons of ministry, must live alone (i.e. outside an established congregational community) or in a community of another congregation to be 'second-class' members of the congregation.[14]

In 1983 the Congregation for Religious published a document called *The Essential Elements of Religious Life*, which sought to summarize the salient points of the Church's teaching on religious life. It aroused controversy since *inter alia* it aimed to reintroduce various attitudes/structures, generally referred to as monastic or conventual (relational), into apostolic congregations that had removed them after Vatican II. Theologian Michael Buckley, while agreeing that there are many insightful and challenging statements about religious life in the document, notes that 'there are really quite serious questions to be raised about the theological adequacy of a number of items'.[15] Here are several examples: as the authority structure of the hierarchy is taken as the model on which all religious authority is to be based,[16] so there must be *personal* authority at all levels of a religious congregation, even though shared authority has been common for centuries in some religious congregations;[17] the relationship with the Church is to be seen mainly as a relationship with the hierarchy;[18] all religious are to have a particular dress;[19] a 'common and constant apostolate is part of the institute's sound traditions' and cannot be altered without detriment to the identity of a congregation;[20] community life is to be structured in monastic or conventual ways.[21]

Benedictine Joan Chittister complains that although Vatican II says that renewal of religious life depends on a return to the charism of the founder, the needs of the members and the signs of the times, the 1983 document defines 'certain past characteristics of religious life as immutable'.[22] That is, according to the document, the process of evolution characteristic of religious life through the centuries must now cease. Religious taking the renewal call seriously turned aside from the impersonality and rigidity of large institutional apostolates and communities to favour small communities in and through which religious could respond prophetically to the most urgent apostolic needs. The document, says Chittister, revokes these reforms by seeking to return religious to 'the identification of the Gospel life with the institutional life'.[23] John Lozano goes to the heart of the issue when he says that the document 'descends from a generic concept of religious life . . . and then adds the apostolic aspect, instead of reflectively following the genesis itself of our institutes in the church, in which we have become religious in order to better develop a ministry required by the People of God'.[24] These criticisms are valid because even the new Code of Canon Law (Canon 605) admits that religious life can be expected to continue evolving and that new forms will emerge. History shows that neither church councils nor curial officials have been able to stop this happening and there is no reason to assume they will succeed today or in the future.[25]

In 1990 Rome published a major document, *Directives on Formation in Religious Institutes*,[26] in which are repeated some of the significant weaknesses of *The Essential Elements of Religious Life*. For example, the ideal religious community is still considered to be either model 1 or model 2 above; that is, community structures need to be predictable or orderly, clearly separating religious from the world beyond. There is more than a hint here of the return to an ideology that the world is evil and to be avoided by religious. The qualities required of candidates are determined primarily by this emphasis on structured community life, not by whether or not the candidates can apostolically relate to people beyond the community boundaries.[27] The charismatic or creative role of religious life within the Church is downplayed.[28]

The 'therapeutic' model of religious life: individualism over community

A new type of religious life community, which I term the 'therapeutic' or 'me-istic' model, has emerged which is diametrically opposed to the values of religious life (see Figure 6.1 on p. 160). It has arisen primarily and understandably as a reaction to the depersonalization of religious life structures of the pre-Vatican II Church, and not because of an awareness of urgent pastoral needs 'out there'. The reaction is long overdue, but we have gone too far if we have adopted this model because it embraces the excesses of Western cultural utilitarian individualism. Acceptance of this model means that the apostolic needs of a rapidly changing world and the aberrations of a restorationist Church are neglected in favour of personal self-fulfilment. Among the indications of chaos listed in the previous chapter there is one symptom particularly characteristic of the therapy model: excessive individualism or 'my rights at all costs'.

When the treatment of those with mental illness and personality disorders is provided on a community or group basis it is sometimes clinically referred to as the 'therapeutic community approach'. Many factors have fostered this form of treatment – for example, dissatisfaction with the consequences of individual psychotherapy, and an awareness of the importance of social experiences in learning and, therefore, in therapy. The therapeutic community is technically designed precisely to respond first and foremost to the individual needs of clients, and only *indirectly* to the needs of the world beyond them. The procedures in these communities have three sources. First, there is a group therapy in which patients expect to receive continuous feedback on how they are behaving as seen by others. Secondly, there is the emphasis on democratic or egalitarian methods: the sharing of facilities, and the frank expression of thoughts and feelings between patients and staff. Thirdly, there is the importance of being a part of a social unit to counteract alienation and promote rehabilitation. For this type of community to function positively it is essential that trained personnel be involved at all times.

Application to religious life

I use the terms 'therapeutic' or 'me-istic' model to describe a new type of religious life, with the following qualifications. First, I do not imply that we religious are mentally ill. However, I believe that some of the assumptions and processes of therapeutic communities, as described above, have been misunderstood and/or accepted uncritically by religious communities, for example:

- the centrality of the human person to the neglect often of the common good; that is, the individual's needs are *the* measure in decision-making; the community must exist solely for the welfare of individual members;

- the use of direct democratic processes in decision-making, when particular constitutions or apostolic circumstances demand instead only consultation by official leaders;

- the denial or downplaying of the principle of subsidiarity/account-ability; hence, an excessive dependence on time-consuming community meetings to decide matters of little importance to apostolic life;

- over-dependence for emotional affirmation on others and the assumption that this is the purpose of community.

Secondly, neither do I imply any condemnation of various forms of psychological therapy that may admirably foster personal/apostolic growth or effectiveness. Rather, I am concerned about the misuse of some therapy methods by amateurs. Thirdly, the new model is an abuse of the relational model described above. I am concerned that some religious communities, with constitutions built particularly according to the apostolic model, have become excessively committed to relational community living so that they neglect the priority of apostolic needs 'out there', actively discouraging individuals from being creatively involved with new apostolic needs. That is, there is a grave myth drift away from the congregational founding vision. Fourthly, I do believe that the characteristics I refer to are evident in the experience of a sufficient number of religious and their communities for a definite new aberrant type to be identifiable. I sense that many religious involved are unaware that they have accepted this new type, even though its introverted value system is radically opposed to the founding mythology of their respective religious communities and obstructs the refounding process.

I believe that the following factors have at least contributed to the model's emergence:

1. Reactions to Vatican II reform

The Council rightly called on congregational leaders to consult religious and communities before making significant decisions. Authoritarianism, as was described earlier, had been all too common in religious life before Vatican II; the dignity of the individual had been abused, the abuse being 'legitimated' by superiors as God's will. However, the meaning of consultation has often become muddled; for example, for some it has come to mean that at all times the majority view must be followed within congregations, even though this type of government is contrary to the founding story.

More serious, however, were the pressures that were placed on religious formed before Vatican II; by a system of detailed rules and uniformity of dress we were trained to be very dependent and conforming people in almost every aspect of our lives. Suddenly we had the chance to be *independent*, to be 'ourselves' for once. We would be able to make decisions unimaginable before the Council, and the new religious culture was to support us in this – at least, so we thought. Little wonder if some of us became over-exhilarated with the liberating experience, like adolescents breaking away to establish our own identity separate from our once intensely controlling congregational cultures.

2. Expectations of religious

Recall the point made earlier (in Chapter 2) that when the Council called us to break away from an undue dependency on our traditional religious cultures, the Revolution of Expressive Disorder was in full force.[29] No value or custom was left untouched by this extraordinary upheaval and the uncritical interiorization of some of the revolution's values has formed the foundation of the therapeutic model, for example:

A cult of individualism/self-fulfilment/'me-ism'/narcissism

The more individualism is encouraged, the more the bonds binding people to the group and to the common good are weakened. Hence Robert Bellah could conclude with deepening sorrow that as the result of the overstress in the United States on individualism, 'marriage, friendship, job . . . church are dispensable, if these don't meet my needs'.[30]

Christopher Lasch speaks of narcissism within the American culture, but his thesis is relevant to other affluent countries. A narcissist is not a self-sufficient egomaniac, but one whose ego is in fact too weak to support an independent self. He/she is a deft manipulator of appearances and feelings, outwardly cool, yet in nervous flight from all commitment and deeply dependent upon others' praise to make up for the emptiness he/she feels within. Because the narcissist's image of self is so poor and envy such a powerful force, there is erected a weak structure of grandiosity through devaluing others. The narcissist is focused only upon himself/herself and others have meaning only as they relate to him/her. Not surprisingly, therefore, a refounding community to be built on the Gospel values of *interdependence* and *collaboration* is impossible if narcissistic values prevail.[31] In a more recent study Lasch analyses the so-called revitalization of 'traditional values' under the Reagan presidency, which in fact became synonymous with unbridled capitalistic economic greed, individualism, the weakening of concern for social justice and the survival of the fittest – reinforcing the culture of narcissism.[32]

The cult of painless/good health

Our cultural value system not only demands that one be healthy, but that one *feel* healthy. The cross or asceticism has no place in this value system. Joseph Tetlow comments on the impact of this value on religious life: 'experienced religious, when they enter what the Church has known as the "dark night" for centuries, think they probably need psychiatric help'.[33]

The cult of immediate pleasure and satisfaction

The ease with which goods can be discarded and replaced by 'better ones' reinforces the feeling that one should not tolerate problems for too long. The tolerance threshold becomes increasingly lower; solutions to problems can be found and there must be immediate results. There is an underlying assumption that what is useful for satisfaction is good. The Gospel call to self-transcendence through faith is seen as irrelevant for personal/group growth or as plain nonsense.

Whatever the source may be, it is certain that the therapeutic religious life community has symptoms rather similar to those just described. The community must be concerned immediately about resolving 'my problems', 'my needs for emotional support in the midst of a rapidly changing world and the chaos of my congregation'. When religious do not feel their needs are being met instantly, they assume the community lacks quality or that its members are not seriously committed to religious life. Lifestyles may become expensive and are legitimated with comments like: 'For too long we religious have been dowdy. We need to express our creative individuality.'

Religious who assume community life must be based on therapeutic values miss the distinguishing quality of the Christ-centred community. Community is formed and is maintained only through conversion to the Lord. Without the Lord as its foundation, there can be no unity, no *communio*, no concern for the welfare of others: 'But now in Christ Jesus, you that used to be so far off have been brought close, by the blood of Christ. For he is the peace between us, and has made the two into one entity and broken down the barrier which used to keep them apart. . . . Every structure knit together in him grows into a holy temple in the Lord' (Eph 2:13, 14, 21). Ultimately, community is not about feeling. Instead, it exists only to the degree that people are prepared to allow Christ himself to be 'the cornerstone' (Eph 2:20) with the asceticism and openness to others that this implies.

3. Culture-shock: reactions to chaos

The disorientation of so many religious, who might well have continued to function satisfactorily within a static ghetto-Church, continues to leave them benumbed and confused over what is happening around them. Some dream and talk incessantly of the congregation's former days of glory – for example, the heroes and heroines of the formation years, its once flourishing schools, well-staffed parishes. These religious look to their congregational leaders and communities to listen to them and 'to put things right' fast; there is little or no awareness of the need to own the chaos themselves.

4. Confusion of congregational leaders

If congregational leaders are unable to claim their own authority to lead in a transforming way, then their own confusion and inadequacies contribute to the therapeutic community style; they become powerless to lead because they are seduced by the self-fulfilment expectations of its members and by their own inability to know what to do.

Once a congregation or community accepts the therapeutic model for itself, religious develop impossible expectations of one another. Religious simply cannot expect to find in communities the level of emotional support and opportunities for intimacy that family life / married life provides. Psychologist Robert McAllister aptly summarizes his own experience of religious with unreal expectations of community: 'Religious communities cannot provide the kind of psychological relationships that healthy families develop, because communities lack the benefit of common origin, the depth of personal attachment, and the closeness of shared life'.[34] The narcissist, emotionally crippled by the need to feel superior to others and to have them constantly at his / her service, inevitably causes conflict in human relationships and no religious community is equipped to solve his / her problems nor the conflicts that result. If the community capitulates to their self-centred disease it becomes trapped by narcissistic values itself.

The following case study illustrates what happens to a congregational leader when he / she unknowingly becomes seduced in the 'me-istic' religious culture.

Case study: the exhausted visitator

An assistant-general of a clerical religious congregation once told me how he felt after the visitation of a province of 200 religious: 'At the end of the three months I began the flight back to Rome; as the plane started its ascent I suddenly found myself in tears, utterly exhausted. I sought professional help to understand my reaction and then I discovered I had unwittingly become trapped in a predominantly narcissistic province. I looked at my notes of the interviews and I found throughout a common pattern. The visitation aimed to help the province to assess its ministry strength, so I constructed the interviews with this in mind; for example, I would ask questions like: "What are the most urgent pastoral needs in your area?" "How are you responding to these needs yourself?" In my notes I found that often those being interviewed would not answer these questions, but instead diverted the interviews back to themselves, their needs, their problems. I would then try to "solve" their problems as an amateur psychologist or give them some pious thought. Above all, I found I was repeatedly affirming them. Now I see that I was trapped in their narcissistic webs and they were draining me of all emotional energy, so by the time I was due to leave the country I was totally exhausted. They had not been helped by the visit and they were waiting for the next visitation for the same thing to happen.'

When a community accepts the model they are apt to choose leaders who are most accommodating to this self-fulfilment model, so a vicious circle develops and little can be done to break it.[35] People trapped in the therapeutic model cannot tolerate energy efforts that seek to direct them beyond themselves to the wider good; at least unconsciously they seek to seduce these efforts inwards for the maintenance of their own lifestyle. In the next case study we see a common reaction of narcissistic religious – to demand of official leaders that they 'tell others to fall into line or else', while denying the need for they themselves to be accountable for their own behaviour.

Case study: the 'get firm' leader learns the hard way

In preparation for a chapter, the congregational leader found that several religious wanted her to become very firm with some members of the province, to insist they conform to the structures of community life. She did so, but quickly found that those who originally complained were not in any way conforming themselves and would take no monition from her on the topic.

One basic thrust of this book is that the Church desperately needs outward-looking, faith-oriented, integrated and creative evangelizers to bring the Gospel into dynamic interaction with the contemporary world. They are imaginative risk-takers for the Lord. But people of this calibre cannot survive therapeutic or neurotic communities; the demands placed upon apostolic innovators by 'me-istic people' are so emotionally suffocating and never-ending that they are either left without energy to create or they move out in order to survive. The process of refounding in therapeutic communities is impossible. Potential refounding persons may grow in ascetical holiness as their imaginative talents are crushed by other religious, but the Church and their religious communities suffer pastoral deprivation in consequence. In apostolic congregations the following question must always be asked: 'What ultimately has priority – the narcissistic needs of individual members or the mission of the Church?'

A community that favours the therapeutic model will attract candidates who fit the qualities of the model and they will be dependent, insecure people, anxious for above-average, on-going emotional support, affirmation, security now and in retirement. The congregation cannot expect from these congregational 'nesters' either now or in the future a vigorous, faith-creative response to new pastoral needs. Such a religious community will be what it recruits: apostolically stagnant and filled with self-centred, over-dependent religious.[36] The following case study shows how a formation programme is undermined because those in authority are committed to the therapeutic model of religious life.

Case study: a community in denial

A province of a clerical religious congregation has many symptoms of chaos, but continues to deny them. It has twelve candidates in training but, with the exception of two, all have already developed signs of religious life dysfunctional behaviour – for example, eating disorders, conservative or fundamentalist views on the Church and liturgy, lack of apostolic concern and sustained interest in theological study, difficulties in personal relationships, little interest in private prayer, desiring middle-class lifestyles. The congregational leader in council continues to call these individuals to the renewal of vows and orders, and remarks when questioned on his policy: 'There is a basic goodness in these men and they will come right. Trust in God. They are no worse than what we have got already in the province and, after all, the people need the priests for the Eucharist.'

The province leader is here blinded by the poverty of his theology of the Church; inevitably, since he has no idea of what the Church should be according to Vatican II, he has no understanding of the role of religious in the Church and consequently the qualities expected in candidates for religious life. He reflects the province's denial of the chaos and thus is merely concerned with living bodies to guarantee the maintenance of the status quo, not with apostolic innovators in the service of the Church. There is no well-founded hope that these candidates have the potential to become prophetic witnesses to the Gospel. For this reason grave injustices are being perpetrated against the people of God, with whom they must later co-operate, and the candidates themselves.

Community and group-oriented cultures

One weakness in the Vatican II documents, especially the Pastoral Constitution on the Church in the Modern World, is that they reflect mainly the concerns of the Western world's cultures. If in the West the tendency is to overemphasize the individual to the detriment of the group, the opposite problem is to be found in most other cultures of the world – for example, Africa, Asia and the South Pacific. Within these latter cultures there is a vigorous ideology that gives priority to group cohesiveness, togetherness and harmony, even if this destroys the rightful demands for the freedom of individuals. In the Philippines, for example, faithfulness to the group, called *bayanihan*, is highly esteemed. A particularly important expression in the culture is *pakikisama*, meaning 'giving in', 'conformity', 'following the lead or suggestion of another' – in other words, 'concession', even when one knows that the concession is objectively the wrong thing to do.[37]

A Westerner, impressed by the façade of harmony and unity in group-oriented cultures and weary of the individualism and polarizations of his/her own culture, may fall victim to cultural romanticism – that is, the disease of thinking that this or that culture in the non-Western world is perfect and its values should be uncritically preserved as though they perfectly enshrined Gospel values. In group-oriented cultures there can be an over-dependency on the group by individuals, not unlike the problems described within the therapeutic community. The challenge is the same: how to foster Gospel-integrated people, motivated for personal growth *and* community growth. No culture is perfect. Every culture has its strengths and weaknesses and thus needs constant redemption.

Fostering refounding communities: practical insights

The need for religious to demonstrate to the Church and the world that true community life is possible has never been greater. Several commentators on contemporary society – for example, Alasdair MacIntyre[38] and Stanley Hauerwas[39] – are rather pessimistic about the possibility of fostering community life on any significant scale. Robert Bellah is a little more hopeful in his reflections on American culture; despite individualism people still have some feeling of commonality having its roots in the Bible and this provides a foundation on which a more informed sense of community can be built.[40]

For Christians, an escape from the world because of the enormity of its problems is contrary to the Gospel for this would be an act of despair, not hope. We cannot adopt, as restorationists would wish, a sectarian Christ-against-the culture orientation. Instead we must be ever open to conscientious and respectful interaction with each other and with cultures, by way of wrestling with the perennial human desires for meaning and belonging in this particular time and place. We religious claim to be a form of Christ-centred discipleship in the service of the Word, and community is integral to this vision. Our task as evangelizers is to foster with the Spirit apostolic communities of praying and active believers, but this cannot be done if we ourselves are not community-oriented in our own lives. We cannot give what we are not ourselves. Unless this vision is sharply defined, frequently articulated and interiorized, we will be seduced into all kinds of by-roads that have little to do with our primary task of evangelizing the

Church and the world. And I believe with Mary Jo Leddy[41] that this seduction by the values inimical to the Gospel continues apace; no longer can we survive as religious in what she calls the 'liberal model' of religious life or what I term variously the 'therapeutic or me-istic model' of religious communities.

Religious wishing to respond to the need to build communities for mission should ask themselves these questions:

- What ministry and model of community are integral to the founding vision of the congregation?

- Are they prepared to co-ordinate, and if necessary sacrifice, personal aspirations and actions for the community's goals and objectives?

- Are they willing to experiment to find the most appropriate structures based on the vision and community model of the congregation's founding person?

- Are they prepared to support one another in mission and regularly share their faith experiences – that is, the ways the Lord is working in their lives and prayer?

- Are they willing to foster an intimacy among themselves that comes from their mutual love of the Lord?

- Are they prepared to be regularly accountable for their lives and ministries to the community?

- Are they open to evaluating regularly the authenticity of their commitment to the community's goals and objectives?

- Are they aware that a commitment to this form of community will demand of them as individuals a level of conversion to the Lord higher than traditional communities generally expect?

If their answers to these questions are affirmative, then the religious are committing themselves to intentional communities in which there will be a Gospel spirit of interdependence and collaboration. Such groupings will be formed according to the axiom 'the new belongs elsewhere' (see Chapter 5) and will be equivalently Basic Christian Communities (as described in Chapter 2) adapted to the requirements of the founding visions of their respective congregations. The following case study shows a refounding community of hope in operation.

Case study: structures adapted to ministry

I once visited an apostolic community of sisters in a New York slum in which its four members were involved in different works with often unpredictable schedules: parish, social work and teaching apostolates. They had clarified their vision and goals as a community, setting aside one evening weekly for shared prayer, an evaluation of the week's work of each sister and an unhurried meal together; they considered this evening sacred and nothing could interfere with it. They set a time for evening prayer for those who would be home, and fortnightly they were able to be together for a eucharistic celebration. After a year they reflected on how things had gone for the community and these are some comments: 'We see now the importance of setting some internal structure realistically based on our different ministerial schedules'. 'After a while we found that our shared prayer became deeper as we prayed out of our experiences of ministry.' 'The idea of setting a time for the weekly sharing of our apostolic experiences I see now as crucial. We would remain isolated from one another without it.' 'I have never experienced such a deep community life of prayer and support in my ministry.'

This community, and others like it, testify to the inner vitality of religious life for those open to radical conversion. We can get out of the chaos, but it means avoiding or discarding anything that smacks of the therapeutic culture.

Summary

Howard Becker perceptively writes that 'Today religionists wonder why youth has abandoned the Churches. . . . I think that today Christianity is in trouble not because its myths are dead, but because it does not offer its ideal of heroic sainthood as an immediate personal one to be lived by believers.'[42] The myths of religious life are alive, but their inner vitality, so frequently suffocated in the pre-Vatican II years through inward-looking and excessively controlling communities, is again in danger of being smothered through confusion over the nature of community. In addition to the traditional models of community, an aberrant, introverted therapeutic type has emerged, one that overstresses individualism and self-fulfilment. Perhaps unwittingly, many religious in recent years assume that religious community life should be synonymous with this therapeutic model.

There is an urgency for congregations to reflect on their founding vision in order to see precisely the type of community that they should be promoting. Most congregations of men and women since the eleventh century have ministry at the heart of their founding. They did not originate, says John Lozano, 'from a desire to live the Gospel together, nor primarily to foster Christian communion or to learn to serve God better, but in order to render apostolic service. Indeed, often the first element to appear in the genesis of these religious families is their apostolate'.[43] As they are communities formed for the purpose of a mission, anything like a therapeutic emphasis is essentially contrary to the founding, and therefore any refounding, faith-shock experience.

If, however, religious are to offer an 'ideal of heroic sainthood' within the Church, then it can only be in and through refounding communities in which interdependence is stressed, based on conversion to the Lord. That is, individuals in faith are prepared to put aside excessive individualism in order to build collaborative relationships to be the Church in miniature. This demands of individuals and communities a prayerful asceticism and the structures that support this.

From the contemporary experience of the religious life, leaders of all ecclesial communities (e.g. dioceses, parishes, Basic Christian Communities) have this to learn: communities cease to be authentically Christian when they exist primarily to serve the personal needs of their members. The harsh truth is that active religious communities die if they turn aside from their primary task of evangelizing outwards. Once leaders cease to challenge, by words and personal example, their followers to follow Christ's missionary vision of faith/justice for the contemporary world, they have lost their prophetic gift of leadership.

Notes

1. Congregation for Religious [1978], *Religious and Human Promotion* (Sydney: St Paul Publications, 1981), p. 11.
2. E. Woodward, *Poets, Prophets and Pragmatists: A New Challenge to Religious Life* (Blackburn, Vic: Collins Dove, 1987), p. 35.
3. J. Padberg, 'Understanding a Tradition of Religious Life' in G. A. Arbuckle and D. L. Fleming (eds), *Religious Life: Rebirth through Conversion* (New York: Alba House, 1990), p. 6; see also J. M. Lozano, *Discipleship: Towards an Understanding of Religious Life* (Chicago: Claret Center, 1980), pp. 197–219.
4. See D. Knowles, *Christian Monasticism* (London: Weidenfeld & Nicolson, 1969), pp. 69–82.
5. See R. W. Southern, *Western Society and the Church in the Middle Ages* (Harmondsworth: Penguin, 1970), pp. 250–99; for a helpful overview of the evolution of religious congregations, see M. Wolff-Salin, *The Shadow Side of Community and the Growth of the Self* (New York: Crossroad, 1989), pp. 3–22.
6. Padberg in Arbuckle and Fleming, op. cit., p. 12.
7. See ibid.
8. See G. A. Arbuckle, *Out of Chaos: Refounding Religious Congregations* (New York: Paulist Press/London: Geoffrey Chapman, 1988), pp. 71–7.
9. J. M. Lozano, 'The Theology of "The Essential Elements" in the Teaching of the Church' in R. J. Daly *et al.* (eds), *Religious Life in the U.S. Church: The New Dialogue* (New York: Paulist Press, 1984), p. 119.
10. See J. Hennesey, 'To Share and to Learn' in Daly, op. cit., p. 61.
11. *Constitutions of the Society of Mary* (1986), para. 12.
12. Ibid., paras 12, 14.
13. Ibid., para. 127.
14. See S. M. Schneiders, *New Wine Skins: Re-Imagining Religious Life Today* (New York: Paulist Press, 1986), pp. 252–5.
15. M. Buckley, 'Reflections on the Document "Essential Elements" ' in Daly, op. cit., p. 273.

16. See *The Essential Elements of Religious Life* (Melbourne: ACTS, n.d.), para. 49.
17. Ibid., paras 50–52.
18. Ibid., paras 40–43.
19. Ibid., para. 34.
20. Ibid., para. 25.
21. Ibid., paras 19f.
22. J. Chittister, 'Rome and American Religious Life', *America*, vol. 155, no. 12 (1 November 1986), p. 257.
23. Ibid., p. 259.
24. J. Lozano, 'The Theology of "The Essential Elements" in the Teaching of the Church' in Daly, op. cit., p. 130.
25. See Buckley, op. cit., p. 262.
26. The document comes from the Congregation for Institutes of Consecrated Life and Societies of Apostolic Life.
27. See H. J. Gray, 'The Structure of the Document', *The Way Supplement*, no. 71 (1991), p. 37.
28. See E. Woodward, 'Images of Community', *The Way Supplement*, no. 71 (1991), pp. 82f.
29. See B. Martin, *A Sociology of Contemporary Culture* (Oxford: Basil Blackwell, 1981), *passim*.
30. R. Bellah, 'Religion and Power in America Today', *Commonweal* (3 December 1982), p. 652.
31. See C. Lasch, *The Culture of Narcissism: American Life in an Age of Diminishing Expectations* (New York: Warner, 1979) and *The Minimal Self: Psychic Survival in Troubled Times* (New York: Norton, 1984); also P. C. Vitz, *The Culture of Self-Worship* (Grand Rapids, MI: Wm B. Eerdmans, 1982), and A. B. Schmookler, *Out of Weakness* (New York: Bantam, 1988), pp. 98–142.
32. See C. Lasch, *The True and Only Heaven: Progress and its Critics* (New York: Norton, 1991), *passim*.
33. J. Tetlow, 'American Catholic Spirituality', *New Catholic World* (July/August 1982), p. 154.
34. R. McAllister, *Living the Vows: The Emotional Conflicts of Celibate Religious* (San Francisco: Harper & Row, 1986), p. 37.
35. See W. R. Bion, *Experiences in Groups* (London: Routledge, 1991), p. 177.
36. See G. A. Arbuckle, *Strategies for Growth in Religious Life* (New York: Alba House, 1986), pp. 203–35.
37. See G. A. Arbuckle, *Earthing the Gospel: An Inculturation Handbook for Pastoral Workers* (London: Geoffrey Chapman/Maryknoll, NY: Orbis Books, 1990), pp. 46–55.
38. See A. MacIntyre, *After Virtue* (Notre Dame, IN: University of Notre Dame Press, 1981), *passim*.
39. See S. Hauerwas, *The Peaceable Kingdom: A Primer in Christian Ethics* (Notre Dame, IN: University of Notre Dame Press, 1983), *passim*.
40. See R. Bellah, *Habits of the Heart: Individualism and Commitment in American Life* (San Francisco: Harper & Row, 1986), *passim*.
41. See M. J. Leddy, *Reweaving Religious Life: Beyond the Liberal Model* (Mystic, CT: Twenty-Third Publications, 1991), pp. 47–78; see also the results of a survey of religious life in the United States by D. Nygren and M. Ukeritis, *Origins*, vol. 22, no. 15 (1992), p. 266.
42. H. Becker, *Escape from Evil* (New York: Free Press, 1975), p. 164.
43. J. Lozano, *Discipleship: Towards an Understanding of Religious Life* (Chicago: Claret Center, 1980), p. 207.

7 Denial, grieving and leadership

This chapter explains:

- that every group, including religious communities, experiences grief;

- why and how groups resist acknowledging loss;

- why mourning rituals are essential for the refounding of religious communities (and the Church) and the avoidance of restorationism.[2]

Grief is experienced by communities or cultures of any type of organization as well as by individuals. Grief is the sorrow, anger, denial, guilt and confusion that so often accompany significant actual or anticipated loss by individuals and/or cultures – for example, the death of a friend, the loss of a job, the closure of an institution, defeat in war, a national sporting failure, economic depression. Yet unless cultures and individuals admit that loss has occurred by experiencing a period of grieving or mourning, and thus formally let go of that which is lost, they remin haunted or entrapped by the past and unable to open themselves to new ways of thinking and acting. Rightly does Ovid claim: 'suppressed grief suffocates' creativity.

In earlier chapters it was explained that cultures react to anxiety-evoking realities such as chaos in ways similar to individuals – for example, scapegoating, denial, groupthink. Chaos is an experience of a massive loss of identity, security or sense of belonging so that the experience of grief can be equally traumatic. I believe that a major reason why religious congregations, parishes or dioceses resist or hesitate about refounding is their failure to mourn or ritually detach themselves from that which is lost or no longer apostolically relevant. Restorationism results simply from the refusal to grieve and risk the new.

Understanding resistances to change

Resistance to change can be overt or hidden. When parents publicly protest over the closure of a school by a religious congregation there is *overt* resistance to the decision. But the most potent forms of resistance are generally hidden. As was seen in Chapter 2, every culture, including that of a religious community, has its own rules that govern its thinking and behaviour and these usually operate at the subconscious level. So when the culture's identity is threatened it is especially within the culture unconscious that various forms of resistances or defence mechanisms emerge, generally leaving people quite unaware of why they react in certain ways. If defence mechanisms become *chronically* embedded in a culture, then they subtly haunt members of that culture and hold them back from facing objective reality. And since these resistances are so deeply rooted in the culture unconscious, it is difficult for people to identify them and counteract their influence. The following case study illustrates how denial is a powerful form of resistance to owning reality; it is used by both individuals and groups.

Case study: personal example of beneficial denial

In mid-1990 I was in the front coach of a commuter train that smashed into a stationary train in an isolated part of Australia. I survived, but, tragically, others were not so lucky. Our coach's survivors escaped into an undamaged coach and there a great spirit of mutual support emerged; people joked and laughed, and some even sang, as though at a party. It took an hour for relief workers to reach us. When the first police officer entered our coach, I heard him exclaim in amazement, possibly even condemnation: 'Don't you people know what has happened?' Having seen the horrific sights in the front coaches and now some of the blood-covered injured among us, he simply could not understand why we could all be so happy. I said to myself: 'Why is he so surprised? Of course I and others know what has happened!' I felt he was insulting our intelligence. Then, as an anthropologist, I realized that a culture of denial had spontaneously emerged in our coach to help the group cope with the enormity of the disaster and this was influencing my own feelings without my being aware of it. The officer had immediately sensed this culture of denial and instinctively reacted against it.

Denial, the pretending that the source of anxiety does not exist, is perhaps the most common form of the defence mechanisms. It is simply the effort to disavow any unpleasant or unwanted piece of external reality. As long as it does not become chronic or habitual, such denial offers individuals and cultures the space to develop resources to cope with loss. The culture deludes itself that nothing has changed; any fact that dares to undermine this delusion is rejected. I and others rejected the policeman's exclamation because, though in our heads we accepted the fact of death and injury, in our hearts our coach culture simply encouraged us to deny the full force of the ghastly reality of death and injury that was surrounding us. The denial evoked regressive behaviour; the jokes and laughter of the adults among us became akin to the behaviour of adolescents. Regression is an attempt to revert to reassuring behavioural patterns more appropriate to earlier stages of development (e.g. childhood). The apostle Peter could not believe that he could ever deny the Lord, but when faced with the fear-evoking experience of being recognized as a companion of Jesus he acted like a little boy caught doing something wrong and repeatedly lied: 'Peter . . . started cursing and swearing, "I do not know the man".' Luckily he was shaken out of his regressive behaviour when 'the cock crowed' and he 'remembered what Jesus had said. . . . And he went outside and wept bitterly' (Mt 26:74–75).

Other forms of individual or cultural resistance to reality are repression and projection. Repression is the forceful rejection from consciousness of impulses, memories or experiences that are painful and generate a high level of anxiety. Memory gaps are its most common expression. The love for firearms makes the United States a nation with 70 million gun owners and 200 million guns, and more than 64 per cent of the 20,000 people murdered in 1990 were shot. Most victims knew their attacker: guns bought to prevent burglaries are often turned on husbands, wives, lovers. However, a high percentage of American voters believe that the private ownership of guns is a constitutional right; the possible loss of private guns is sufficiently anxiety-evoking for the culture to repress the shocking murder statistics. And so the deaths continue.[3] The Eucharist is the heart of a believing community, yet more and more communities are being deprived of this gift of the Lord because of the rapid decline in the number of priests, and there is no well-founded hope that the trend will be halted. But Rome represses this information every time it insists that the issues of married clergy and women priests should not be openly discussed. Cultural projection exists when groups of people seek to reduce their feelings of guilt and anxiety by blaming other people or circumstances for the chaos or anxiety-evoking situations; whatever is dangerous or painful from within is passed on to outside agencies (see the analysis of witch-hunting in Chapter 3).

A culture or group in chronic denial cannot, at least at the culture unconscious level, tolerate people who are honestly in touch with reality; such people must be seduced into the existing state of denial or marginalized lest they win converts to the truth. This is a basic anthropological assumption throughout this book.

The stages of cultural/individual grieving

Grieving or mourning is a process whereby *ideally* loss is formally acknowledged, together with the resistances to reality, and the future is confronted with all its uncertainties, fears and hopes. Though the process involves several identifiable stages, the grieving journey is nonetheless extremely complex and no one model of stages can possibly encompass its complexity. Moreover, the process of movement through the stages is by no means automatic. In fact, individuals and cultures can become locked in at one stage and even regress to an earlier stage. Cultures can even attempt to jump stages in order to avoid painful experiences.

At least three major stages of cultural grieving can be identified (see Figure 7.1). The first stage is marked by a feeling of sadness together with the symptoms of resistance (e.g. denial, repression, projection) to the reality of loss as described above. Thus there can be a yearning or nostalgia for what has been lost, a restlessness, despair, and an anger that can be directed indiscriminately – for example, against friends, God, another culture/or superiors as the assumed cause(s) of the grief.

In the second stage, that is the liminality phase, a culture feels both attracted by the security of the past and the call to face the future. It is a period of sometimes anxious reflection, a search into mythological roots to obtain a sense of identity and self-worth. This can lead to outbursts of localized excessive nationalism or delusions of grandeur, a widespread repression or denial of the realities of loss. This is a risky time because the temptation is for the culture or organization to cling tenaciously to what has been lost and simply refuse to face the future; the group can initiate a spectacular project that is totally out of touch with reality. For example, a Third World country in the midst of economic and social chaos starts its own international airline to give itself the feeling that 'we are as good as anyone else', or a parish that is in grave financial debt decides to refurbish the church 'to make parishioners feel good'. If these resistances to reality continue, chronic grief takes over and it is extremely difficult, if not impossible, for a culture to move out of the escapist depression. People may then come 'to love being miserable' and this gives the particular culture its warped sense of identity or belonging; on the other hand, people can become so feverishly busy that the pain of loss is repressed.

The third stage may be called the recovery or reaggregation phase. The bereaved culture or organization is able to look with some marked detachment at what has been lost. It is realized that life must now go on with the best of the past being carried over into the future.

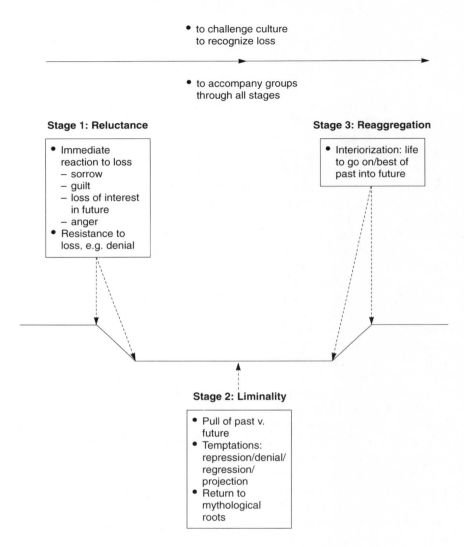

ROLE OF RITUAL/PROPHETIC LEADER:

- to challenge culture
  to recognize loss

- to accompany groups
  through all stages

Stage 1: Reluctance

- Immediate
  reaction to loss
  – sorrow
  – guilt
  – loss of interest
    in future
  – anger
- Resistance to
  loss, e.g. denial

Stage 3: Reaggregation

- Interiorization: life
  to go on/best of
  past into future

Stage 2: Liminality

- Pull of past v.
  future
- Temptations:
  repression/denial/
  regression/
  projection
- Return to
  mythological
  roots

Figure 7.1 Cultural grieving and role of ritual leader

Understanding the need for rituals of mourning

The way in which a people's culture deals with physical bereavement sets the pattern for how people cope with other significant losses. In traditional societies people are especially aware of the fact that a community has a life of its own. When for example a death occurs, the entire community, not just particular individuals, is affected. A set of social relationships has been destroyed by the death, and a new set must be established if the community is to hold together and survive. If the death is not acknowledged, the new order of relationships cannot emerge. Emile Durkheim, a founding father of sociology, wrote earlier this century that 'Mourning is not a natural movement of private feelings wounded by a cruel loss; it is a duty imposed by the group'.[4] No member of a traditional culture is allowed to be indifferent to a death in their midst because, when one person dies, in a sense the entire group dies, and this needs to be formally acknowledged. Those who feel no personal sorrow will nonetheless be expected to weep, and even inflict suffering and inconvenience on themselves. By collectively mourning, the members express their belief that the group itself is in grief and in doing so they overcome and repair the loss that has occurred. Durkheim's comment may appear to be rather cynical in denying to the mourners spontaneity of feeling, which must often be real enough, but he is right about the need for the community itself ritually to mourn.

From the study of traditional cultures, including the cultures of the Old and New Testaments,[5] we learn several lessons of significant importance for personal and group life everywhere; these lessons can be summarized as follows:

- all change is 'felt as catastrophic even when it is rationally recognized for the better, since it threatens the established and familiar order and requires new attitudes and behaviour, changes in relationships, a move into a comparatively unknown future';[6]

- rituals formally articulate that loss affects not only an individual within culture, but the culture itself;

- without these rituals naming the reality of loss and articulating what the culture should become through a new set of internal relationships, the group is in considerable danger of being trapped in or haunted by the past;

- unarticulated grief is like a powder keg waiting to be ignited into all kinds of culture-destroying behaviour, and that cannot be tolerated, so the following axiom is inherent in rituals of grieving: 'holding on kills, letting go heals';

- ritual leaders, by directing individuals and cultures through the stages of grieving, show that it is possible for anxiety to be mastered in constructive ways so that realistic order is achieved while due respect is paid to the past.

By *ritual* we mean the stylized or repetitive, symbolic use of bodily movement and gesture within a social context, to express and articulate meaning. And ritual action occurs within a social context, where there is potential or real tension/conflict in social relations, and it is undertaken to resolve or hide it. Rituals in traditional cultures, by not hiding the reality

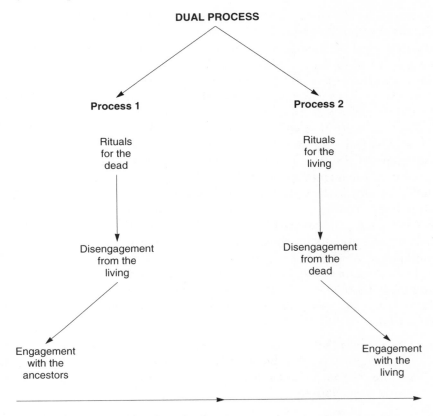

Figure 7.2 Disengaging and engaging for newness

of loss, seek to resolve the tensions and conflicts to allow new life to emerge.

There are normally two levels of oppositional, disengagement/engagement processes at work within traditional death rituals (see Figure 7.2). First, there is a ritual process that is directed at the deceased. The dead are formally *disengaged* from the living; they are given permission, as it were, to leave this world and become *engaged* in relationships with other spirits elsewhere. They are assigned to a new, esteemed and safe status: tradition. Among the Australian Aborigines, for example, although the spirit is independent of flesh, in the sense of outlasting their disunion, a spirit is thought to haunt its former 'home'. It must be formally encouraged to 'move on' if it is to become an honoured ancestor in tradition. The second set of disengagement/engagement rituals relate directly to the living. They must formally become *disengaged* from the negative influences of the deceased and *engage* themselves in forming a new set of social relationships or culture.[7] Often in traditional cultures these two processes take place within a span of three stages, the pattern being the same as described earlier: the separation stage in which the rituals vigorously encourage the community to admit that death has occurred; the liminality stage in which the community particularly concentrates over a lengthy period of time on the two processes of disengagement and engagement. Finally, rituals mark the end of mourning and the community must now concentrate on living out the new set of social relationships.

Denying loss in Western cultures

I was once working with a congregational leadership team and encouraging them to identify and admit to quite obvious symptoms of chaos within their province. For two days I was puzzled that the team kept holding back from acknowledging the symptoms until one member of the team identified the major source of their reluctance. He said 'I think we are concentrating too much on the negative. Our task is not to bemoan what is lost, but to concentrate on only the good things in the province. I find even the word "grieving" is too negative! Our culture is one of hope, not of death!' Others agreed with him. They resisted admitting the chaos in the province basically because they did not see that mourning was an essential Christian virtue. They did not want it in their own personal lives nor as leaders of their province, and for this reason they were seriously failing as a congregational team. Until they owned up to their own need for grieving it would be impossible for them to lead the province constructively through its chaos into genuine renewal and refounding. In their present state they would not be prepared to sanction those religious in their province who could act as the agents of this faith journey. As I listened to the team's resistance and denial, I identified a little with how Jesus must have felt when the Pharisees would not admit to, and grieve over, their failings:

> 'We played the pipes for you,
> and you wouldn't dance;
> we sang dirges,
> and you wouldn't be mourners.'
> (Mt 11:17)

The team in their refusal to admit the need to grieve mirrored the cultural values of much of the Western world. Much has been written on the fact that, unlike traditional cultures, Western societies do everything they can to camouflage death and repress it from consciousness. The English anthropologist Geoffrey Gorer summarized his own research into the decline of grieving rituals in Britain and the United States: 'Mourning is treated as if it were a weakness, a self-indulgence, a reprehensible bad habit instead of a psychological necessity'.[8] People in the affluent world have been deprived of their own deaths and the right to grieve over loss. Of the three stages – separation, liminality and reaggregation – only the *third* is stressed, thus the dual oppositional processes of disengagement/

engagement cannot be realized. That which is lost remains socially unburied. The past haunts us and we simply have lost the cultural art of knowing how to exorcize its powerful hold on our emotions and memories.

Loss and congregational cultures

The following case studies exemplify what happens when religious congregational cultures do not tackle the realities of loss and hold on to their grief 'as others do who have no hope' (1 Thess 4:13).

Case study: a consultant's experience with group denial

During the two decades after Vatican II, I was often invited to conduct for religious congregations and dioceses in-depth surveys of attitudes and personnel resources. Very often, participants denied in a variety of ways disturbing truths about themselves in the surveys' findings.

Generally, denial would show itself first by a personal attack, for example: 'Who do *you* think you are? Stop wasting our time. There is nothing wrong with our province, until some fool like you comes around and tells us otherwise!' A good example also of anger and projection because the questions raised anxiety about the future for the surveys' participants. Another comments: 'How could you possibly write such harsh things about the congregation? Your criticism shows that you lack charity and compassion!' When the personal attack failed, an assault was made on my professional competence: 'I cannot accept your conclusions because the way you phrased the questions shows professional incompetence'. (Neither he nor any other member of the community had training in the social sciences.) Then there were other escapist statements like: 'Your report has been received, but it has been decided that the time is not right to act on its conclusions' (i.e. the *straight rejection approach*); 'We are most grateful for your fine report, and we expect to act on it in due course' (i.e. *the bottom-drawer method* – nothing is done); 'God is never tied down by the findings of surveys. You can never reduce religious life to a statistic' (i.e. *spiritual escapism* – the ultimate flight from reality); 'There are some minor inaccuracies in your report. Kindly explain' (i.e. the *'minoritis'* method: such inaccuracies provide an excuse to reject the total report).

Case study: a 'group-minder' articulates the 'madness'

A lengthy study had been jointly commissioned by several dioceses into the pastoral needs of several minority groups. *Inter alia* it was discovered that these minorities were underrepresented in Catholic high schools and that the level of prejudice was significantly high among Catholic teachers.

The report, in addition to being presented to relevant bishops, was tabled by its author at a provincial chapter of a clerical religious congregation, as the latter maintained several of the high schools surveyed. After the report was formally presented, a chapter member rose and severely attacked the report's findings without, however, offering any proof for his allegations: 'This is a most unscientific report. . .'. Silence descended on the chapter and no one – including the provincial who had asked for the report to be tabled, and the chapter president – rose either to defend the report or to question the validity of the condemnatory comments. The chapter then passed to other business as though the report had never been tabled.

This case study has several interesting features. The report showed clearly that the country in which the dioceses were located was about to experience a violent breakdown in race relations. This, and the evidence of prejudice among teachers within the congregational schools, evoked so much anxiety that the chapter instinctively wanted to deny the facts. The person who attacked the report – that is, the 'group-minder' or the informally group-approved censor of troublesome incoming information – articulated the deep anxieties within the chapter culture unconscious and conveniently found a scapegoat in the author and his report. Having disposed of the anxiety-evoking report, the chapter was able to get down to much less threatening issues that it could easily control. The chapter president did nothing, nor the provincial who had personal and position authority to call the group-minder to order. They colluded with the denial in the chapter culture. Within five years the racial violence predicted by the report occurred, but it took a further eight years before another chapter admitted the congregation must acknowledge the country's multicultural/racial issues. By then, this large congregation had missed the chance to make a major contribution pastorally and educationally to racial harmony. Ignorance may be bliss for those refusing to claim their own authority/power, but not for those who must suffer its misuse.

Case study: an administration loses touch

A provincial congregational team felt the pressures of chaos and decided they had to do something 'spectacular' to lift morale immediately. On the invitation of a bishop, they opened a new school and explained to the province that 'all must have faith'. Shortly afterwards, the administration started another apostolate. For a while the province felt good about the new initiatives, because, said the congregational leader, 'they show we are alive and well'. However, morale collapsed again later, but the team still felt all would be well if they could find yet another grand gesture to undertake. They were wrong.

189

In the above case study the team refused to confront constructively the province's deep grief, in itself a symptom of the chaos. Opening two houses, they thought, would be sufficient to remove the province's sense of drifting and low morale. All they did was to distract the province for a short time from the distress of the chaos; eventually people recognized that the projects alone would do nothing to assuage their sense of loss. The team acted like the poor debt-ridden country establishing its own international airline for prestige reasons. Disaster was inevitable. I find that the turning to the spectacular gesture with the hope that it will solve morale problems is particularly common within religious congregations today. It takes various forms, for example the taking on of new works (see the above example), an unnecessary building or refurbishing spree, or the establishment of formation programmes when there is no possibility of attracting recruits. Anything to hide the inner pain and the need to confront it in faith.

Case study: a general chapter in grief

A general administration prepared over a two-year period its congregation for a general chapter and the assistance of a facilitator/discernment expert was found for the preparation and the chapter itself. The theme of the preparatory period was 'integral conversion for mission'. During the chapter, at the request of the provincials, the faith-oriented discernment process was to be given particular emphasis rather than the customary parliamentary debating system. The congregation's provincials had approved of this several months prior to the start of the chapter.

When the chapter opened, two important events occurred. The facilitator, at the instigation of a small national group, was subtly, but effectively, told he was no longer needed. Delegates accepted this decision without hesitation. Secondly, the participants were invited to discuss over several days the implications of the superior general's detailed and thorough report on the state of the congregation. However, discussion was far more brief than had been originally planned and critically important issues in the report were ignored (e.g. declining membership, clericalism, the poverty of conversion and pastoral creativity). Participants moved quickly to the writing of visionary documents; delegates enjoyed debating (according to well-known parliamentary rules) minutiae within the documents that took no account of the existential conditions as detailed in the superior general's report. Chapter committees became exceedingly busy producing innumerable reports. In the large committee established to write the mission statement, threatening topics (e.g. liberation theology or inculturation) were avoided. On several occasions individuals attempted to introduce these themes for reflection, but they were quickly marginalized as 'dangerous leftists'. In the evaluations of the chapter members, most considered the chapter 'a great success', 'an experience of congregational fraternity at its best'.

This case study highlights the resistances to anxiety-raising reality within the chapter culture unconscious. The facilitator and the superior general's report were too fear-creating. Once the appointed facilitator had been skilfully marginalized into a powerless position, the way was open for regressive behaviour – that is, the return to the traditional methods of conducting their chapters and to a theological language that did not threaten the security of participants. The sheer busyness of the chapter committees falsely assured delegates that the gathering was realistically confronting the *real* issues; in fact, it was yet another way for the chapter to avoid reality.[9]

There is an element of truth in Durkheim's view that religion is the act whereby a group worships itself.[10] In a burst of corporate denial, groups become entrapped in their own dreams of a grandiose present and future, believing their dreams or fantasies are the reality. This happened at the above chapter. The chapter's visionary statements became verbal and enthusiastic acts of 'self-worship'. In this atmosphere of fervent self-congratulation, it is very difficult – in fact, often quite impossible – for any member, other than a chapter's elected officials or a facilitator, to call the group back to reality.

Anne Shaef and Diane Fassel see grandiosity as one of the symptoms of the addictive society; it is the pretending that the group is greater, or something other, than it is. They write:

> Grandiosity keeps the mission lofty and frequently unattainable. We have found that the helping professions often refuse to make their statement of purpose realistic . . . partially because of their inability to deal with the feelings of pain and frustration they experience when they see so few real changes . . . [Grandiosity] can reassure us that we are important and do important work.[11]

The chapter culture in the above case study, with its visionary rhetoric, became itself an addictive substance leaving its members unable to recognize the death symptoms within its own organizational culture and the congregation at large. Chapter members became hooked on their own visionary statements. They chose not to see that, without radical individual and congregational conversion in and through the darkness of faith and beginning with themselves in the chapter, the chapter rhetoric would be of no value.

Sometimes I meet such powerful denial in the cultures of religious communities that I sense the presence of evil. A strong statement, but no other word can fittingly describe the reality. Take the example above of the congregational team that kept denying for two days the very obvious symptoms of the chaos, and consequently the need to grieve over them. No human skill seemed capable of breaking their defences.

Theologians commonly distinguish between moral and non-moral evil. Moral evil is the breaking of the moral law or, when faith is present, an act of disobedience to the will of God. Non-moral evils are those ills that do not come directly from human sin. It is this latter type of evil I particularly, though not exclusively, have in mind since people are generally unaware at the conscious level of what is happening. The evil is this: these are *good* religious, but they refuse to struggle to be *better*. Religious are called to strive for the more or the better, not to be satisfied with just the good. Contentment with the good and the fear of what the better might demand of people blocks the Spirit from entering and transforming their lives through the gift of grieving. There is disobedience here, again not necessarily culpable, but there is at least an objective refusal to heed the call of the Spirit. All I can do in this situation is to wait and pray with St Paul: 'Do not be mastered by evil, but master evil with good' (Rom 12:21). And the admonition of Jesus: 'this kind [of evil], it is cast out only by prayer and fasting' (Mt 17:21). We cannot push people into conversion – that is a gift of the Lord to be freely accepted or rejected by them.

Case study: a province in depression

I quote from an observer's description of her province which is denying the need for bold and creative apostolic action. This cannot happen until the province acknowledges that the past cannot be restored. 'Up to a decade ago we were receiving many candidates into our formation programme. The future seemed really bright. Then quite dramatically the numbers dropped off. Our provincial chapters made many statements about this and these made people feel fine; they believed that there would be change because the documents said there would be. But nothing happened. We began later to have a sinking feeling that we might even die out as a province. Last year the congregational leadership team asked all houses to have meetings to discuss the last chapter statements about the future in the light of declining numbers. Well, we had meetings and more meetings . . '. but we got nowhere. If there is another meeting to discuss the future, we will scream. The meetings just drifted.

'Recently we suddenly decided to close several of our hospitals. This has led to a lot of anger and ill-feeling between members, because one hospital being closed is the foundation community of our province. "If that goes", many say, "that is the end! We must do everything we can to keep it going!" Many of us claim our congregational leadership is doing nothing. When they visit they just speak of good things. Frankly, we are confused, even paralysed, in the presence of all the problems. One group in our province wrote a paper recently and said that there is no real problem, provided we returned to our old apostolates and did things just as we did them before. I really don't know what to think . . .'

In this case study the province's culture has never known periods of numerical decline or apostolic confusion; from the time of its foundation several decades earlier, recruits entered annually in good numbers and new apostolates developed. This pattern no longer exists. The culture now is in grief and defensive mechanisms are evident, chronically insulating the province against the realities of dying and death. The official leadership in the province is paralysed, believing that documents and 'smooth words' alone will help the province out of the chaos.

The following experience comes from a religious who was appointed bishop after spending most of his priestly life in ecclesiastical administration. His diocese contains extremes of rich and poor; on becoming bishop he moved into the luxurious episcopal residence within a wealthy suburb. He tells his own story and no commentary is needed.

Case study: a religious bishop benefits from grieving

'In the early years of my administration I enjoyed the prestige and comfort of the task. It never occurred to me that the poor would never visit me in the rich section of the city. I would visit the slums in my chauffeured car, accompanied by the episcopal symbols of power. One day one of my priests in the slums was murdered at the request of powerful political forces for they feared his growing criticism of their corruption. I then saw the poverty of his house and the tears of the poor as they mourned his loss. Would these people cry if I, the bishop, died? What had I ever done for them? Then I realized how remote I had become from the marginalized, the Lord's favourites! I hesitated to give up my symbols of prestige . . . I prayed for the strength to move out into the unknown. It was so hard to let go.

'Then I transferred into the slum myself to live where the murdered priest had been. No more chauffeured car! No more symbols that hide me from the pains of the poor! Now the poor freely approach me, talking of their sufferings, their joys, their love of Mary and the saints. For the first time in my life I am beginning to know what it means to live by faith; yet the Lord rewards me because now I see his face in the poor. What more could I ask of him!

'I have become marginalized by most of my fellow bishops now. Perhaps they see in me what they should be themselves . . . I pray for them. At long last I think I know what the role of religious must be: to challenge the Church to be Christ to the poor!'

The leader's role: to challenge denial ritually

John Keats describes the dynamic of loss and newness characteristic of the mature person (and culture):

> Most like the struggle at the gate of death
> Or liker still to one who should take leave
>   of pale, immortal death
> And with a pang as hot as death is chill
> With fierce convulse, die into life.[12]

Authentic grieving is that time in life in which we are called to 'die into life'. This message is powerfully and repeatedly presented throughout the

Bible, for example in the lamentation psalms, Jeremiah, and the lives of Mary and Jesus.[13] Even Yahweh through Jeremiah is pictured as grieving; he sorrowfully admits the loss in order to permit the unimaginably new to enter:

> Incurable sorrow overtakes me,
> my heart fails me . . .
> The wound of the daughter of my people wounds me too,
> all looks dark to me, terror grips me . . .
> Prepare to call for the mourning women!. . .
> Let them lose no time in raising the lament
> over us!
>
> (Jer 8:18, 21; 9:16–17)

Yahweh so feels the anguish of his people's loss that he cries in pain, yet in the midst of the sorrow the new is already being dreamed about:

> Look, today I have set you
> over the nations and kingdoms,
> to uproot and to knock down,
> to destroy and to overthrow,
> to build and to plant.
>
> (Jer 1:10)

A radically new people will emerge from the chaos provided they admit that without Yahweh they are powerless. The story of Ruth and her mother-in-law Naomi is touchingly one of mourning for newness. Two women experience and admit to Yahweh their considerable loss – Ruth her homeland and Naomi her husband and two sons. Neither has lost hope in Yahweh, and the impossible happens; Ruth finds a kind husband and Naomi a grandson, whom she later adopts (Ruth 4:16).[14]

This theme of loss, leading to the admitting of chaos, which then leads to newness, carries through into the New Testament in the message of Christ and in his personal example – from death freely accepted, the liminality of the tomb, to the incredible newness of the resurrection. Mary acknowledges her own nothingness in faith and experiences in consequence the 'impossibly new' – 'the child will be holy and will be called Son of God' (Lk 1:35). The healing of Bartimaeus, just as Jesus is to enter Jerusalem for the last time, functions as a parable of the paradox of loss/newness (see Mk 10:46–52). When the blind beggar cries out in anguish over his loss of sight, people around him are embarrassed by the shrill honesty of his plea and command him to keep quiet. They want to deny that he has lost his sight. But Jesus hears him and says: 'Call him here' (v. 49). Bartimaeus 'throwing off his cloak . . . jumped up and went to Jesus' (v. 50). Note the liminality stage of Bartimaeus' ritual of grieving because he does two things: he runs to the Lord while still blind, risking injury to himself, and in faith he lets go of the cloak, which is the symbol of his status/security as a blind beggar. He trustfully journeys in darkness towards the new, but not yet attained, gift of sight. Then the impossible happens for Jesus restores to him his sight. Once Bartimaeus could see, he who earlier was seated *beside* the road is now *on* the road *following* Jesus (the reaggregation stage of grieving), an example of what it means to be a disciple of the Lord – a radical letting go of the old in faith, humanly risky though it be, so that the new may enter.

The loss/newness paradox is at the heart of Paul's spirituality: 'If we have been joined to him by dying a death like his, so we shall be by a resurrection like his' (Rom 6:6). He exhorts the Ephesians: 'You were to put aside your old self, which belongs to your old way of life and is corrupted by following illusory desires. Your mind was to be renewed in spirit so that you could put on the New Man that has been created on God's principles, in the uprightness and holiness of the truth' (Eph 4:22–24). Paul knows what this means in his own life; for example, he admits that it cost him his Jewish status to be a follower of Jesus (see Phil 3:5–8). In admitting his losses and weaknesses Paul discovers strength beyond his imagination, but he keeps coming back to the key precondition for newness – namely, the need to let go of the old: 'that is why I am glad of weaknesses, insults, constraints, persecutions and distress for Christ's sake. For it is when I am weak that I am strong' (2 Cor 12:10).

Since we Westerners have culturally lost the art of dying we must build appropriate rituals of loss so that the new and creative may enter into our lives, our congregations and the Church itself. Mourning rituals of traditional cultures, including the cultures of the Old and New Testament, are able to guide us. Notice in the text of Jeremiah on p. 194 where Yahweh calls on the mourning women to start the formal rituals of grieving for Israel; by their cries these women summon the people to grieve openly. In traditional cultures the community's leader(s), either directly or through delegated people (e.g. mourning women), exercise a pivotal role in challenging the culture to recognize loss and the dangers of chronic denial in all its devious forms.

Walter Brueggemann defines the task of biblical prophets: 'The task of prophetic ministry is to nurture, nourish, and evoke a consciousness and perception alternative to the consciousness and perception of the dominant culture around them'.[15] The authentic ritual leader in grieving needed at every level of the Church does precisely this because those in grief are in a *betwixt-and-between* stage: they experience loss, but the new is as yet unknown to them. A new world in hope must be articulated for them, an alternative to the one they had become used to but that is now no longer available to them. In leading the people out of oppression and bondage under the Egyptians, Moses as ritual leader inspires the travellers in the wilderness with the vision of an entirely new world, 'a land of streams and springs' (Dt 8:7). He repeatedly articulates the conditions they must fulfil if this alternative world is to be reached; they must let go of all that obstructs their journey into the promised land – their nostalgic yearnings for Egypt, their sinfulness, the enticing attractions of the surrounding pagan cultures: 'Be careful not to forget Yahweh your God, by neglecting his commandments . . .; he was the one who gave you the strength to act effectively' (Dt 8:11, 18).

In Jesus, the role of ritual grieving leader and prophet reaches perfection: 'It is true that Moses was trustworthy in the household of God, as a servant is . . . but Christ is trustworthy as a son is, over his household. And we are his household as long as we fearlessly maintain the hope in which we glory' (Heb 3:5–6). To show us the vision of a Kingdom beyond human understanding and the way to reach it, it was 'necessary that [he] should suffer before entering into his glory' (Lk 24:26). His entire life is a ritual of letting go, a pilgrimage of faith in liminal darkness on his way to God the Creator; all the while he remains his own ritual leader. At Emmaus Jesus himself is the ritual leader, challenging the two disciples to own up to their loss and that of their community in a creative way. Jesus leads them through the first stage of separation in which they freely express their anger and sadness that things had not turned out as they had so sincerely hoped. Jesus does not judge or condemn their anger (Lk 24:17–24). They then enter the liminality phase of their ritual journey; here Jesus, having obtained their trust, strongly challenges them to recognize and accept their loss. They will then be open to a community and personal newness beyond human imagination, resulting from the death and resurrection of Jesus (Lk 24:25–32).

In Jesus, and Moses before him, we have a model for us not just of the role of congregational (and *all* church) leaders, but also of the qualities required of them. They are future-oriented or hope-filled people, since they believe their primary task is to challenge a culture to interiorize a vision not yet realized. They recognize that the group is trapped in an unconscious denial of loss; they believe they must publicly articulate this refusal to face uncomfortable realities, even though the process of confrontation may isolate them as leaders. Their task, difficult though it be, is to empower the group to assume responsibility for its own mourning because the group is tempted to become overly dependent on the ritual leader. Neither Moses nor Jesus succumbs to this temptation. As the reaggregation stage for the Israelites is about to begin – the entrance into the promised land – Moses slips away in a spirit of remarkable patience and detachment to die alone on a mountain and to rest in an unmarked grave (Dt 34:1–7). When the two disciples at Emmaus are in danger of becoming over-dependent on Jesus' presence, Jesus suddenly withdraws to allow them to test their new-found apostolic strength by returning to Jerusalem – the reaggregation phase of their ritual of loss (Lk 24:30–35).

Religious commit themselves to live radically Gospel values. Their vows publicly proclaim that they aim to rely on God's power instead of depending on the ordinary means of development acceptable to most people. At the heart of their reliance on God is the imperative that religious grieve over their own sins and failings, those of their congregations, the Church and the world. They claim to be specialists in the process or ritual of letting go so that the impossibly new may enter. Prophetically they must challenge the Church (including the hierarchy) and the world to enter in faith the same process of grieving. Many hesitate to take on the task to which they have committed themselves. It is too awesome and risky a duty, and marginalization and suffering are the inevitable consequences.

In the above case studies of chaos and denial by religious congregations, those with authority/power refuse to exercise their ritual functions integral to their leadership role. At the provincial chapter at which the report on prejudice was tabled, the people with authority/power to challenge the chapter to face the report's implications for the province failed miserably as ritual leaders. When the report's author expressed concern to one leader over the implications of the denial within the chapter, the comment was made: 'Let things be. This is not the time to disturb the status quo.' At the general chapter the officially appointed moderators were aware of its denial, but refused to claim their authority/power to confront the group with this unpopular, anxiety-creating fact. They hoped that things would turn our right in the end, if allowed to drift long enough; but that did not happen, thus intensifying the malaise within the rank and file of the congregation and further exacerbating their distrust, and even growing cynicism, over the poverty of congregational leadership. The leadership team that established two new houses wanted to spare the province the pain of confronting its own chaos before God, wishing it to move immediately into the reaggregation stage without passing through the terrifying purgation of liminality. The team colluded with the province's denial, thus failing to claim their authority/power as ritual leaders.

In the case study about the province in depression, congregational leaders thought documents alone would lead to group conversion, an aberration that also flourished among participants at the above general chapter. Instead, they should have developed their role of ritual leadership of a grieving process within the province culture, both personally and through delegates. As long as they fail to do this, the province will not face the task of fostering bold apostolic initiatives adapted to the most urgent needs of today. The same is true of any religious community or the Church refusing the challenge to grieve because without it there can be *no* refounding.

A ritual of group grieving

The following ritual[16] has been developed specifically to assist religious communities in the art of grieving. I have used the ritual many times with groups as large as four hundred and as small as five; its simplicity, the use of the loss/newness paradigm, and periods of meditative silence invariably evoke in communities a freeing experience of letting go to allow the new to enter.

Preliminary instructions

- As participants enter in silence into the darkened room they are given a lighted candle and move into groups of eight (or fewer) in circles; the paschal candle is alight in the centre of the room; meditative background music can be played.

- It is advisable not to extend the ritual beyond approximately one hour.

- If the ritual is to be a community experience, then ideally the ritual leader should be the community leader or someone elected by the community as its representative.

Process

1. *Leader*: Reads Isa 45:7. Invites all to enter into the darkness of the tomb so that they may discover the newness of the resurrection.
2. *Reader*: Reads Ps 143.
3. *Leader*: Invites all to ponder the question 'What significant thing do I feel I have lost personally or communally?'
   Pause for a few moments.
   Invites participants to name some loss or grief that they have experienced, advising them to keep their naming to one word or a phrase. There is no discussion on what is named. (If it is not possible to sit in small groups, participants may be invited to write their loss on large sheets of paper fixed to walls or tables.)
   After each participant names a loss, then he/she extinguishes their candle; the paschal candle and lights are extinguished by the leader.
   Silence for a short period.
4. *Reader*: Once all have extinguished their candles, Ps 88 is read. Silence for a lengthy period.
5. *Leader*: Invites participants to identify some newness or joy that has entered the group or their ministry; the paschal candle is lit. After a short time the leader invites them to name the newness in the group (or write it on sheets around the room). Each participant, having named a newness, then lights his/her candle from the paschal candle.
6. *Leader*: After all candles have been lit, there is a short period of silence, followed by the leader reading Rev 21:1–7. A resurrection hymn follows. All are then invited to give the sign of peace.

Summary

To be human is to experience loss daily, for example through illness, ageing, on the death of friends. Grief following loss is also a normal human occurrence; it does not need to be treated, but its pain needs to be recognized – thereby allowing people, organizations or cultures the right to acknowledge their loss in order to permit the new to enter. As Brueggemann says: 'The public sharing of pain is one way to let the reality sink in and let death go'.[17] The human tendency, especially in Western cultures, is to resist acknowledging that loss has occurred; there is a fear of letting go of the known and tried and of having to enter into the new unknown. Mourning is a psychological and cultural requirement for healthy and creative living, but even more so it is a Gospel imperative.[18] We remain spiritually stunted unless we are prepared to die with Christ in order to rise with him.

Within the Church the ideology of restorationism is a symptom of the failure to grieve; that is, the refusal to let go of the irrelevant and allow the apostolically new to enter. Religious by vocation are called to be specialists in the art of letting go of the old to allow the 'impossibly new' to enter; therefore religious must prophetically be challenging the Church to enter constructively into the grieving process. However, religious congregations are experiencing massive grief, but I believe very few are admitting it. As long as they delay doing so, the Church is deprived of a much-needed challenge and model of Christian grieving. Mirroring the loss-denying secular society, many religious communities have deep-seated pathological problems, such as chronic denial, that are holding back these communities from pastorally creative action or refounding. Congregational leaders cannot lead others through grief into the 'impossibly new' if they are not themselves journeying with the Lord prayerfully through darkness in faith, love and hope (Lk 9:24). The same must be said of all leaders in the Church – be they bishops, pastors or animators of faith communities. Let these people learn from the sad experience of congregational leaders who personally hold back from entering the paschal mystery for mission.

Notes

1. J. Gardner, 'How to Prevent Organizational Rot', *Harper Magazine* (October 1965), p. 23.
2. A fuller account of the rituals of grieving are in my book *Grieving for Change: A Spirituality for Refounding Gospel Communities* (London: Geoffrey Chapman, 1991), pp. 1–58. The American edition of the book is *Change, Grief, and Renewal in the Church: A Spirituality for a New Era* (Westminster, MD: Christian Classics, 1991). See also my book *Earthing the Gospel: An Inculturation Handbook for Pastoral Workers* (London: Geoffrey Chapman/Maryknoll, NY: Orbis Books, 1990), pp. 103–5.
3. See *The Economist* (UK) (7 September 1991), p. 20.
4. E. Durkheim, *The Rules of Sociological Method*, trans. S. Solovay and J. Mueller (New York: Free Press, 1965), p. 31.
5. See Arbuckle, *Grieving for Change*, op. cit., pp. 61–139.
6. I. Menzies Lyth, *The Dynamics of the Social* (London: Free Association, 1989), p. 34.
7. See K. Maddock, *The Australian Aborigines: A Potrait of their Society* (Harmondsworth: Penguin, 1974), pp. 158–76.
8. G. Gorer, *Death, Grief and Mourning in Contemporary Britain* (New York:

Doubleday, 1965), p. 85. See also Arbuckle, *Grieving for Change*, op. cit., pp. 43–58.

9. See the helpful comments by D. Fassel, *Working Ourselves to Death: The High Cost of Workaholism and the Rewards of Recovery* (London: Thorsons, 1992), pp. 103–6 and *passim*.

10. See E. E. Evans-Pritchard, *Theories of Primitive Religion* (Oxford: Oxford University Press, 1965), pp. 48–77.

11. A. Shaef and D. Fassel, *The Addictive Organization* (San Francisco: Harper & Row, 1990), pp. 123f.

12. J. Keats, 'Hyperion' in *The Complete Poetical Works of Keats*, Book III (Boston: Houghton Mifflin, 1899), pp. 211f.

13. See Arbuckle, *Grieving for Change*, op. cit., pp. 86–107.

14. See A. L. Laffey, *An Introduction to the Old Testament: A Feminist Perspective* (Philadelphia: Fortress Press, 1988), pp. 205–10.

15. W. Brueggemann, *The Prophetic Imagination* (Philadelphia: Fortress Press, 1978), p. 13.

16. This ritual has been constructed by Gerard Whiteford SM.

17. Brueggemann, op. cit., p. 111.

18. See C. Parkes, *Bereavement* (New York: International Universities Press, 1972), p. 142.

8 Collaborative government: practical hints for authority dissenters

On their return the apostles gave him an account of all they had done. Then he took them with him and withdrew towards a town . . . where they could be by themselves.

(Lk 9:10)

When change is driven from the top of the organization – without significant across-the-board participation – it is a recipe for failure. . . . Participation empowers the vision.

(James Belasco)[1]

This chapter explains:

• the theory of collaborative government;

• the nature and the experience of collaborative government in religious life;

• in practical terms how this form of team leadership should emerge and be sustained.

A fundamental theme in this book is refounding. Whether in a diocese, parish or religious community, this is the process whereby a believing community, under the inspiration and leadership of pastorally creative people, is relating the Gospel message to the critically challenging problems within contemporary cultures. These imaginative pastoral people cannot emerge and act, however, if official leaders (i.e. authority dissenters) are not fostering an atmosphere conducive to pastoral creativity. The latter need a transformative, organic style of leadership and the type of government they initiate is sometimes called 'collaborative'.

However, considerable confusion exists in the Church today regarding the precise meaning of 'collaborative government'. Though some of this complexity has been removed earlier (in Chapter 4), in the following pages I analyse the nature of collaborative government in more detail and offer some practical guidelines to encourage this form of administration. I concentrate particularly on the practical dynamics of collaborative leadership *within* the officially appointed congregational leadership teams at the provincial and general levels. By extension, what is said of the collaborative process within these teams will apply *mutatis mutandis* to all other congregational leadership groups and to the hierarchical Church itself.

Collaborative government: definition and some practical insights

Collaborative or team government is the result of a high level of *interdependency*; that is, each person in the team has his/her role clarified and feels responsible for, and is supported in, its achievement, but works to combine his/her actions with those of others in view of a commonly accepted vision and mission. The stress is on interdependency, not dependency or counterdependency. In a dependency or power form of government, the authority person dominates and other administrative officials passively receive his/her commands; counterdependency exists when there is resistance or rebelliousness against authority. And independence operates when individuals do not work in alliance with others, a problem highlighted in Chapter 5.[2]

The following are some conclusions that have come from the shared experience of many congregational administrations:

1. The need to model collaborative government

Collaborative leadership is needed throughout a religious congregation, but unless its officially elected leaders are prepared to model this style of government, no amount of rhetoric will persuade a congregation as a whole to accept it. This means getting the theology behind this form of government right from the beginning. The early Church especially understood itself as the sacred people of God's possession, a people with a way of life differing from that of other cultures around them, a people supportive of one another for life *and* mission. St Paul defines what this different way of living must mean:

> And to some, his 'gift' was that they should be apostles; to some prophets; to some, evangelists; to some, pastors and teachers; to knit God's holy people together for the work of service to build up the Body of Christ, until we all reach unity in faith and knowledge of the Son of God and form the perfect Man fully mature with the fullness of Christ himself. . . . If we live by the truth and in love, we shall grow completely into Christ, who is the head by whom the whole Body is fitted and joined together, every joint adding its own strength, for each individual part to work according to its function. (Eph 4:11–16)

And 'pray constantly' (1 Thess 5:17).

A congregational leadership group, if it is to become a collaborative team for government, must struggle to *be* what Paul describes for the Church at large.

2. Leadership functions must be balanced

The leadership team cannot be proactive or apostolically prophetic unless it can achieve a balanced tension between its four essential functions,[3] namely:

- to keep in touch with the founding vision and the congregation's traditions;

- to nurture itself; that is, to foster intra-group communication;

- to provide improving maintenance services; that is the day-to-day administration;

- to be prophetic; that is, to be future-oriented, or proactive, challenging the congregation to accept the process of refounding.

It will be a struggle to develop and maintain the balance, since the temptation will be to put more energy into some functions to the neglect of others. For example, too much stress on nurturing produces a de-energizing therapeutic model of government; and too much emphasis on congregational traditions or maintenance requirements will hold the team back from its primary purpose – that is, encouraging the congregation to prophetic action.

3. Congregational leadership is 'messy'

Collaborative leadership is generally very messy, because it is a human activity involving cultural change, and the personalities, emotions and quirks of many creative people. It certainly is not functioning well if there is no dissension before important decisions are made.[4]

4. Open government for information

Since the congregational team exists to respond to the pastoral needs of a rapidly changing world, the communication about these needs and the creative responses to them must be fast, two-way and accurate. The leadership team is concerned to get the right information at the right time and to pass it on to the people who need it, to get the message understood and acted upon. However, the temptation to spend an excessive amount of time on analysis of the information being received must be resisted. Organizations can become so caught up in more and more analysis and information gathering that they become paralysed. On the other hand, paralysis can also develop if organizations are consistently rushing into decision-making without sufficient research/information. Creative risk-takers become de-energized not only with excessive, introverted meetings and analysis, but also by having to interact with leadership groups that are constantly failing to listen to essential information.[5] Whatever way group paralysis occurs, we have a recipe for organizational suicide.

5. Remaining open to the new: The need for reality-testing skills

Even the most creative leadership teams can develop middle-life weariness. They can lose their drive and enthusiasm and adopt a mechanistic leadership or managerial style; they fall victims to the deadly disease of spending their time solving the problems of yesterday rather than anticipating the challenges of tomorrow. Bureaucracy, red-tape and complacency are the symptoms of this mortal sickness and so teams must develop methods to counter this, some of which will be explained.[6]

Case study: the over-confident team

A congregational leadership team was elected with a clear mandate by a province wishing for some long-overdue prophetic challenging. For two years the team lived up to this expectation, but by the third year the team was felt to be losing touch with reality, causing anger and disillusionment within the province; team members frequently spoke of their need to be open to new apostolic needs, but this was not happening. The team finally sensed the gap between themselves and the province and sought the help of a consultant. It was found that the team had become victims to the seductiveness of certainty, as one said: 'We knew the needs of the province when we assumed office and we knew what to do about them, but we keep forgetting to keep listening to what people were saying about new pastoral needs. We have been too certain of our "rightness".' Their leadership remained effective only as long as the needs remained the same. They had to relearn the art of listening.

Every leadership team needs skills for interpreting what is happening within its own group and the wider society it seeks to serve. If a team is unable to be honest and courageous enough to be reflecting on the strengths and weaknesses of its own inter-relationships, it will remain insensitive to key aspects of what is taking place within the wider organizational culture.[7]

Achieving collaborative leadership: practical hints

1. Clarify the team vision/mission, goals and objectives

> Write the vision down,
> inscribe it on tablets
> to be easily read.
> For the vision is for its appointed time,
> it hastens towards its end and it will not
> lie.
>
> (Hab 2:2–3)

Yahweh's command through the prophet Habakkuk is as relevant to leadership teams as to provinces or congregations as a whole; namely, they must have a vision for themselves and it needs to be frequently referred to in decision-making. Recall that a vision statement (see Chapter 4) articulates a mutual purpose or the place where everyone agrees to go in response to the question 'What do we want this team to look like within a set period of time?' A realistic vision fulfils three criteria:

- it must be sharply focused; if not, strategic planning to realize the vision is fuzzy;

- it must be inspirational or hope-raising to empower people to act;

- each member of the team must be involved in preparing the vision, otherwise it will not be owned by the entire team.

The vision statement is short – preferably no longer than a paragraph – but the mission statement is longer because it sets out the primary task of the team; that is, what the team must do to realize the vision. Here is a hypothetical vision statement: 'Our congregational leadership agrees that by the end of two years we will be a fully operative collaborative team in which members will: feel they are communicating with each other; know that their talents are accepted and being used for the good of the team; have their roles clarified and respected; be accountable to the team itself and to the wider religious community we serve.'

The mission statement will set out the goals and objectives or strategies that must be adhered to if this vision statement is to be realized. For example, the mission statement could contain, *inter alia*, the following: 'Within six months team member X will report to the team with practical alternatives for developing effective accountability structures . . . and team member Z will lead the evaluation discussion on the proposed alternatives'. The mission statement is not worth the paper it is written on if timetables are not set for the implementation of the statement's stages and people specified to carry specific responsibilities.[8] Finally, members must be committed to implementation of the mission statement; they must feel in

205

the pits of their own stomachs, as it were, that there is an urgency about the vision and the implementation of the mission statement, but this will happen *only* if all the team members are intimately involved in its formulation. One cannot write a mission statement for someone else to put into practice!

Case study: failure to articulate goals and objectives

A provincial leadership team of a clerical religious congregation was asked to provide its mission statement, goals and objectives as part of an evaluation process. They said they did not have one because it was unnecessary. 'All we need is the knowledge of what the provincial chapter tells us to do in our team', said one member and others agreed. 'Our theological assumptions of Church and religious life are implicitly present in all our decisions; we work so well together that we do not have to articulate them', said another. They all agreed that one of their major strengths was their ability to think alike: 'there are no significant dissenting views in the group when we make decisions'.

In this case study the leadership team accepted intellectually the rhetoric of their chapter documents – namely, that the leadership group should model collaborative teamwork for the province – but this contradicted reality. They had regressed unknowingly to a pre-Vatican II hierarchical model of organization in which the councillors saw themselves purely as advisers to the provincial. They also did not see themselves as having a team prophetic role in the province, because their task was only to fulfil the duties set out for them by the chapter. In other words, they opted to be managers, not a leadership team with a transforming or prophetic thrust. They had attended several workshops that stressed the need for vision/ mission statements, but this had not influenced their behaviour – even though they said the workshops were 'valuable and enjoyable'. The group was so overwhelmed by the fears of the new that the disturbing information of the workshops was repressed. Thus the case study highlights both the need for theological clarity and on-going evaluation of a team's performance. This group discovered only at the end of its administration that theologically they were *attitudinally* pre-Vatican II in their under- standing of Church and religious life and that this had negative effects on their decision-making. Regular evaluations would have revealed the marked discrepancies between the ideals of their congregational documents and their own performance as leaders.

2. Appreciate diverse forms of collaborative leadership

The collaborative approach means that all team members share in the decision-making processes. They do this in one of several ways: for example, discussion leads to consensus or a majority vote *or* the team leader or his/her delegate decides after consultation with other members. The preference is the first option: full involvement in decision-making through consensus. However, there must be flexibility. The group should learn what option is the most appropriate at a given time; for example, the urgency for decisions and action may allow only the last option – that is, a decision is made by the one with the most authority. If lengthy/wide consultation or majority voting is made the unchanging rule, then decisions may never be made and urgent apostolic needs are left unattended. The consequence is that an organic style of leadership is turned into an oppressive mechanistic one.

Earlier I clarified what is meant by consensus – that is, when a particular decision is finally made after all parties feel they have been involved at each stage and that their views have been listened to.[9] There may be disagreement over the details of the decision, but all believe it is the best decision in the circumstances. However, if consensus decision-making is pursued at all costs – that is, if it is made into a rigid ideology – then points of conflict and disagreement can be forced underground. If these issues remain unattended to, then all kinds of unresolved negative feelings or hurts will haunt the group and threaten to split it apart at some point. The same danger exists if the majority voting option is pushed through too quickly, because then disagreements and differences of opinion also remain unresolved. A final word of warning. Sometimes there is unnecessary tension when team members are not told *before* their advice is sought what form their participation is to take: is it simple consultation, consensus or majority vote? False expectations can be raised, and then distrust – the enemy of collaboration – emerges.

Pseudo-consultation is to be avoided; this involves the illusion of participation without the substance. Decisions have already been made by leaders, but other team members are then 'consulted to keep them happy'. There is no intention of changing the original decisions. This leads to disillusionment, disaffection, cynicism and comments like: 'I know he had made his mind up before he even asked me. What's the use of trying!'

3. Clarify roles; delegation and subsidiarity

The principle of subsidiarity can be summarized thus: whatever team members are able do for themselves ought not to be removed from their competence and taken over by other people (e.g. by the congregational leader). In other words, decisions should not be made at higher levels if they can be made lower down. This means that the team leader must establish boundaries for other team members so that people are not interfering needlessly in what others are delegated to do. If the boundaries of respective competencies are smudged, all kinds of quite unnecessary tensions and conflicts will emerge, draining energy inwards that should be going outwards to the realization of the team's mission. The task, then, of the team leader is to guard these boundaries so that team members can concentrate on their tasks in the service of the group.

Canon law/constitutions will set out precisely those decisions that must be made by the team leader (i.e. major superior) with the consent or consultation of the council. In other matters, he/she can lawfully delegate authority to congregational team members. I find, however, that subsidiarity can fail to operate for one of several reasons. First, whenever team members are unsure precisely who has the delegated authority or authorization. Team members and the province or congregation as a whole must be told which person has the right to make decisions and to take responsibility for them. Secondly, the principle is broken when the major superior or the congregational leader attempts to take back the authority without justification, or when other team members try to interfere without due reason. Team members then feel used, irrelevant and de-energized as persons. Thirdly, there can be occasions when the leader does not intervene when he/she should do so because the one to whom the authority is delegated is unable or unwilling to act.

Case study: the reluctant leader fosters injustices

Sister X has delegated Sister Y on her leadership team as the one responsible for the educational apostolate of the province and the extent of the latter's authority/power has been publicized throughout the province. Y initiated a review of one of the province's high schools, which concluded that the school should merge with a school a short distance away run by another congregation willing to co-operate in the plan. Failure to accept the plan would mean that the congregation would have to subsidize the running of the school with ever-increasing amounts of money. The entire leadership team accepted the plan to merge the schools, but Y kept finding excuses to stop the decision being implemented – hoping that the impossible would happen and allow the congregation to maintain the status quo. The team's leader refused to intervene, saying: 'We must wait until Y learns from her failure to act. If I step in she will never learn and she will be badly hurt.'

By failing to intervene, the congregational leader assented to a series of injustices resulting from Y's on-going hesitancy to act – for example, the misuse of the congregation's limited financial resources reserved for the care of its ageing members and for apostolic projects based on more urgent needs. The hopes of teachers, parents and students were also falsely kept alive so that when the closure finally came they were seriously inconvenienced. The congregational leader placed the importance of Y's personal growth above the rights of the congregation and others. The failure of X to assume her rightful responsibility to lead evoked anger among other team members and concerned individuals within the province itself. The province rapidly lost confidence in the entire leadership group.

If the principle of subsidiarity is to be adhered to then agendas for meetings need to be carefully screened. No matter should be coming to team meetings that can and should be dealt with at lower levels. If this screening does not take place, the team is back to the limitations of direct-democracy procedures; namely, that no decisions are to be made unless all *fully* participate with every piece of information being made available to them. Transforming leadership is impossible in these circumstances; members become bogged down by irrelevant minutiae and the critically important issues of building the future are crowded out.

4. Ensure team members are accountable

St Luke records Christ's missioning of the apostles: 'He called the Twelve together and gave them power and authority . . . he sent them out to proclaim the kingdom of God and to heal' (Lk 9:1–2). He instructs them how to proclaim the message and then sends them out for an apostolic experience. On their return, he draws them aside to give 'him an account of all they had done' (Lk 9:10). Here we see Jesus clarifying the mission for the apostles, setting them their primary task and then calling them to evaluate their experience.

Likewise in a congregational team, every team member must be accountable on the basis of the team's vision/mission statements for his/her performance to the group. The team itself, through appropriate channels, must similarly be accountable to the whole province/congregation. The team leader's primary task in imitation of Jesus is to keep articulating the team's vision/mission statements and to call the members to be accountable for their respective tasks. In addition, he/she must check to see if the boundaries of delegation are adequate or suitable: Do the boundaries need changing in view of the vision and circumstances? Are the boundaries being needlessly transgressed? Jesus at times would take an incident where the disciples had failed to keep to their primary task and use it as an occasion of learning; for example, their confusion over his vision of servant leadership (see Lk 9:46–48). So also in a congregational team. The leader needs to use failures in delegation to help members to discover the nature of subsidiarity in more depth.

5. Guarantee commitment to the refounding process

Integral to the primary task of a leadership team is its concern for the future of the group. Hence the team will be concerned to find, empower and support renewal and refounding persons, placing them according to the axiom 'the new belongs elsewhere' (see Chapter 5). In brief, the leadership team make it their priority to encourage the 'pastorally innovative eccentric' – never a popular priority in a religious community suffering from calcified chaos.

6. Foster skills for teamwork

Congregational leadership groups must learn to see themselves as teams, not as a set of individuals. In a team, members must be aware of each other's strengths and weaknesses so that they will act in a manner that uses their diversity to serve the group as well as the individual. The group needs to ask itself four basic questions if it is to assess the quality of its teamwork:

- Do members feel they are communicating easily with one another?

- What skills are needed for the team to fulfil its primary task?

- What skills do members in fact have, in the light of its primary task?

- What skills must be 'bought-in' from outside to make up for the group's lack of necessary qualities?

The research of Ned Herrmann pinpoints the need to clarify the preferred mode of thinking of each team member, since this will avoid a good deal of unnecessary tension and conflict. Herrmann divides the way people think into four patterns and shows that while an individual uses all four patterns he/she clearly prefers in practice one mode of thinking.[10] The four categories are what he terms: 'machine-gun thinkers', 'detail thinkers', 'storytellers' and 'dreamers'. Machine-gun thinkers are highly rational and quick thinkers – analytical, factual and precise – and emphasize the major points of issues. People like lawyers, physicians, financial officers and scientists tend to be machine-gun thinkers; if they are chairpersons at meetings they keep people to the agenda and discourage any kind of diversion, even though it might in the long term be helpful to the group. Detail thinkers are present-oriented people, logical and slow thinkers, concerned with detailed information, but poor at seeing patterns in such material. They make good accountants, middle managers, quality-control agents, manufacturing foremen. A machine-gun thinker will tell people the nature of the end product, but the detail thinker explains step-by-step how the product is to be realized. Storytellers are intuitive, deeply concerned with the feelings of people, stressing teamwork, relationships and participation in group activities. They are past-oriented people, avid recounters of anecdotes, the stories having no particular purpose other than the pleasure of recounting them. Social workers, nurses, teachers and personnel officers tend to be storytellers.

Dreamers, however, are far more intuitive than logical and factual. They are future-oriented, highly imaginative persons, with new ideas springing from a mind that organizes experiences, facts and relationships to discern a path that has not been taken before. Somewhere along this uncharted path, intuition compresses years of learning and experience into an instantaneous flash.[11] They are rarely able to provide before a project begins all the concrete details for its implementation; they act in short stages, then evaluate and change direction with ease if it appears that is the right thing to do. As their thinking does not follow predictable patterns, they feel oppressed by routine or the acceptable order of 'doing things around here'. Artists, architects, entrepreneurs, strategic planners, path-finding dissenters or refounding persons in secular and religious affairs are 'dreamers who act'; that is, they have the added gift of being able to strategize their vision through concrete action. Herrmann highlights the inevitable tensions existing between people having different thinking modes, for example dreamers and storytellers cause considerable anxiety and annoyance to machine-gun and detail thinkers – and vice versa! Yet each mode of thinking is essential for good teamwork.

The relevance of Herrmann's analysis for effective congregational team leadership may seem obvious, but my experience is that particularly among male religious there is a hesitancy to clarify the diverse skills and preferred modes of thinking of team members. Moreover, in male congregations – as in the Church at large – the tendency commonly is to elect machine-gun and detail thinkers as their leaders, since they are generally status quo-oriented and distrustful of people with anxiety-evoking ideas and dreams. Also, not uncommonly, in both male and female communities, I find that if a dreamer is elected as the community head, the community then takes fright and quickly elects *strong* machine-gun and detail thinkers 'to keep a check on "that dangerous dreamer"'! Of course for a dreamer to be an effective doer, he/she needs analytical and logical skills within his/her team. But the latter must be open to, and supportive of, the dreamer's innovative mode of thinking. Dreamers, and to a lesser extent storytellers, as team members in religious congregations, can normally expect to suffer periods of intense loneliness, even marginalization, unless the team becomes aware of what is happening. Hence the importance of discovering the skills of each member of the team and compensating for what is lacking. In the case study earlier in this chapter the provincial administration that considers its chummy cohesiveness a major strength does not recognize it is in fact a grave weakness. The members of the administration are either machine-gun or detail thinkers; as there are no responsible dreamers within the group, team members have no felt need for prophetic leadership.

Case study: A dreamer experiences marginalization

A dreamer had been elected as a congregational leader, but the majority of team members were strong machine-gun and detail thinkers. Team meetings with the leader as chairperson rambled on without direction, causing intense pain to all but himself. Some considered resigning as they could not function in this chaotic situation, but finally the leader was persuaded to step down as chairperson in favour of a machine-gun team member. Tensions lessened, but not for the leader who felt increasingly isolated and frustrated, because she was unable to share her vision for the congregation with other team members as they were unwilling to appreciate her talents as a dreamer.

Incidents of this kind can be personally and apostolically tragic. The congregational leader was marginalized by her own team for several years until she was able to convince her colleagues of the need for a review of their effectiveness as a team. With the help of an outside facilitator her own position was better understood, but it did not make up for the years of frustration experienced as leader or the paralysing effect it had on the congregation's efforts at refounding.

Trust between team members is essential because without it members communicate inadequately; they will censor the information given to one another. Maybe the lack of trust comes from conflict or the fear of it happening, but conflict is unavoidable even within the best teams. It is important not to hide it, but to recognize its causes and develop methods of conflict resolution. The congregational leader in the above case study lacked these skills and the team suffered in consequence. Robert Bolton distinguishes between the emotional and the substantive dimensions of conflict. The former include anger, distrust, defensiveness, fear and resentment. Substantive dimensions involve conflicting needs, disagreements over policies and practices, and divergent views of roles and the uses of resources. These substantive issues cannot be resolved until the emotional aspects are faced up to and the team may require an outside facilitator for this to happen.[12]

Case study: confidentiality breakdown causing mistrust

A leadership team had been slowly developing good intra-communication over a two-year period. Unexpectedly, one team member heard that a team colleague had revealed to an outsider a matter confidential to the team. For months the former felt he could not raise the issue with the one who broke the confidentiality. The more he held back, the angrier he became; eventually, he no longer felt confident in bringing to the team's attention matters of considerable urgency for for the province as a whole; fearing that the needed confidentiality would not be preserved. Other team members felt something was wrong but felt powerless to act.

In this example one incident in which confidentiality is broken undermines the functioning of the entire team, because once trust is undermined communication breaks down. Ideally, the team member should have approached the offender and resolved the tension between them. The team leader did feel that something was wrong in the group, but lacked the confidence to raise his concern within the team itself, so team meetings became increasingly strained and formal. Finally, another team member convinced the team that it was time to bring in the services of an outside facilitator; the process entered into by the team was necessarily a painful one, but ultimately trust was restored. The team now employs the facilitator regularly to help them evaluate the effectiveness of their intra-communication.

7. Use consultants and facilitators

You will recall that people commonly resist change because they fear to lose something of value to them, or they do not understand change and its implications, or they fear they do not have the capacity to learn the new attitudes and skills that change will require of them. The skills of consultants and facilitators are often essential to help individuals and groups confront constructively their lack of knowledge and their fears of change. The task of the consultant 'lies in helping insights to develop, freeing thinking about problems, helping the client to get away from unhelpful methods of thinking and behaving, facilitating the evolution of ideas for change, and then helping him/her to bear the anxiety and uncertainty of the change process'.[13] There are as many kinds of consultants as there are disciplines. For example, a theological consultant can be employed by a congregational team for the precise purpose of assisting members to understand better the mission of the Church, because if they are unclear about this their team decisions will be faulted throughout.

The consultant will have specialized knowledge that the team needs, but the facilitator's task is concerned with the ways this knowledge can be interiorized by the team members. The facilitator's skill is to keep the group focused on the topic, ensuring that all opinions are heard, fostering good communication methods, and assisting the group to identify resistances to dialogue. Though sometimes the roles of consultant and facilitator can be combined, I personally feel their tasks are so difficult that generally they should be kept separate. In this book I keep coming back to a major anthropological insight – namely, groups resist change (even if intellectually they accept its necessity) and will do everything possible to prevent it. Facilitators and consultants are concerned to help a group be more change-oriented. Therefore they become good targets for the group's fears and various unconscious conspiracies commonly develop to prevent these specialists from accomplishing their tasks.[14]

Case study: a consultant becomes trapped by group denial

A congregational leadership team met for several days to evaluate their experience of working together. A consultant agreed to assist them with information on the overall state of religious life, but she quickly found the group somewhat passive and unreflective – although one team member aggressively attacked the consultant, accusing her of something she had not in fact said. For the remainder of the evaluation this team member maintained a passive aggressive stance. The evaluation continued for three days with the group's passivity intensifying. The consultant found the experience draining and, though she was aware of considerable denial in the group, she did not know how to deal with it constructively.

Later the consultant reviewed her role in the evaluation with a skilled supervisor and discovered the following: first, though members of the group kept insisting they related well together and enjoyed one another's company, in fact they were deeply divided theologically on critical issues of ecclesiology and religious life but feared to admit it openly to one another; secondly, the group was projecting its own inner chaos on to the consultant who unknowingly began to carry the group's weariness and malaise. The group was displaying what the psychologist W. R. Bion terms fight/flight reactions. Most members were so frightened of unaddressed divisions between them that they grasped every possible opportunity to flee from co-operating with the consultant.[15] Thus the group remained passive throughout the evaluation. The member who spoke harshly to the consultant represents the 'fight' reaction: confront vigorously, but avoid listening. On reflection, the consultant recognized that at the end of the first day she should have described to the group her impressions of what was happening. If the group's attitudes still did not change, she should have withdrawn immediately from any further involvement. Because she had not withdrawn, the group continued to punish her for its own inability to face internal divisions.[*]

---

8. Support conferences of major religious superiors

These conferences were established following the Council so that, according to the New Code of Canon Law, 'by combined effort they may work to achieve more fully the purpose of each institute, while respecting the autonomy, nature and spirit of each' (Canon 708). These conferences may

---

*For some guidelines on the use of consultants by leadership teams within the Church, see Appendix 1.

restrict themselves to a managerial style of leadership, for example the provision of informational and insurance services. However, I believe the conferences provide religious with the opportunity for an *enhanced* prophetic role in the Church, and in some instances, as is the case in Ireland,[16] this is happening. Executives, mandated by their conferences and equipped with research and mass media comunication services, are able to respond to some of the most urgent apostolic needs, for example the highlighting of injustices within a country and/or in government policies. This dissenting action may evoke negative reactions from bishops' conferences, but this should not dissuade religious from their prophetic role. A religious conference that fails to provide this leadership will, I believe, slowly disintegrate because there is no inspiring vision to hold individual congregations together in any form of worthwhile partnership.

9. Nurture group life humanly/spiritually

A task-oriented congregational team expends considerable energy. Unless individuals and the group have space and time to restore this energy, then individual/group burn-out, bickering, excessive tiredness, denial of reality, poor concentration on problems inevitably develop.

The group can revitalize its own energies in a variety of ways and the options chosen will depend on what the group enjoys doing. One team, for example, may enjoy a regular meal together well away from their place of meeting; another team may receive energy through open-ended discussion on particular topics. A group that has fun together is more likely to be a group that can stay and work together. The spiritual life of the group must be nurtured. A group in which members are able to share their faith experiences will possess an inner freedom for honesty and openness. I have seen the energy of individuals and groups rise with extraordinary rapidity as a consequence of members being able to share in faith their deepest concerns. The level of sharing is not something that can be pushed. It grows under the power of the Holy Spirit as members become more comfortable with one another and with the presence of the Lord in their midst.

Case study: an administration uncomfortable with faith-sharing

---

A general administration believes that one of its major strengths is the friendliness of its members. Yet their common prayer life does not reflect this optimism as it remains very formal and rubrically exact. Prayers are said in common, but there is a marked lack of spontaneity or inspiration.

On investigation it is found that deep, unacknowledged theological and cultural divisions exist within this administration. Members relate to one another at a superficial level, making sure to gloss over the painful issues dividing them; their common prayer life reflects this superficiality and repression of division. Until they acknowledge the truth about themselves, they cannot share their faith experiences at any meaningful level and their public prayers will continue to convey a note of artificiality.

Members of leadership teams need to realize that the primary concern of team building is not the individual needs of the group's members, but the welfare of the congregation and the Church it serves. People can become so concerned to achieve collaboration and cohesion that these qualities become not means, but an end in themselves. The team style then changes from an organic to a mechanistic one, and a rigid conformity to rules predominates. The creative dissension of individual team members is then stifled or crushed. This is what William G. Dyer means when he writes: 'Creativity is often at odds with the conditions that foster collaboration. It is possible to increase team work while inhibiting creativity, which seems to stem from the less fettered individual.'[17]

Summary

Three things are required for people to become a leadership team at any level of the Church: opportunities, competency and conversion. An awareness of apostolic opportunities is not difficult – not so the achievement of competency and conversion. Competency in ecclesiology and the history/theology of religious life is essential, if right policy decisions are to be made consistently; competency also involves the acquisition of skills by team members themselves and/or the 'buying-in' of the necessary skills of other people. One set of skills that will normally need to be 'bought-in' are those of the facilitator/consultant to help the team to formulate its vision/mission statements and to evaluate its performance regularly in the light of these statements.

The commitment to use knowledge and skills, however, comes from conversion. No leadership group within the Church will ever be prepared to face its own powerlessness and need for outside help if it is not open to an on-going conversion to the Lord and his mission. It is only through a shared faith in the resurrected Lord that members can learn to find 'joy in the truth . . . to make allowances, to trust, to hope, and to endure whatever comes' (1 Cor 13:7).

APPENDIX 1: The use of consultants/facilitators – practical hints

From experience I offer the following guidelines to:

(A) *Leaders of religious communities*

- Before contracting with a consultant/facilitator, find out if he/she has the skills you need;

- Check out with each member of your group if he/she is prepared to become intimately involved in the interaction of the group under the guidance of the consultant/facilitator;

- A group evaluation or consultancy should not take place if any one member cannot be present, because it is the *group* that evaluates itself, not just individuals in the group;

- Work out a precise brief with the consultant/facilitator before the evaluation is to take place; if there is need for the brief to be changed, then renegotiate it – remembering that the consultant/facilitator is free to accept or reject it.

- Following sessions with the consultant/facilitator, plan ways in which new insights can be put into practice.

(B) *Consultants/facilitators*

- Insist on a clear brief; if your skills do not fit the brief, decline the request;

- Indicate to the group when it strays from the brief; if they continue to do so and no new brief has been negotiated, then withdraw from the consultancy;

- Only rarely should you work alone, for the dangers of being trapped by the group's denial are too great; when working in pairs one is able to observe from the group's margin what the consultant in the frontline cannot see happening;

- Normally, consultancy should not end as soon as information has been imparted; the group will need assistance during the liminal period – that is, the stage when the old is being let go of and the new is not yet well established.

A leadership team, like any human group, can lose touch with reality. Thus the team needs regular reality-testing sessions in which questions like the following are asked:

- Are the usual staying-in-touch-with-reality methods still working?

- Have they outlived their usefulness?

- Are they blocking the flow of information in and out of the group?

- Are members of the team continuing to listen and communicate with one another?

- Are the vision/mission statements being adhered to?

Since the group will not normally have the objectivity to do the evaluation by itself, it is advisable to seek the services of an outside facilitator.[18]

The most commonly named obstacle to creativity is constraint. Constraint includes the lack of freedom in deciding what to do or how to do it, and lack of control over one's own ideas. Hence it is advisable to be flexible regarding the format of team meetings. Formal meetings with well-prepared agendas are essential and at these gatherings the machine-gun and detail-thinking people flourish. Yet formal meetings constrain creativity. Thus for inspiration and creativity to emerge, at times a more relaxed meeting style is beneficial (e.g. when there is no fixed agenda to be followed). Members are free to reflect on all kinds of issues bothering them as team members and gatherings of this kind are generally times for energy-creating interaction, the chance for the dreamers and storytellers to be actively involved and stimulating the imagination of the group. In these invaluable sessions people can dream about the future of the province/congregation, brainstorming about strategies for action, without having to worry about the details of implementation. For the first few sessions of this type a skilled facilitator may be required to help the team develop confidence in the process.

Notes

1. J. Belasco, *Teaching the Elephant to Dance* (New York: Penguin, 1990), p. 220.
2. See W. G. Dyer, *Strategies for Managing Change* (Reading, MA: Addison-Wesley, 1984), p. 124.
3. See A. L. Kelley for an excellent clarification of these functions in *Your Church: A Dynamic Community* (Philadelphia: Westminster Press, 1982), pp. 43–59.
4. See K. Albrecht, *The Creative Corporation* (Homewood, IL: Dow Jones-Irwin, 1987), pp. 46f.
5. See G. Pinchot, *Intrapreneuring* (New York: Harper & Row, 1985), pp. 224f.; see also helpful insights of I. Briggs Myers, *Gifts Differing* (Palo Alto, CA: Consulting Psychologists Press, 1980), pp. 69–75.
6. See P. Drucker, *Innovation and Entrepreneurship: Practice and Principles* (New York: Harper & Row, 1986), p. 149.
7. See E. H. Schein, *Organizational Culture and Leadership: A Dynamic View* (San Francisco: Jossey-Bass, 1987), pp. 137–47, 270–96; and D. Graves, *Corporate Culture: Diagnosis and Change* (New York: St Martin's Press, 1986), pp. 120–44.

8. See J. Alvarez, 'Focusing a Congregation's Future', *Human Development*, vol. 5, no. 4 (1984), pp. 25–34; A. J. Lindgren and N. Shawchuck, *Management for Your Church* (Nashville: Abingdon, 1977), pp. 45–59.
9. See N. Conway and J. Alvarez, 'Decision Making by Consensus', *Human Development*, vol. 9, no. 2 (1988), pp. 41–6.
10. See P. G. Neuhauser, *Tribal Warfare in Organizations: Turning Tribal Conflict into Negotiated Peace* (New York: Harper Business, 1988), pp. 73–83.
11. See R. Rowan, *The Intuitive Manager* (New York: Berkley, 1986), pp. 11ff.
12. See R. Bolton, *People Skills* (Brookvale: Simon & Schuster, 1987), p. 217; see also J. F. Benson, *Working More Creatively with Groups* (London: Tavistock, 1987), pp. 130–145, 119f.
13. I. Menzies Lyth, *The Dynamics of the Social*, vol. II (London: Free Association, 1989), p. 33; see also Benson, op. cit., pp. 244–7.
14. See R. H. Schaffer, *The Breakthrough Strategy* (New York: Harper & Row, 1988), pp. 18–38.
15. See W. R. Bion, *Experiences in Groups* (London: Routledge, 1991), pp. 63–5.
16. See report in *Catholic International*, vol. 3, no. 6 (Paris, 1992), pp. 294f.
17. W. G. Dyer, *Strategies for Managing Change* (Reading, MA: Addison-Wesley, 1984), p. 176.
18. See helpful insights by M. F. Kets de Vries and D. Miller, *The Neurotic Organization: Diagnosing and Changing Counterproductive Styles of Management* (San Francisco: Jossey-Bass, 1985), pp. 15–45, 133–205; and E. H. Schein, *Process Consultation: Lessons for Managers and Consultants* (Reading, MA: Addison-Wesley, 1987), *passim*.

Epilogue

Carefree, I used to think,
'Nothing can ever shake me!'
Your favour, Yahweh, set me on unassailable heights,
but you turned away your face and I was terrified.
To you, Yahweh, I call . . .
What point is there in my death, my going down to the
abyss? . . .

(Ps 30:6–9)

The first three lines of the above passage from the Bible aptly describe the self-confidence of the Church and its constituent bodies (e.g. dioceses, parishes, missionary organizations, religious congregations) in the years leading up to Vatican II. Especially in the Western world, the Church was a mighty self-contained fortress, on unassailable heights of power and prestige – secure in a never-ending supply of recruits to the priesthood and religious life, its churches, universities, colleges and schools. It never dawned on us that anything could ever shake this edifice of the Lord.

Now the euphoria of the refounding Council has gone for many in the Church. Now we are the poor Church of sinners, shaken by massive defections from the ranks of the priesthood, religious life and laity, financial and sexual scandals, internal polarizations. We feel burdened by the escapist uselessness of restorationist and fundamentalist forces in the Church, as well as by the brashness of secularists in our midst who would squander the richness of our ascetical and civilizing traditions. We have been cast down from seemingly unassailable heights of religious power and grandeur – all in the space of a few short years. We feel the Lord has turned his face away from us and we are terrified of the darkness, of our powerlessness. We cry: 'How long, Yahweh, will you forget me? For ever? How long will you turn away your face from me? How long must I nurse . . . sorrow in my heart day and night?' (Ps 13:1–2).

Why are we so surprised by the darkness, by this dramatic turn of events? We rejoiced when the Council reminded us that we are a pilgrim people, yet we did not stop to read the guidelines that go with this inspiring title: 'God led the people a roundabout way through the desert of the Sea of Reeds' (Ex 13:18). Those who sincerely wish to be a pilgrim people soon come to realize, as did the Israelites of old, that the way to the Kingdom is not straight. It is the roundabout way, a detour, in which there is a darkness of an Exodus or a Gethsemane.

Surely one of the most powerful images used by Yahweh, and reaffirmed by the words and life of Christ, is that of the chaos.[1] Yet I find in workshops on refounding the Church and religion congregations that people commonly hold back from using the word 'chaos', preferring a softer or less threatening term to describe their sense of loss. However, the fact is that we cannot escape experiencing what the Bible means by chaos, no matter how we seek to disguise its reality with the language of doublespeak. Consider how Yahweh uses instructively the theme of chaos in the Book of Job, a remarkable text about the universal human struggle for meaning within an often muddled world. In that book the two mythical figures, Leviathan and Behemoth, represent the primeval chaos created by Yahweh and from which he moulds order and meaning in the world (see Job 40:19).[2] When Job suffers afflictions he returns, like these two figures, to God-formed chaos and there experiences the timely lesson of the powerlessness of humankind (Job 40:15). The entire creation is constantly in danger of falling back into this state of chaos; by ourselves we can do nothing to stop this backward slide from taking place. Only God as Creator can ultimately control chaos and order. Yet, as Yahweh so beautifully explains to Job, when the Lord turns his face away from us and we encounter the fear-evoking force of darkness and uncertainty, then as creatures of God and as stewards of his gifts we come into contact with the chaos out of which we were made and the lessons it symbolizes. That is, we can encounter afresh – if we freely choose to do so – the roots of our being, our own powerlessness, and at the same time the saving, the re-creative and energizing power of God in Christ. The roundabout way, then, becomes salvific.

To be salvific, therefore, the experience of darkness must be openly acknowledged and personally/corporately owned – immensely difficult though this may be; we cannot learn from this ordeal if we deny it is happening to us. This is what we mean by conversion to the Lord's way of living. His way to the light of the resurrection is through the asceticism of dispossession:

> But he emptied himself,
> taking the form of a slave . . .
> And for this God raised him high . . .
> (Phil 2:7, 9)

Having embraced the powerlessness of humankind, Jesus opened himself to the re-creative energy of God the Creator. Chaos was not embraced for itself alone, but as the roundabout way to the humanly inconceivable life of the resurrection. St John of the Cross grasps this chaos/creation dialectic in inspiring language:

221

> When the soul frees itself of all things and attains to emptiness and
> dispossession concerning them, which is equivalent to what it can do of
> itself, it is impossible that God fail to do His part by communicating
> Himself to it, at least silently and secretly. . . . God will enter the soul
> that is empty, and fill it with divine goods.[3]

Alice told the Queen that 'one can't believe impossible things'. To which
the Queen replied confidently: 'I dare say you haven't had much practice.
When I was your age, I always did it for half an hour a day. Why,
sometimes I've believed as many as six impossible things before
breakfast.'[4] The Queen's words contain, like the Book of Job, a timely
lesson for us. Before the Council the Church had become an ageing culture,
thoroughly certain about itself and destiny, secure in its prestige and past
achievements. It had lost the art of appreciating the necessity of the roundabout way; it needed to become young again, to get in touch with its roots
in chaos and its inner powerlessness before God.

The dreaming of impossible things in the Lord is the act of hope. The
act of hope does not ignore the chaos within and without, nor is it a dream
for everything to be returned to the secure ways of the old status quo. To
be authentic, hope emerges out of an acknowledgement of our own
powerlessness to act without the Lord. It is the act of trust in the Lord that
if we struggle to put aside our own attachments, he can work humanly
impossible things through us for his glory. Those impossible things may
not be what we want, but they will be what God wants. That may well
mean the death of ways of evangelizing that make us feel comfortable. It
may well involve the death of existing pastoral structures or the religious
congregation we have given our lives for. The way of refounding the
Church is the roundabout route: the way of asceticism, of darkness, of
dreaming and doing the 'impossibly new' in the, Lord.

The truly hopeful in the Church name the pain of the chaos and of their
myriad losses. When the pain has been named it can be let go in order to
give space for the impossibly new to enter. This process of salvifically mourning for the newness of the resurrection can be stopped, however, in
various ways. Once we have begun to mourn we can become so frightened
of the darkness that we take refuge in the securities of worldly visions; or
the communities we belong to are so weary and introverted that they refuse
even to allow the public expression of pain. Or there are those within the
Church who see no chaos or pain at all; they offer people false hopes
embodied in restorationism because they will not acknowledge the fact that
authentic hope is founded in admitting to our inner powerlessness.[5]
Jeremiah's words can be applied to them: 'Without concern they dress my
people's wound, saying "Peace! Peace!" Whereas there is no peace. . . . And
so as others fall, they too will fall' (Jer 6:14–15).

Today in the Church there are people acknowledging the salvific power
of loss, but there is particularly little support for them among official
leaders of the Church. Restorationism is a denial of the rich possibilities of
grief. It is a denial of the call of the Lord to dream impossible dreams of

evangelization within a secularizing world or of the salvific potential of a faith-acknowledged chaos.

Restorationists should ponder the early history of the Israelites. The journeying of the Israelites in the desert or wilderness is a fundamental and most powerful symbol for them of chaos – the dramatic breakdown of the predictable. This period in the wilderness after leaving Egypt is the archetypal experience of what chaos means: travellers without a sense of direction, bickering with one another, angry at Yahweh and Moses his spokesman, hungry, a prey to all kinds of diseases and witch-hunting crazes, without landed roots that would give them an abiding sense of belonging. They yearned for land they could again call their own and for the chance to grow their familiar, good-tasting food. Egypt suddenly became highly attractive – the evils of oppression forgotten! So the restorationists in their midst vigorously demanded that Moses lead them back to the securities of the past: 'Was it for lack of graves in Egypt, that you had to lead us out to die in the desert? What was the point of bringing us out of Egypt? . . . We prefer to work for the Egyptians than to die in the desert!' (Ex 14:11–12). 'Why did we not die at Yahweh's hand in Egypt, where we used to sit round the flesh pots and could eat to our heart's content!' (Ex 16:3). If these restorationists had had their way, then the people would never have entered the chosen land nor have discovered, on letting go of their attachments to the former securities of Egypt, that Yahweh is a 'God of tenderness and compassion' (Ex 34:6). They would never have experienced the humanly impossible vision that Yahweh had for them: 'You of all the nations shall be my very own' (Ex 19:5, JB).

The Church is in the dangerous liminal stage of change, like the Israelites under Moses – the darkness of the betwixt-and-between period; the pre-Vatican II Church has yet to be boldly assigned to the noble state in history and the new Church of Vatican II values has yet to take confident shape. It is a phase of uncertainty, bickering, scapegoating and intense pain. Restorationist forces will not let the old Church go. If only the rich potential of this liminal darkness could be grasped: for 'now is the real time of favour, now the day of salvation is here' (2 Cor 6:2). Unless we die to the old and risk the new in the Lord, Vatican II will be a waste of time.

We desperately need more and more authority and pathfinding dissenters. They dare to challenge the Church's hierarchy and others to accept the inevitability of death, or the need to let go of that which apostolically is no longer relevant, as the condition for the humanly impossibly new to emerge. These prophetic people, weary of more and more escapist rhetoric, witch-hunting and denial in the Church, daily remind us by their words and actions that the ultimate source of Paul's hope arises from his acceptance of his own powerlessness:

> But we hold this treasure in pots of earthenware, so that the immensity
> of the power is God's and not our own. We are subjected to every kind

of hardship ... we see no way out but we never despair; ... always we carry with us in our body the death of Jesus so that the life of Jesus, too, may be visible in our body.... That is why we do not waver; indeed, though this outer human nature of ours may be falling into decay, at the same time our inner human nature is renewed day by day.

(2 Cor 4:7, 8, 10, 16)

Notes

1. See G. A. Arbuckle, *Out of Chaos: Refounding Religious Congregations* (New York: Paulist Press/London: Geoffrey Chapman, 1988), pp. 146–62.
2. See D. Cox, *Man's Anger and God's Silence: The Book of Job* (Middlegreen: St Paul Publications, 1990), pp. 102–4, 125–7.
3. 'Living Flame' in *The Collected Works of St John of the Cross*, trans. K. Kavanaugh and O. Rodriguez (Washington, DC: ICS Publications, 1979), para. 3.46.
4. L. Carroll, *Alice in Wonderland, Through the Looking Glass and Other Comic Pieces* (London: J. M. Dent, 1929), p. 149.
5. See W. Brueggemann, *Hope within History* (Atlanta: John Knox Press, 1987), pp. 86f.

Index

accountability 101, 104, 152
addictive society 191
Adizes, I. 55
Arnold, P. 46
authority/power
 defined 78
 types 79
'authority' dissenters 6f., 98–125, 223

Basic Christian Communities (BCCs) 30,
 54, 91f.
Bellah, R. 89, 98, 115
Benedict of Nursia, St 159
Bennis, W. 67
Berger, P. 36, 50
Bion, W. 120, 214
Bishops of England and Wales, submission
 to 1985 Synod of Bishops 35, 61, 73
Boff, L. 74f., 97
Brueggemann, W. 195, 224
Buckley, M. 167
Bühlmann, W. 16, 28

chaos
 calcified chaos and refounding 143
 defined 45, 143, 180, 221
 religious congregational chaos
  symptoms 136f.
Chittister, J. 167
collaborative government 202–18
collegiality 33, 60
community 158f.
community life, religious 158–63
 individualism 170
 intentional communities 90, 103
 models 158–63
 therapeutic or me-istic model 168f.
Conferences of Bishops 19, 60f.
Congregation for the Doctrine of the
 Faith 74
congregational leaders
 and 'new belongs elsewhere' 149–54
 'seduction' by group 145, 150
consensus 111, 207
consultants, role of 213f., 217f.
Crosby, M. 11
cultural anthropology 10

cultural models of Church 81–93
cultural shock 45, 171
culture(s)
 defined 37f.
 group/grid 80
 growing–organic/ageing–mechanistic
  55–7
 life-cycle 43
 open/closed 27
 power/role/person/mission types 125
 revitalization 43–8

deficiencies in the Church 30ff.
denial 182, 191, 193
'detail thinkers' 210
dialogue 111
*Directives on Formation in Religious
 Institutes* (1990 document) 167
dissent 1, 2f., 9f., 113
dissenters 2, 30, 110, 113, 123
 'authority' dissenters 6f., 98–125, 223
 'pathfinding' dissenters 6f.
Douglas, M. 68, 80
Dulles, A. 15, 77, 83

Enlightenment 22, 49
envy 139f.
Essential Elements of Religious Life (1983
 document) 166f.
evil 191f.
Expressive Cultural Revolution (1960s)
 46, 51

facilitators, role of 213f., 217f.
fundamentalism
 defined 46f.
 in the Church 53f.

Ganey, M. 107
Gardner, J. 180
Gorbachev, M. 47, 48
Greeley, A. 52, 87
grief 180
grieving, stages of 183
groupthink 112

Hall, E. 37
Hebblethwaite, P. 64, 65f., 95

Hornsby-Smith, M.   87, 96f.
Hunter, J.   47

Inquisition   30
Instruction on the Ecclesial Vocation of the Theologian   9, 77

John of the Cross, St   46, 145, 221
John XXIII   24, 48, 49, 91, 108
John Paul II (also as Cardinal Wojtyła)   3, 33, 58f., 60f., 79, 87

leaderless communities   99ff.
leadership
   collaborative   99, 202, 205–16
   and management   102, 125
   primary task   102, 108, 125
   servant   122f.
   situational   99
   transactional   99, 102
   transforming   99, 101ff., 105, 107
Leddy, M. J.   131, 176
Loyola, St Ignatius   113, 162f.
Lozano, J. M.   131, 177
Lyth, I. Menzies   150, 199, 219

McBrien, R. P.   11, 76
McCarthy, Senator J.   68f., 71
McCormick, R.   11, 76
McDonagh, S.   40
'machine-gun thinkers'   210
Major Superiors Conferences, prophetic role of   214f.
Malina, B. L.   96
management   102
Merici, St Angela   31, 162
Metz, J.   132, 143, 145
millenarian movements   46, 145
mission statements   205
myth/mythology   38, 135
   polar opposite myths   39f.

Neal, M. A.   61
Neo-Catechumenate   52f., 62
neurotic communities/cultures   43, 140f.
'new belongs elsewhere'   119f., 149

O'Malley, J. W.   41, 142
Opus Dei   52, 53, 62
orthodoxy
   show trials   72
   and witch-hunting   68–78

pastoral planning   149
Paul VI   28, 50, 51, 58, 129
Pilgrim Church   18
Pius IX   23, 57

Pius X   22
Pius XII   2, 4, 23f.
popular religiosity   19, 86
primary task   25, 105, 164
Provost, J.   74

Rahner, K.   26, 27, 94, 98
Ratzinger, Joseph Cardinal   59f., 73, 77
reformation in the Church   21
refounding   4, 32, 201
   defined   21f., 144
   founding/refounding   143
   'new belongs elsewhere' and schism   153f.
refounding persons   146–9
religious congregations
   brothers   141f.
   clerical religious   142
   ministry and religious life   177
   types   160
   women's congregations   141
religious life
   chaos   135–41
   prophetic function   20, 131
renewal and refounding compared   149
resistance to change   181
restorationism   3f., 94, 125, 166f., 199, 222
Ricci, M.   31
rituals of mourning/grieving   184ff.

'scapegoating'   67, 180
Schaef, A. W.   191
schism and refounding   153f.
secrecy, role of   69, 75f., 94
sects/cults   46, 85, 134
Shorter, A.   28, 59
'story-tellers'   210f.
subsidiarity, principle of   207ff.
Swidler, L.   32
symbol, definition of   38f.
Synods of Bishops   61

Teresa of Avila, St   145, 153
Theissen, G.   91
Thomas, K.   12

vision statements   205

Ward, M.   31, 133
'witches'/'witch-hunting'   68, 73, 78ff., 93
Wittberg, P.   153
Wojtyła, Cardinal *see* John Paul II
Woodward, E.   158